HALACHA AND CONTEMPORARY SOCIETY

HALACHA AND CONTEMPORARY SOCIETY

edited by
Rabbi Alfred S. Cohen

KTAV PUBLISHING HOUSE, INC.

RABBI JACOB JOSEPH SCHOOL PRESS

Library of Congress Cataloging in Publication Data
Main entry under title:

Halacha and contemporary society.

   1. Jewish law—Addresses, essays, lectures.
2. Orthodox Judaism—Addresses, essays, lectures.
3. Judaism—20th century—Addresses, essays, lectures.
I. Cohen, Alfred S.
BM520.2.H34   296.1′8   84-741
ISBN 0-88125-042-2
ISBN 0-88125-043-0 (pbk.)

CONTENTS

Introduction

הלל הזקן אומר ... אם ראית דור שהתורה חביבה
עליו פזר (ברכות סג.)

Hillel the Elder said: "If you see a generation which
holds the Torah dear, then disseminate (learning)."

The American Jew of today is unquestionably a person with a
seemingly unquenchable thirst for Torah knowledge. In America
and Israel, yeshivot flourish, and new ones are constantly being
opened to meet the burgeoning demand. *Shiurim* in *Daf Yomi* are
organized in the most unlikely places. Along with the surge of
interest in Jewish thought and learning has come a tremendous
desire to be well informed in practical Jewish halacha, and in
particular on those matters which represent a new challenge in
finding an accommodation between Jewish values and modern
social realities. However, many sincere persons find themselves
unable to navigate the heavy waters of talmudic polemic and
rabbinic erudition; the technical difficulties in mastering Aramaic
and Hebrew texts and in comprehending esoteric legal terminology
have effectively put a vast area of Jewish knowledge out of the
reach of many.

It was to fill this need that the *Journal of Halacha and
Contemporary Society* came into being. The amazingly enthusiastic
response to the *Journal* in the short time it has been published is a
source of deep gratification to its editors and publishers. The
Journal of Halacha and Contemporary Society focuses in each issue
on a select number of situations which confront the Torah-
committed Jew in modern society, and offers a synoptic analysis of
halachic thinking on that topic. We try to make the reader aware
of areas wherein a potential halachic problem exists, and to trace
the authentic Jewish approach to such problems. Every effort is
made to present a lucid, objective survey of the subject; our goal is
never to render a halachic decision (psak) but to inform the reader
of the opinions of the leading halachic decisors of the past and
present. Every word is checked and rechecked by talmudic scholars
for accuracy, and we seek the advice of *Gedolim* in setting policy
for the *Journal*.

A publication of this sort is not one to be undertaken lightly. Some of the questions raised are of an extremely delicate nature; a false impression or inadequate explanation might, G-d forbid, lead someone to inadvertent error in observance of mitzvot. Much of the material appearing herein was heretofore known only to the scholars who were able to master it in the original, and thus there was some trepidation in making it available to the public, whose reactions could not be gauged in advance. However, the decision was made to proceed with this venture, based on the precedent of the Chafetz Chaim.

In setting down the laws of *lashon hora* in *Sefer Shmirat HaLashon*, the Chafetz Chaim admitted his hesitation, realizing that some people would seize upon certain paragraphs as a *heter* for *lashon hora*, or that they might unjustifiably elaborate upon or draw conclusions from what he wrote. Nevertheless, he decided to set down the halachot so that those honestly seeking the truth might find it. He relied on an incident in *Bava Bathra* 89b: Rabbi Yochanan ben Zaccai was perplexed, for he had become aware of the devious business practices employed by some Jewish merchants. If he were to denounce these activities publicly, some heretofore honest persons might possibly find out how to cheat their customers; but were he to remain silent, people would lose respect for the Rabbis, as being unaware of the realities of life. The Gemara concludes that he decided to discuss the cheating publicly, despite the possible pitfalls, relying on the verse

ישרים דרכי ד' ... צדיקים ילכו בם ורשעים יכשלו בם

"The ways of God are straight; the righteous will walk in them, the sinners will stumble on them."

Despite this, every issue goes to press with the Editorial Board's prayer echoing the prayer which Rabbi Nechunya ben Hakanah said daily as he entered the Beth Midrash, "May it be Thy will, O G-d, that no mishap occur through me and that I make no error in a matter of halacha" (Brachot 28a).

יהי רצון מלפניך ד' אלקי שלא יארע דבר תקלה על ידי ולא
כאכשל בדבר הלכה.

This book represents a selection of essays which have appeared in the *Journal of Halacha and Contemporary Society* in the past three years, and focuses on three major areas of concern: the family, the community, and the individual. However, each article is independent of the others in the same unit and can be read without them.

Neither the *Journal of Halacha and Contemporary Society* nor this book would have been possible were it not for the vision and courage of the Board of Directors of Yeshiva Rabbi Jacob Joseph, which agreed to sponsor this undertaking. In particular, I owe an incalculable debt of gratitude to the President of the Rabbi Jacob Joseph School, Dr. Marvin Schick, for his unswerving support, for his foresight and trust, and for the many valuable suggestions he has made in the course of publication. My thanks also to the members of the Editorial Board of the *Journal of Halacha and Contemporary Society* for their advice and assistance. I am indebted to the loyal staff of the *Journal* for typing and proofreading assistance beyond the call of duty.

Rabbi Alfred S. Cohen
Editor

THE FAMILY

Halachic Aspects of Family Planning

Rabbi Herschel Schachter

In order to be certain that our Journal falls well within the parameters of the halacha, it was decided from the outset that all articles published herein would receive the scrutiny of Gedolei Yisroel.

In a discussion last year with one of the outstanding Roshei Yeshiva regarding certain articles for inclusion in the Journal, we were strongly urged by him to print an article on M'niat HaHerayon (Birth Control). Not only did this Godol request this article, but he also specifically requested that it include all Heterim available. His feeling was that it is important for people to have knowledge, so that they will be able to approach their Rov for advice.

The Editor

Introduction

The halacha forbids public lectures on matters of *Gilui Arayot*, for fear that some of those attending such *Drashot* will misunderstand the fine points of the law and do forbidden acts thinking that they are permissible.[1] Many years ago, Rabbi

---

1. Chagiga 11b.

Rabbi Herschel Schachter, Rosh Yeshiva and Rosh Hakollel, Yeshiva University

Feinstein ruled in a responsum[2] that the issue of family planning is included under the broad heading of *Arayot*, and therefore may not be treated in journals available to the public.

Nevertheless, over the past twenty years this topic has been dealt with at length in both public forums and popular journals. Its treatment, unfortunately, has been less than satisfactory, with presentations often being incomplete and inaccurate. Several Gedolim felt that a new halachic paper on this subject in English would be appropriate, and it is upon their insistence that this paper is being written.

The halachic issue involved in family planning touch on many areas; this paper will introduce the reader to these various areas, without attempting to exhaust the halachic discussion involved.

It should be stressed that this essay is not intended to be a source of practical halacha; each family situation is different, and questions must be referred to a qualified Rabbinic authority.

Piryah V'rivyah

With the words "*Pru U'rvu*," the Torah charges every Jewish male to be fruitful and multiply. The exact number of children one must have in order to fulfill the mitzvah is debated among the Tannaim, with the accepted view being that of Bais Hillel, who require at least one son and one daughter.[3] According to the Talmud Yerushalmi, Bais Hillel actually agrees with Bais Shammai, that even one who has two sons has fulfilled his obligation. The mitzvah, says the Yerushalmi, consists of having either two sons or a son and a daughter. The Talmud Bavli, however, clearly disagrees, and its opinion is accepted by the *Shulchan Aruch*, which lists a son and a daughter as the minimum requirement.[4]

But it is not sufficient to have given birth to these two children. They themselves must be capable of having offspring.[5]

---

2. *Igrot Moshe*, Even Hoezer Vol. 1, pg. 163.
3. Yevamot 61b.
4. *Shulchan Aruch*, Even Hoezer (1, 5). See, however, *Avnei Nezer* (Even Hoezer, 1 and Choshen Mishpat, 127) who tends to accept the opinion of the *Yerushalmi*, based on a passage in the *Zohar*.
5. Even Hoezer (1, 5).

Therefore, if they should die before having had children of their own, it will turn out retroactively that their father has not fulfilled his obligation of *P'ru U'rvu*[6].

Underlying the mitzvah is the idea that every male Jew should participate, at least partially, in the perpetuation of Klal Yisroel.[7] This, however, was not always the rationale. Until *Mattan Torah, P'ru U'rvu* was required of all nations.[8] At that time, the nature of the mitzvah clearly was to personally participate in the perpetuation of the human race.[9] Since *Ma'amad Har Sinai*, the

---

6. Yevamot 62a.
7. The Talmud (ibid.) states that a convert who has had non-Jewish children before converting, has thereby fulfilled the mitzvah of *Piryah V'rivyah*. When the Rambam quotes this statement of Rabbi Yochanan (Ishus 15, 6) he qualifies the halacha: The convert only has fulfilled his mitzvah provided the children convert as well. The *Magid Mishna* points out that this condition is obvious since today, after *Mattan Torah*, the mitzvah no longer is to perpetuate the human race, but rather to perpetuate Klal Yisroel.

   It is with this understanding of the mitzvah in mind that several contemporary *Gedolim* have pointed out that in our particular generation, with such a large portion of the Jewish people having been annihilated during the war years, it is more important than ever for couples to have larger families, in order to help perpetuate Klal Yisroel. (See *Chelkat Yu'ukov* Vol. 3, no. 62.)
8. *Mishneh Lamelech* (Melachim 10,7). This is not in accordance with the opinion of Maharsha (Sanhedrin 59B) that both before and after *Mattan Torah*, this mitzvah did not apply to other nations. See *Avnei Nezer* (Even Hoezer, 79) for a discussion of this point.
9. According to the *Bach* (beginning of *Hilchot Sukkah*), whenever the Torah commands us to perform a mitzvah and explicitly gives the reason, we can only fulfill it if the performance of the act of the mitzvah (*ma'aseh hamitzvah*) is accompanied by *Kavana* (intention) for the reason given. According to Rabbi Hersh Melech Shapiro of Dinov (*Derech Pikudecha* pg. 39), the mitzvah of *Piryah V'rivyah* is one such mitzvah, as the Torah explicitly spells out its reason (Bereishis 1:28): the preservation of mankind.

   One could argue with Rav Hersch Melech's analysis, based on the Gemara mentioned above: Until *Mattan Torah*, one can argue, the mitzvah applied to all nations, and the nature of the mitzvah was indeed to preserve mankind. But after *Mattan Torah*, the nature of the mitzvah shifted. When G-d commanded the Jewish men that "they must all return to their wives" (Devorim 5, 27), no reason was mentioned. It can be argued that this verse, which cites no reason, is the basis of our observation of the mitzvah today, and the reason given in Breishis - the perpetuation of mankind - is no longer the true rationale of the mitzvah. Therefore, the mitzvah of *Piryah V'rivyah* would not fall into the category of mitzvot described by the *Bach*, where the reason for the mitzvah is specified.

nature of the mitzvah has changed: it now applies only to the Jewish people and consists of perpetuating Klal Yisroel.

If one is physically unable to have children, some *Poskim* feel that the act of adopting a boy and a girl and raising them as Jews can serve as a secondary form of fulfilling the mitzvah.[10] This view is based upon the Talmudic statement that "the Torah considers one who raises another's child as if he himself had given birth to that child."[11] The Talmud obviously does not mean to say that a non-Jewish child can become a Kohen, Levi or Yisroel in this manner; the remark is limited, rather, to the mitzvah of *Piryah V'rivyah*.

The mitzvah of *Pru U'rvu* is considered by the Talmud to be more important than most other mitzvot. Thus, although one is not allowed to sell a Sefer Torah, if it will enable someone to marry and start a family, the sale is permitted.[12] Likewise, although ordinarily a Kohen living in Israel may not set foot outside the land, (the Rabbis having declared *Chutz Lo'oretz* to be a place of *Tumah*,) nevertheless, for the purpose of marrying and raising a family he may leave.[13] Furthermore, *Pru U'rvu* is one of the rare instances in the Talmud where the Rabbis actually advocate the commission of a minor sin in order to gain the ability to observe a very great mitzvah. Tosafot labels *Pru U'rvu* as a "Mitzvah Rabbah"[14] because it involves the perpetuation of Klal Yisroel.

A couple who decide not to have children are in clear violation of this most fundamental biblical mitzvah. Moreover, if a wife refuses to have any children, her husband has the right, and even the obligation, to divorce her, and he need not pay her *Kesuba*.[15] Since having children is considered one of the essential components of a marriage - "*Ein Isha Ella L'Bonim*"[16] the wife, with her

---

10. *Chochmat Shlomo* (of R. Shlomo Kluger) to Even Hoezer (1, 1).
11. Sanhedrin 19b.
12. Megillah 27a.
13. Avodah Zarah 13a.
14. Gittin 41b, and Tosafot.
15. See K'subos 72a regarding the wife who does not keep her *nedarim*, and *Rosh*, *ibid*.
16. *Lev Aryeh* (Grossnass), Vol. 1, #30 in the name of R. Boruch Ber Leibowitz.

refusal, is therefore at fault for the breaking up of conjugal life,[17] and consequently forfeits her monetary privileges.

The same idea is the basis of another mishna. If a man marries, and later discovers that his wife is an *Eilonis* (unable ever to bear children), the marriage is considered to have been based on error, and is null and void with no *Get* required.[18] Thus, the inability of the wife to have children is considered a great enough blemish to annul the entire marriage.

Putting Off The Mitzvah

The more common situation confronting us today is not so much the case of a couple desiring not to have any children at all, but rather that of the couple who haven't yet completed their schooling, or are financially insecure and therfore are interested in postponing the starting of a family. What is the halacha's opinion on putting off the fulfillment of a mitzvah for a year or two? Obviously, with respect to mitzvot like *Tefillin* and *Lulav* which have prescribed times, the person who waits until an entire day passes has irretrivably lost his opportunity to perform the particular mitzvah. But regarding *Piryah V'rivyah*, where the Torah does not stipulate any time, one might think that the couple who have their children a year or two later fulfill the same mitzvah as if they had begun their family at the start of their marriage.

There is a rule governing the performance of all mitzvot that, as a biblically-derived recommended enhancement of the mitzvah, one should zealously perform the mitzvah at the earliest opportunity. This is known as the *Hiddur Mitzvah D'oraiso* of *Zrizim Makdimin L'Mitzvot*.[19] Were this the only issue involved in delaying the raising of a family, there might be ample ground to allow postponement, based on the consideration of inconvenience. Because of pressing circumstances we often postpone a *Bris* or a *Pidyon HaBen* to a later hour in the day,[20] foregoing this *Hiddur Mitzvah D'oraiso* of *Zrizim Makdimin*.

---

17. Taanit 31a.
18. Yevamot 2b and Tosafot.
19. Pesachim 4a.
20. We are assuming that just as a *bris* done on the eighth day is a more enhanced

It should be noted, though, that once the designated day for the mitzvah has passed, with no secondary time having been set by the Torah, many *Poskim* rule that it is implicit in the obligation of the mitzvah that it be taken care of as soon as possible. This is no longer merely a *Hiddur Mitzvah*, but rather an essential condition of the biblical command.

A case illustrating this point is recorded in the responsa of Rabbi Yechezkel Landau, the *Nodah B'Yehudah*. In Rabbi Landau's time, first-born Jews used to avoid fasting on Erev Pesach by attending a *Seudah* of a *Bris*. Even if no baby were born a week before Yom Tov, the last boy born during that season of the year whose *Bris* had to be delayed, would have his *Bris* held over until Erev Pesach for the benefit of the first born.

The *Nodah B'Yehudah*[21] opposed this practice. He pointed out that when the *Bris* cannot be performed on the eighth day proper for medical reasons and must be delayed, one may not postpone it for an additional day unnecessarily. Such a *Bris* must be performed on the earliest possible day.

A possible source for the *Nodah B'Yehudah's* opinion can be seen from the Gemara in *Makkos* (13b): If a person unintentionally violates a commandment whose intentional transgression carries the punishment of "*Kareth*," he is required to

---

mitzvah than the *bris* which is postponed, so too the *pidyon haben* done on the thirty-first day constitutes a more enhanced mitzvah. This is clearly the opinion of the *Geonim* (quoted by Ramban to Bechoros 63a) that if the *pidyon haben* is done after the thirty-first day, the father must add one-fifth extra. They obviously feel that just as there is a special mitzvah of having the *Bris* on the eighth day *(bizmano)*, so too there is a special mitzvah of having the *pidyon haben* on the thirty-first day. Other *Poskim* disagree and feel that the mitzvah of *pidyon haben* is really the same, whether done on the thirty-first day or afterwards, the only difference being that *Zrizim Makdimin L'mitzvot* dictates that it be done on the earliest possible day. (See *Imrei Yosher*, Vol. 2, no. 132.) This question is a most relevant one in the instance of a baby born on a Thursday, whose *pidyon haben* should take place on Shabbos. Do we allow a *pidyon haben* on Shabbos? If the thirty-first day is the proper time of the mitzvah (similar to a *milah bizmanah*, whose time is the eighth day), then it should be permitted to do the *pidyon* even on Shabbos. See *Orach Chaim* (339,4); *Yoreh Deah* (305, 11) and *Likutei Pinchos* (Schwartz).

21. *Yoreh Deah*, Vol. II, no. 166.

bring a special sin offering *(Korban Chatos)* to the Temple. The Talmud derives from a verse that this special sacrifice is not brought by one who unintentionally failed to circumcise himself, although the sin of not observing *Bris Milah* is punishable by *Kareth.* The difficulty in understanding this Talmudic passage is obvious: If we are discussing the bringing of a *Korban Chatos,* clearly the one bringing it is alive, for no *Chatos* may be brought on behalf of a dead person. In that case, how can we say that, by mistake, this person has not fulfilled the mitzvah of *Bris Milah?* As long as he is alive, he can always rectify the situation by having the *Bris* performed upon himself! The simple reading of this Gemara has led several *Rishonim*[22] to conclude that if one delays the performance of the *Bris Milah,* even if only for a short period of time, and even though he ultimately does fulfill the mitzvah later on in life, the *mere postponement* constitues an act of *Bitul HaMitzvah.*

If we accept this premise, we might then logically extend it to apply to all mitzvot with no biblically-specified time of performance. It would be self-understood that the proper time for the performance of a mitzvah is the earliest available opportunity, and one who delays doing a mitzvah, but ultimately does perform it, has been both *m'vatel* and *m'kayem* the mitzvah. Hence it should follow that if one postpones having a family after already having had the opportunity, even if he were later to fulfill the mitzvah, the delay itself would constitute a *Bitul HaMitzvah.*

However, one could still argue that there is a major point of distinction between these cases. In the situation of *Bris Milah,* there originally was a set time for the mitzvah. Having failed to do the mitzvah at the proper time, we are obligated to make it up at the earliest opportunity. But in the case of *Piryah V'rivyah,* there never was a fixed time for the mitzvah. Perhaps in such a case the only problem involved in postponing the mitzvah would be that of *Zrizim Makdimin L'Mitzvot.*

---

22. See Rambam and Ravad, Hilchot Milah, (I, 2).

Chazon Ish

Nevertheless, a further complication arises from the Chazon Ish's interpretation of a Gemara in *Moed Katan* (7b). The Gemara there derives from a verse that the mitzvah of *Re'iyas Negaim* (showing suspected cases of *Zora'as* to a Kohen) may be postponed in certain special cases. The mitzvah of *Re'iyas Negaim* is similar to that of *Piryah V'rivyah* in that both have no biblically-set time for their performance. The implication of this Gemara is clear: if not for the special verse, we would not have allowed the postponing of the mitzvah. The Chazon Ish writes[23] that he is unsure just what violation such a delay would have constituted. Does the Gemara mean to say that whereas in other mitzvot we insist that *Zrizim Makdimin L'Mitzvot*, here, with respect to *Re'iyas Negaim*, the Torah never required *Zrizus* even as a *Hiddur L'chatchilah*? Or perhaps the Gemara meant something more significant - that whenever the Torah requires us to do a mitzvah, but mentions no specific time, it is understood that the proper time for the mitzvah is the earliest opportunity, and only with respect to *Re'iyas Negaim* has the Torah made an exception.

The Chazon Ish prefers the second interpretation. According to his opinion, then, a young married man would not be allowed to postpone the raising of a family, as such a delay would constitute a *bitul* of the mitzvah.

Maharam Schick

Another major objection is raised by the Maharam Schick. Biblically, he writes[24], a person need not fear that he will die before he has a chance to do the mitzvot required of him. But rabbinically it is ruled that such a fear is in place when a long time interval is involved. This is the rabbinic principle that *"Chaishinon L'miso L'zman Merubah."*[25] A married person who delays having his

---

23. Commentary to the end of Negaim.
24. Responsa, Even Hoezer, no. 1.
25. The Torah allows one to wait until the next Yom Tov to bring the previous Yom Tov's sacrifices to the Temple, and no fear is expressed that the individual may not live that long. But rabbinically we do not allow postponement for seven days or more, as this is considered *"zman merubah."*

family for a year or two would clearly violate this principle; he must take into account the chance that he may die in the interim and forever forfeit his opportunity to fulfill the mitzvah.

But whatever the source of the prohibition be, whether biblical according to the Chazon Ish or rabbinic according to the Maharam Schick, the halacha is stated quite clearly, in both the Rambam[26] and *Shulchan Aruch:*[27] Postponing the mitzvah of *Piryah V'rivyah* is not allowed.

Spacing

If the couple's first pregnancy resulted in a set of twins, a boy and a girl, then the husband has fulfilled his mitzvah of *Piryah V'rivyah*. However, if only one child is born first, the question now becomes whether the same two considerations mentioned previously (of the Chazon Ish and the Maharam Schick) still apply to prohibit any delay in having the next child.

Of course, if it is medically feared that the wife may become ill if she has the second child too soon after the first, there is no question that one is permitted to postpone fulfilling the mitzvah. It is a generally-accepted rule[28] that one is not obligated to do any mitzvah that will be hazardous to his health.

However, if the wife is perfectly healthy, and the couple is interested in delaying having their next child for non-health reasons, what could possibly be a reason to negate the two considerations mentioned above?

In the collection of Responsa entitled *Bnai Bonim,*[29] Rav Yosef Henkin is quoted as having allowed a wait of even four years or more between children. According to the suggestion of his grandson, Rabbi Herzel Henkin, the reason for this lenient decision runs as follows: In the Talmud we find[30] that a woman may nurse

26. *Ishus* (15, 1).
27. *Even Ho'ezer* (76, 6).
28. See *Sha'arei Teshuva* to Orach Chaim, chap. 640, end of section 5, *Igrot Moshe* Orach Chaim, vol. I, no. 172.
29. Jerusalem, 1981, no. 30.
30. Ksubos (60a).

her child for up to four or even five years. In Talmudic times a nursing mother would be unable to conceive. Why didn't the Rabbis forbid this practice of nursing for such an extended period of time on the grounds that it prevents the husband from fulfilling his mitzvah of *Piryah V'rivyah* earlier? Obviously, the answer must be that since the extra-long period of nursing is beneficial to the baby, we do not insist upon rushing to do *our* mitzvot at the expense of well-being of the child. So, today as well, if the mother is interested in delaying having her next child so that she will be able to take better care of her first child, and devote more attention to him, then the situation might be comparable to a mother nursing her baby for four years in Talmudic times. If, however, the mother plans to go to work, or to school during the free time, and is not delaying having her second child for the benefit of the first child, then Rabbi Henkin sees no justification for allowing the husband to delay the fulfillment of his mitzvah.

Others claim that the practice in Lithuania before the war was to allow for a pause of up to two years between the birth of one child and the conception of the next.[31] The rationale for this time period seems to be based on the following reasoning: the Talmud tells us[32] that a nursing mother does not fully regain her strength until a full two years after having given birth. Therefore the nursing mother has a partial status of a *Choleh She'ein Bo Sakonoh* - a sick person whose life is not in danger. Whereas with respect to more serious rabbinic laws we are not lenient on her behalf, and therefore require the nursing mother to fast on Tisha B'av and other serious fast days, regarding less serious rabbinical laws we assign this woman the status of a *Cholah*, and allow her to eat on Shiva Asar B'Tamuz and other minor fast days.[33]

The Talmud in another concept awards the same status to all mothers who have given birth within the last two years, whether they are nursing or not.[34] According to the Maharsham, quoted by

31. Quoted in *Igrot Moshe*, Even Ho'ezer vol. I, beginning of no. 64.
32. Niddah (9a).
33. Taanis (14a); *Orach Chaim* (550, 1; and 554,5).
34. Niddah (9a). See *Igrot Moshe*, Yoreh Deah, vol. III, pg. 287, that this is no

Chief Rabbi Ovadia Yosef in his responsa,[35] this is also true,
regarding the woman's status as a semi-*Cholah*. Hence, he rules,
any woman who has given birth need not fast on minor fast days
for two years, even if she is not nursing. This ruling affirms that a
woman is a partial-*Cholah* for two years after childbirth.

Chaishinon L'misoh MideRabbanan

Let us return now to the aforementioned principle *Chaishinon
L'misoh MideRabbanan:* the Rabbis ruled that a person must fulfill
a mitzvah at the earliest opportunity for fear that he might die
unexpectedly and be unable to perform it at a later date. Assuming
that the only problem involved in postponing having a family is
the issue of *Chaishinon*, as presented by the Maharam Schick, one
might argue that if we were to divide all rabbinic laws into two
general groups of (a) the more serious laws and (b) the lighter
ones, then this principle of *Chaishinon L'misoh MideRabban*
would belong to the second category. The fact that we allow a
Yeshiva student to postpone his marriage in order to advance in his
Torah studies,[36] although this means foregoing the rabbinic

---

longer true today. Obviously Rabbi Feinstein would also not accept the lenient
view of Maharsham regarding fasting on *Shiva Asar Be'Tamuz*.

35. *Yechaveh Da'as*, vol I, #35.

36. Kiddushin (29b). According to the Chazon Ish, that postponing any mitzva
constitutes an act of *bitul hamitzva*, we must understand why the yeshiva
student is allowed to delay getting married in order to advance in his Torah
studies.

Perhaps the idea behind this is, that since the whole mitzva of *piryah
v'rivyah* is for the purpose of perpetuating klal yisroel, the ultimate purpose of
which is *masores ha-Torah*, passing Torah from one generation to the next, and
his learning is also for the purpose of perpetuating Torah for klal yisroel, it may
be permissible to delay marriage on that ground. Indeed the gemara tells us
(Sanhedrin 19b) that one who teaches someone else's child Torah is considered
as if he fathered him. In his writings, the Chofetz Chaim urged childless couples
to support yeshivot, in order to have this partial fulfillment of the mitzvah of
piryah v'rivyah. And in fact, in a certain sense, those who teach others Torah or
support yeshivot have fulfilled this mitzva of perpetuation of *masores ha-Torah*
in a much greater fashion than others who merely biologically give birth to a
son and a daughter. In the words of the prophet Yeshaya, 56:4,5, "So speaks

principle of *Chaishinon L'Misoh*, would seem to indicate that the principle is of a less serious nature.

By combining the two assumptions — (a) postponement of the fulfillment of the mitzvah is a rabbinic law of a lesser degree, and

---

Hashem to the childless who ... support Torah: 'And I shall give them in my home a ... name which shall be greater than sons and daughters.' "

If the yeshiva student feels that by marrying early his ability to transmit Torah to future generations will be weakened, then in his situation the mitzvah of *piryah v'rivyah* would dictate postponing marriage for the sake of learning Torah.

According to the *Bais Shmuel* (beginning of Even Hoezer) this is the reason for the delay of this mitzva from the age of 13, the usual age when one becomes obligated to fulfill all other mitzvot, until the age of 18. If young boys would be obligated to marry at 13, their ability to transmit Torah to future generation would be hampered, and the entire goal of this mitzva would be undone. We wait until the age of 18, at which time we assume the young man has already had a chance to become sufficiently oriented in Torah learning.

In connection with this point, it is interesting to note that although the mishna in Avot (סוף פרק ה') requires that a man marry at 18, the gemara in Kiddushin mentions the age of 20 (29b). The רש"ש (in כתובות נ.) suggests that perhaps this discrepancy reflects a fundamental dispute the *Tannaim* had as to how long it might take one to develop an approach to Torah learning. In Chulin 24a, the gemara quotes a controversy among the *Tannaim* regarding this point, whether three years or five years might be required. Since the mishna in Avot recommends that boys only begin study of Talmud at age of 15, then it should take either until 18 or 20 to pick up the *derech halimud*, depending on the views of the individual *Tannaim*.

A completely different approach to this problem is presented by the N'ziv (in his commentary to the *Sheiltot*, 5:4) and after him by Rabbi Elchanan Wasserman *(Kovetz Shiurim* II, no. 19). Both understand that it is permitted for the *talmid chacham* to postpone any mitzva, not just *priyah v'rivyah*, if he feels that observing the mitzva sooner would interfere with his learning. The gemara in Moed Katan 9a derives from a *posuk* that one should interrupt his Torah studies only to perform a mitzva which cannot be taken care of by others. Regarding such mitzvot that can be attended to by others, the *talmid chacham* is instructed not to interrupt his Torah studies.

Here, although the mitzva of *piryah v'rivyah* cannot be performed for him by anyone else, nevertheless the ability to delay the mitzva until a later time puts it into the same category as a mitzva which the *talmid chacham* need not do now, and which may be taken care of by others; and the halacha says that in such a case, the *talmid chacham* need not interrupt his learning, and may rely on his intention to perform the mitzva later, just as in the other case he may rely on others to do the mitzva.

(b) all new mothers within two years of childbirth, whether they
are nursing or not, have the status of *Cholah* with respect to this
lesser category of rabbinic laws — we may conclude that if a
woman chooses to postpone having her next children for two
years, feeling that she would like to first regain her full strength,
she may do so.

However, if we assume, as the Chazon Ish does, that
postponing the fulfillment of any mitzvah is regarded biblically as
an act of *Bitul Hamitzvah*, (nullifying the mitzvah) even if one
ultimately does fulfill the mitzvah, then this explanation for
allowing the two-year delay would not be valid.

Despite the two views outlined above, which allow spacing at
either two or four year intervals, Rabbi Moshe Feinstein, in a
responsum,[37] vehemently opposes the practice. He denies that it
was ever the common practice in Lithuania to allow up to a two-
year pause.

Al Tanach Yodecha

It is now several years into their marriage, and our couple has
already been blessed with a son and a daughter. What now? The
Talmud tells us[38] in the name of Rabbi Yehoshua that even after
one has fulfilled the biblical obligation of *Pru U'rvu*, he is still
required to continue to have children in his later years. This idea is
derived from the words of Koheles (11:6) בבוקר זרע את זרעך
ולערב אל תנח ידך, *v'loerev al tanach Yodecho* - 'In the morning
you should plant your seed and in the evening, as well, you should
continue to do the same." The consensus among the *Poskim* is that
this law of Rabbi Yehoshua is not biblical in nature, but only
rabbinic.[39]

According to the *Aruch HaShulchon*,[40] the Rambam's view is
that לערב אל תנח ידך does not constitute an *independent* rabbinic
mitzvah, but is rather a *Hiddur Mitzvah Min Hamuvchar* (a very

37. see above, note 31.
38. Yevamot (62b).
39. See *S'dei Chemed*. חלק ה עמוד 141.
40. Even Hoezer (1, 8).

desirable enhancement) of *Piryah V'rivyah*. Hence it follows, as the Ramban has pointed out,[41] that although one who violates any rabbinic law is considered wicked (a *Rosho*) and may be referred to by other people as such[42], one who refuses to observe this ruling of Rabbi Yehoshua regarding *Lo'erev al tanach yodecha* would not be considered a sinner. And although Beth Din could force someone to get married even if he did not want to, Beth Din would not force one to observe this mitzvah of having more children than the minimal two. This principle of Rabbi Yeshoshua is a statement of the proper mode of behavior *(derech eretz)* rather than an official rabbinic enactment *(takkanah)*.

In fact, the Talmud relates that when the Romans intensified their religious persecutions against the Jewish people, there was a popular feeling among the pious Jews that it would be proper for our nation to refrain from having families. Why bring more Jews into this world just to be persecuted and prevented from observing the laws of the Torah? But the Rabbis felt that it would be much too difficult to impose such a rabbinic prohibition on all the Jewish people, and therefore they refrained from instituting this *Gezaira* (decree).

Exactly what were the Rabbis thinking of forbidding? According to Tosafot,[44] they never had any thoughts of doing away with the biblical mitzvah of *Piryah V'rivyah*. Although the Rabbis do have the authority to require of us that we not perform biblical mitzvot,[45] nevertheless, any rabbinic decree aimed at completely abolishing and negating an explicit mitzvah in the Torah is beyond the scope of their authority.[46] Therefore, Tosafot explains, the discussion in the Talmud revolved about instituting a *Gezaira* that no one should have more than a son and a daughter. In other words, the Rabbis considered this mitzvah of *Lo'Erev al Tanach Yodecha*.

41. *Rif*, Yevamot (62b).
42. Shabbos (40a).
43. Bava Bathra (60b).
44. ibid. starting "din". See *P'nai Shlomo*.
45. Yevamot (90b).
46. See *Taz*, Orach Chaim end of תקפ"ח

Other *Rishonim*[47] disagree with Tosafot and interpret the Gemara according to its literal meaning: The Rabbis were actually contemplating enacting a *Gezaira* to completely abolish the mitzvah of *Piryah V'rivyah*.

In actuality, however, the Rabbis never did enact this decree. As previously mentioned, they felt it would be practically impossible for the masses to observe such a strict prohibition. "It is preferable for the people to violate the laws unintentionally rather than knowingly and on purpose." Based on the terminology used by the Gemara, there is a minority opinion quoted in *Shulchan Aruch*[48] that runs as follows: Since refraining from having a family is the more proper thing to do, therefore, any individual who chooses to do so by never marrying at all or by not having more than the bare minimum of one son and one daughter (depending upon the two interpretations mentioned above), should not be faulted, since he is really acting in the more proper fashion. And certainly the Beth Din may not force that individual into observing the mitzvah which he refuses to fulfill.

This opinion of the Mordechai has only been accepted by the *Shulchan Aruch* with respect to the inability of the Beth Din to enforce the observance of the mitzvah. However, it is assumed by the majority of the *Poskim* that since the Rabbis have in fact not enacted any prohibition against raising a family, large or small, both of the basic mitzvot, *Piryah V'rivyah* of biblical origin, and *Lo'Erev al tanach yodecha* of rabbinic origin, still remain in full force, and must be totally and properly observed by all Jewish men.

Postponing Lo'Erev

Our young married couple, who has already had a boy and a girl, would now like to know if they must have the rest of their family at the earliest opportunity, or whether they may postpone fulfillment of the mitzvah of *Lo'Erev al tanach yodecha*.

---

47. See *Biur Hagra* to Even Ho'ezer, Chap. 1, section 10.
48. Even Ho'ezer (1,3) in Ramo.

In response to this question, the *Birkai Yosef*[49] cites a clear implication from the Rambam that, in this mitzvah, *temporary* postponement *is* allowed provided that the couple does not plan to completely discontinue having children.

Hastening the Coming of Moshiach

According to one opinion in the Talmud,[50] the reason for the mitzvah of *Piryah V'rivyah* is to hasten the coming of Moshiach: "The son of David will not come until all of the souls in heaven (in the *'Guf'*) have been born." Every time another child is born to Klal Yisroel, the coming of Moshiach is thereby hastened.

Although this opinion has not been accepted insofar as it explains the nature of the mitzvah of *Piryah V'rivyah*, the other two premises upon which it is based are indeed accepted: a) Every individual has an obligation to do whatever is in his power to hasten the coming of Moshiach and b) the birth of each new child into Klal Yisroel is considered another step towards the coming of Moshiach.

Having Children

The Talmud stresses the importance of the mitzvah of rejoicing at a Jewish wedding. If one rejoices properly, it is considered as if he had rebuilt part of the ruins of the destroyed city of Jerusalem. But what is the connection between the two?

When a young couple gets married, we assume that they will soon be having children. Every new child born into the Jewish people hastens the coming of Moshiach. The halacha tells us that there is a special mitzvah to celebrate upon the occasion of the building of the Temple.[52] Even in advance of the actual building, on the occasion of a significant historical event which will lead up

---

49. Even Ho'ezer, chap. 1.
50. Yevamot (62a).
51. Brochos (6b).
52. Ramban to Bamidbar, end of *Parshas Noso*. See *Or Hamizrach 5734*, "*Regarding Megillat Ta'anit.*"

to *binyon habayis*, it is also proper to celebrate the *aschalta d'geula*[53] (beginning of the Redemption).

It is for this reason that every Jewish wedding is considered, in a sense, an *Aschalta D'Geulah*, for we know that the young couple will soon be having children, and will thus hasten the coming of Moshiach and the rebuilding of the Temple.

Based upon the combination of these ideas, some *Poskim*[54] have pointed out that even one who has already fulfilled his basic mitzvah of *Piryah V'rivyah* should still try to raise a larger family for the sake of hastening the coming of Moshiach. This, too, is our responsibility and obligation.

Sirus

Our couple has already been blessed with a number of children and now decide that they would not like to have any more. What may they do to prevent having additional children?

The common American practices of "tying the tubes" of a woman or performing a vasectomy on the man are biblically forbidden.[55] A Jew may not surgically sterilize any human, animal, or even insect.[56] Not only is this prohibited when the actual operation is performed by a Jewish doctor, but also when a non-Jew is engaged to do the act of sterilization. The Talmud states[57] that if a Jewish person brings an animal to a non-Jewish veterinarian to be sterilized, the Rabbis penalize the violator and force him to sell his animal to someone else so that he does not benefit from his sin. Both the Gemara and the *Shulchan Aruch*

---

53. Commentary of *Nesivos* to Megillat Esther (9-19); *Sfas Emes*, Chanukah 5644; *Or Hamizrach*, mentioned in note 52.
54. *Mishneh Halachot* (R. Menashe Klein), vol. 5, no. 210.
55. Shabbos (110b).
56. Rabbeinu Gershom to Bava Bathra (80a).
57. Bava Metzia (90b).
58. The Gemara in Bava Metzia tries to determine exactly what prohibition has been violated in this situation. One opinion suggests that just as *Amirah L'nochri* (asking a non-Jew to perform a prohibited act for a Jew) was forbidden by the Rabbis on Shabbos, Yom Tov, and Cholo Shel Mo'ed, it was similarly proscribed for all Torah prohibitions. According to Ravad, Hilchot Kilayim (1;3) one would also not be allowed to ask a non-Jew to plant *kilayim* for him in his

rule[59] that it is forbidden to engage a non-Jew to perform any act of sterilization.

The Torah verse[60] forbidding sterilizing animals speaks specifically about male animals. Although the *Sifro* there comments that this prohibition does not apply to female animals, the Rambam states[61] clearly that the *Sifro* only excluded the sterilization of female animals from the *punishment* of *malkot* (lashes) but that the *act* itself is nevertheless prohibited. According to the Vilna Gaon,[62] this prohibition, applying even to female animals, is biblical in nature.

When the sterilization is effected through the taking of medication, orally or by injection, the Rambam and the *Shulchan Aruch* distinguish between a male and a female animal. To cause a

---

field, or according to Tosafot Rosh Hashanah 24b, have a non-Jew make a sculpture of a human figure.

The other view in the Talmud is that the Rabbinic edict forbidding *Amirah L'nochri* is limited to Shabbos, Yom Tov, and Cholo Shel Mo'ed, but the Torah law forbidding *Sirus*—castration of animals—applies even to non-Jews in accordance with the view of the *Tanna* Rabbi Chiya. Therefore, a Jew asking the non-Jew to perform the act of sterilization for him constitutes a violation of *Lifnai Eveir*, inasmuch as the Jew abets the non-Jew in the commission of a sin.

The Rambam has a unique opinion on this matter. He explicitly allows having a non-Jew plant *Kilayim* in one's field. This obviously indicates that *Amirah L'nochri* is only forbidden in the areas of Shabbos, Yom Tov, and Chol Ha-Moed. At the same time, the Rambam seems to assume that asking a non-Jew to castrate an animal may possibly constitute a biblical violation. According to the Rambam, the Gemara in Bava Metziah drew a comparison between the two prohibitions of *Sirus* (castrating animals) and *chasimah* (the law forbidding one to muzzle an animal while it threshes grain). In both instances the Torah forbids the *result* brought about *(Issur Chalot)* and not merely the actual act itself *(Issur P'eulah)*. (See *Beis Efraim*, Orach Chaim no. 56, *Tshvos Zofnas Paneach*, N.Y., no. 131 and 233). Because of this distinction, even *Gromo* (indirectly bringing about the result) would also be forbidden in these two cases. It is for this reason that the Talmud raises the possibility that even asking a non-Jew to muzzle one's animal and thresh with it for him, or to castrate one's animal, may also be *Gram-Sirus* and *Gram-Chasimah* which would be biblically forbidden.

59. Even Ho'ezer (5:14).
60. Vayikra (22, 24).
61. *Issurei Biah*, (16, 11).
62. Even Ho'ezer end of chap. 5, nos. 25 and 28.

male to become sterile is forbidden even by non-surgical methods, while such methods are permissible with a female. However, the permissibility of sterilizing a woman through medication is explained by the Talmud[63] to apply only in such a case where the husband will not be prevented thereby from fulfilling his mitzvah of *Piryah V'rivyah*. Even in that case, the *Acharonim* debate the nature of this permissibility. Most feel[64] that non-surgical forms of sterilization are not forbidden for women. Some, however, rule that there still exists a rabbinic prohibition which may only be lifted if the woman is known to suffer unusual pain at childbirth. According to this view, this *Heter* (lenient ruling) is similar to the law allowing violation of *rabbinic* prohibitions on Shabbos for the sake of a sick person *(Choleh She'ein bo Sakona)* even though there is clearly no danger of life or limb. "In a situation of pain *(tza'ar)* the Rabbis did not insist upon the observance of their prohibitions."[65]

The Talmud relates[66] that the wife of Rabbi Chiya suffered unusual pain during childbirth. She drank a special potion of herbs to make herself sterile, without the previous consent of her husband. The Chasam Sofer[67] points out that such action would only be allowed in Talmudic times, when her husband would have the option of marrying another wife if he desired more children. The wife's causing herself to be sterile did not interfere with his ability to fulfill his mitzvah. Today, however, since we no longer allow polygamy or divorce without the wife's consent, it is understood that when a couple marries, the wife obligates herself to assist her husband in fulfilling both his mitzvot of *Piryah V'rivyah* and *Lo'Erev al tanach yodecha*.[68] She may therefore not

63. Shabbos (111a).
64. See *Otzar Haposkim* to Even Ho'ezer in note 77.
65. Ksubos (60a).
66. Yevamot (65b).
67. Quoted by *Pischei Teshuvah* to Even Ho'ezer (5, 11; and 232). See also *Avnei Nezer*, Choshen Mishpot, no. 127, where the same distinction is made.
68. See *Lev Avraham* (#99) where this point of the Chasam Sofer is explained at length. See also *Avnei Nezer*, Even Ho'ezer, no. 79 where he assumes that even during Talmudic times the same was true.

cause herself to become sterile or practice any form of
contraception without the consent of her husband.[69]

Temporary Sirus

Modern medicine has developed an oral medication to be
taken by the man which causes temporary sterility. Since causing
sterility in the male is forbidden even by "drinking a potion,"
would causing temporary sterility also be included under this
prohibition? Dayan Ehrenberg has written a lengthy responsum,[70]
concluding with a lenient decision. Rabbi Moshe Feinstein
assumes[71] that causing sterility is only forbidden when the potion
the male drinks affects the reproductive organ directly. But to
cause even permanent sterility by affecting other parts of the body
would not be prohibited.

Other contemporary *Poskim* question the validity of
both of these lenient decisions.

Chavoloh

It should be borne in mind that the case specifically mentioned
in the Talmud allowing non-surgical sterilization of a woman was
in a situation where this was medically recommended. Rabbi
Chiya's wife sufferd great pain during childbirth. However, if the
non-surgical sterilization is done for non-medical considerations,
some *Poskim*[72] have pointed out that this would constitute a
separate violation of *Chavoloh* — one is not allowed to mulitate his
own body.[73] Even the slight act of self-mutilization involved in
donating blood to the Red Cross is a serious question dealt with by
contemporary *Poskim*.[74]

---

69. Regarding *temporary* use of contraceptives by the wife, without the permission
    of her husband, see *Chavazelet Hasharon*, Even Ho'ezer pgs. 229-231.
70. *D'var Yehoshua*, vol. III, Even Ho'ezer, no. 7.
71. Even Ho'ezer vol. III no. 15. See Chazon Ish, Nashim 12.
72. See *Torat Chesed*, Even Ho'ezer, no. 44, section 41.
73. Bava Kamma (91b).
74. See *Igrot Moshe*, Choshen Mishpot, no. 103; *Pischei Teshuvah* to Yoreh Deah
    chap. 157, section 15.

Hashchosas Zera And Contraceptives

The Halacha forbids *Hozoas Zera L'vatola* — the needless emission of semen. Not only does this prohibition apply when no cohabitation takes place at all, but even when a man has had relations with his wife and interrupts the act in middle so that the emission of the semen will not take place in the vagina.[75]

It is generally accepted that both of these forms of *Hashchosas Zera* (the wasting of semen) are biblically prohibited,[76] notwithstanding a strong minority opinion[77] that this law is only rabbinic in origin. Even in situations of danger to the life of the woman should she become pregnant, the accepted view among the Tannaim is to forbid coitus interruptus.[78]

This does not mean that *Tashmish* (intercourse) is allowed only when there exists a possibility of its leading to pregnancy. Tosafot[79] points out that even when a woman is pregnant or is too young or too old to conceive, her husband is permitted to have normal relations with her. The *Igrot Moshe*[80] points out that even if a woman has had a hysterectomy, her husband may still continue to live with her. Whenever *Tashmish* is performed in a normal fashion, even though it is clear that no pregnancy can

---

75. Yevamot (34b). There is, however, a difference between the two examples of "השחתת זרע". In the case of masturbation, the violation is more severe, and is considered a form of "niuf." In the second case of coitus interruptus, however, the violation is less severe, and consists only of wasting the seed. (In the first case there is really a double violation — a) *niuf*, and b) השחתת זרע). The difference would be in a case where the doctors insist on making sperm tests, to see how to enable the husband to become fertile. We would only allow the second form, for in this type of situation the seed is not being wasted at all; this test will lead to the possibility of having children. The *Poskim* have very detailed guidelines regarding these cases. See אחיעזר כ׳ג כד׳ז׳ה: and *Igrot Moshe* אה׳ע־ח׳׳א, and others in אגר׳מ.

76. *Igrot Moshe*, Even Hoezer.

77. See *Otzar Haposkim* to Even Ho'ezer chap. 23; *Torat Chesed* no. 43; *Chavatzelet Hasharon* (pg. 230) quoting *Ezer Mikodesh* (to chap. 23); *Mishneh Halachot* vol. 5, pg. 315.

78. See *Igrot Moshe*, Even Ho'ezer Vol. I, pg. 155.

79. Yevamot (12b) beginning "shalosh".

80. Even Ho'ezer, vol. I, no. 66.

possibly result, this does not constitute "wasting of the husband's seed"

The hysterectomy case is a most significant one. We consider the act one of *Tashmish kiderech kol ho'oretz*, marital relations performed in a normal fashion, even though the semen cannot possibly enter the woman's womb for she has no womb to speak of. Based on this case, many *Poskim* have concluded that women who so choose may insert a cloth *(Moch)* in their body before *Tashmish* to prevent pregnancy. If the *moch* is inserted deeply enough so that it doesn't interfere with the act of *Tashmish*,[81] and, in the words of Maharshal,[82] "the bodies derive pleasure one from the other," this too is considered *Tashmish kiderech kol ho'oretz*, and would therefore not constitute a violation of *Hashchosas Zera*.

One could still argue the point and distinguish very simply between the cases: Only in the situation of the pregnant wife and the woman too young or too old to have children, etc., where the *Tashmish* on its own will not lead to pregnancy, is it considered *Tashmish Kiderech Kol Ho'oretz*. But when the woman inserts a *moch* and the obstruction blocking the semen from entering the cervical canal is an unnatural one, perhaps then relations would not constitute *Tashmish kiderech kol ho'oretz*, and would therefore be forbidden?

This point of distinction, however, does not seem to be valid. We know that even if a woman caused herself to become sterile by drinking a potion of herbs, she may continue to be with her husband. Clearly then, even an intentional and unnatural induced inability to become pregnant would not automatically label the *Tashmish* as *Hashchosas Zera*.[83]

It is based on this line of reasoning that Maharshal,[82] Rabbi Shneur Zalman of Lublin,[83] and many other great *Poskim* ruled that use of a *moch* during *Tashmish* to prevent pregnancy is allowed.

81. *Igrot Moshe*, Even Ho'ezer vol. I, no. p. 163.
82. *Yam Shel Shlomo*, Yevamot, chap. 1, section 8.
83. See *Torat Chesed* (pgs. 116d-117a).

In the words of the Chazon Ish,[84] "Use of a *Moch* during *Tashmish* is allowed for all women (even when pregnancy would pose no danger to their lives) ... This was the decision of our great teachers who attained divine inspiration, Maharshal of blessed memory ...

The issue of the use of the *moch* is based on an interpretation of the Gemara in Yevamot (12b): in three special cases, when there exists a possibility that pregnancy may occur and cause danger to the life of the mother, Rabbi Meir allows the woman to use a *Moch*. The contemporaries of Rabbi Meir disagree and argue that "heaven will have mercy" and that "G-d will protect the foolish people who do not look after themselves."[95]

According to Rashi, the Rabbis (whose opinion was accepted in their argument with Rabbi Meir) forbid the use of a *moch*, even though the woman's life is in danger. Other *Rishonim* ask how this can possibly be the view of the Rabbis? Do we not know that even in a doubtful case of danger to human life *(safek sakanat nefashot)* we are allowed to violate almost all Torah laws?

Rashi obviously holds that use of a *Moch* during *Tashmish* is forbidden under normal circumstances. In these three situations the Rabbis disagree with Rabbi Meir, disregarding the possible danger to life. Since the threat to life is not even considered a 50/50 possibility,[86] and the general attitude of people is not to worry about the danger involved in these special situations,[87] therefore the Rabbis did not consider these cases as constituting *sofek sakana* to permit the violation of any prohibitions.

Were the danger more obvious (50/50 or a greater probability) or were it the general reaction of people to be concerned even about a minimal threat to life, then even the Rabbis would agree

---

84. Even Ho'ezer, chap. 37.
85. Tehillim 116, 6.
86. See *Ahiezer* vol. I, no. 23; *Zemach Zedek* quoted there; *Torat Chesed*, no. 44; *Avnei Nezer*, Even Ho'ezer, vol. I, no. 81. It is surprising that Rabbi Moshe Feinstein *(Igrot Moshe* Even Ho'ezer, vol. I, no. 64) rejects this widely-accepted opinion. See also next note.
87. *Mishneh Halachot*, vol. 5, pg. 314. See also *Pe'er Hador* (biography of Chazon Ish) vol. 3, pg. 184, that this was also the view of the Chofetz Chaim and the Chazon Ish.

with Rabbi Meir in permitting the use of a *moch* during *Tashmish*.

Most other *Rishonim*[88] disagree with Rashi's understanding of Rabbi Meir. They feel that Rabbi Meir not only allows the use of a *moch*, but *requires* it. Since Rabbi Meir considers this a situation of *sofek sakana*, he rules that one is *not allowed* to be stringent. If the doctors assess someone's condition as dangerous and think that he must eat on Yom Kippur, that person is *not allowed* to fast.[89]

It is a bit unclear exactly how much of Rashi's interpretation of the Gemara is rejected by the other *Rishonim*. The Maharshal (and his group of *Poskim*) understand that the other *Rishonim* hold that use of a *moch* during *Tashmish* is always allowed, and in this case of the far-fetched *sofek sakanah*, Rabbi Meir and the *Chachomim* only disagree as to whether the *moch* is obligatory.

Rabbi Chaim Ozer Grodzensky[90] (and his group of *Poskim*) understand that the other *Rishonim* also agree with Rashi that use of a *moch* during *Tashmish* would normally be forbidden, for since it does partially interfere with the *Tashmish*, this would not be considered *kiderech kol ho'oretz* and would therefore constitute *hashchosas zera*. Only in the situation where the wife's life is in danger did the other *Rishonim* mean to say that there is no violation of *hashchosas zera*. In this situation, it is most natural for the husband to do something to protect his wife from any possible danger resulting from the *Tashmish*, and therefore use of the *moch* is considered *kiderech kol ho'oretz*.

Even the Chazon Ish, who assumed the Maharshal's view to be more correct, in practical application only allowed use of the *moch* during *Tashmish* in the case of *sakana*.[91] "And even if we

---

88. Quoted by *Shitta Mekubetzet* to Ksubos (39a).
89. *Be'er Heitev* to Orach Chaim chap. 618, section 3; *Torat Chesed* pg. 112c. See, however, *Avnei Nezer*, Choshen Mishpat, no. 193, who questions this premise.
90. *Ahiezer* vol. I, no. 23; vol. III, no. 24, 5.
91. According to the *Pischai Tshuva*, (Even Hoezer 23:2) two great *Poskim*, Rabbi Akiva Eiger and the Chasam Sofer, forbid the use of any *moch* during *tashmish* even when the woman's life would be endangered in the event of a pregnancy. The overwhelming majority of the later *Poskim* have not accepted this view, and have attempted to explain away the two responsa as being misunderstood by the *Pischai Tshuva*:

should choose to be more strict regarding all healthy women, and forbid the use of a *moch* during *Tashmish* just as we forbid its use after *Tashmish*, still in a situation of hazard we should allow the use of the *moch* only during *Tashmish* and not after." And thus he concluded his *Psak:* (ruling) "According to the Din it would appear that in an instance of hazard to the woman's life, we may allow the use of a *moch* during *Tashmish*.[92]

The case dealt with by Rabbi Akiva Eiger in his responsum did not really concern a woman whose life was in danger, but rather one who would suffer extreme pain during childbirth. Rabbi Akiva Eiger apparently felt that with respect to our issue, this woman should be treated the same as any other normal healthy woman and, therefore, not be permitted to use a *moch*. But in the event that there would be a real threat to a woman's life if a pregnancy were to result, even Rabbi Akiva Eiger would allow use of the *moch* during *tashmish*. (*Igrot Moshe*, Even Hoezer, Vol. I, no. 64.)

The Chasam Sofer, in his responsum, dealt with a case where the husband had not yet fulfilled his mitzva of *piryah v'rivyah*, and the doctors forbade this woman from every having normal relations (non-contraceptive). If one were to follow the logic of R. Chaim Ozer, that only in an instance of *sakana* is the *tashmish* with a *moch* still considered *kederech kol ho-oretz*, then in this case, where the husband has no children and his wife is medically unable ever to bear him any children, since the halacha would require the husband to divorce his wife and marry another woman who would be able to bear children, we no longer have the right to declare this as תשמיש כדרך כל הארץ. See p.230 חבצלת חשרון חלק אבן עזר. But in a case where the husband does have some children, and the halacha would not require him to divorce his wife (even if he had not yet fulfilled *pirya v'rivya* (See פתחי תשובה אבן העזר קנד ס'ק כ'ו אבני נזר אה"ע ס' א) or in a situation where the doctor temporarily forbid her from becoming pregnant, then even the Chasam Sofer would probably have allowed use of the *moch* during *tashmish*.

See however חבצלת השרון volume 3 p. 101 that Rabbi Babbad himself feared to issue a *psak* against the simple reading of the decision of the Chasam Sofer, although he was really convinced that the Chasam Sofer would have agreed to allow use of the *moch* in his special case.

92. Rabbeinu Tam disagrees with Rashi's interpretation of the gemara. He understood that the *moch* spoken of was to be used *after* tashmish, to wipe away all the semen and thereby prevent pregnancy. Since according to Rabbeinu Tam all women may do this (even if pregnancy would not pose a danger to their lives), and this type of *moch* is sufficient to prevent pregnancy, Rabbi Meir would never allow the woman whose life is in danger to use a *moch* during *tashmish*, as this would be a violation of *hashchosas zera*. We only allow violation of Torah laws in a situation of *sakanas nefashos*, if the goal of saving the life can not be accomplished in a permissible fashion. (See Ahiezer Vol. 1, no. 23.)

Nowadays, instead of a *moch*, a diaphragm is used. The diaphragm is placed in front of the cervical opening and prevents the sperm from entering. Since the diaphragm interferes virtually not at all with *Tashmish*, it might follow that its use should be allowed even according to Rabbi Chaim Ozer and his group of *Poskim*. This case should certainly be considered *Tashmish kiderech kol horetz*. Such indeed was the view of Maharsham.[93]

It should be noted, however, that use of a diaphragm may cause a new problem in *Hilchot Niddah:* The inexperienced woman may scratch her body either with her fingernails or with the plastic disc, and may later be unable to ascertain whether the blood before her is *dam makoh*, from a cut, or *dam niddah*. In such instances, a competent Rabbi must be consulted.[94]

Even Maharsham however, practically speaking, *halacha l'maaseh*, only allowed use of the diaphragm in a situation where the woman's life would be placed in danger in the event of pregnancy.

What about use of a condom? Is this considered a normal act of *Tashmish* since "both bodies derive pleasure one from the other,"[92] or, since the semen does not even enter the vaginal area at

---

The majority of the *Rishonim* disagree with Rabbeinu Tam, and interpret the gemara as Rashi, that the *moch* spoken of is used *during* tashmish. Exactly what aspect of Rabbeinu Tam's *p'shat* do they reject?

Most *Poskim* assume that the other *Rishonim* felt that the medical facts were not correct. The use of the *moch* after *tashmish* would not suffice to protect the woman's life. The use of the *moch during tashmish* would be much safer. But even according to the other *Rishonim*, use of a *moch* after *tashmish* would be allowed by all women, even where pregnancy would pose no danger to her life. (*Toras Chesed*, no. 42; *Avnei Nezer, Even Hoezer* no. 79 and 81).

The Chazon Ish disagrees and is of the opinion that, although Rabbeinu Tam felt use of a *moch* during *tashmish* was forbidden even in the situation where pregnancy would pose a danger to the woman's life, and use of a *moch* after *tashmish* is *always* allowed, the other *Rishonim* held just the opposite — that use of a *moch* after *tashmish* is always forbidden, even in the situation of danger to life. This controversy has practical relevance today regarding use of a douche after coitus.

93. Responsa vol. I no. 58
94. See "*Halochos of Niddah*," Shimon Eider, pg. 122, quoting Rabbi Moshe Feinstein.

all, this certainly is not *Tashmish kidarko* and therefore a violation of *hashchosas zera?*. Rabbi Chaim Ozer is quoted[95] as having assumed that even this case is considered *kiderech kol ho'oretz*. But the overwhelming majority of *Poskim*[96] following him have *not* accepted his view. According to the majority opinion, even if the woman's life would be endangered in the event of pregnancy, we would not allow the husband to use a condom.

In reality, even the lenient view of Rabbi Chaim Ozer has probably been quoted out of context. In his responsum,[97] he deals with a special case where the woman's life would be in danger if she were to become pregnant again. According to his opinion (as explained above), use of a diaphragm during *Tashmish* in such circumstances is considered *kiderech kol ho'oretz*. To this Rav Chaim Ozer adds that even use of a condom under such circumstances would also be considered *kiderech kol ho'oretz*. However, if the woman is perfectly healthy, Rabbi Chaim Ozer would most probably agree that a condom would not be allowed. If, according to Rav Chaim Ozer, use of a diaphragm is not *kiderech kol ho'oretz* (if the wife is healthy), even though the sperm enters the vagina since it is artifically blocked from passing through the cervical canal, certainly he would agree that use of a condom, which artifically prevents the sperm from even entering the vagina, would not be considered *kiderech kol ho'oretz*.

According to Rabbi Menachem Manesh Babbad of Tarnapol[98] and Rabbi Meir Arik[99] and many other *Poskim*, spermicidal jellies or foam sprays do not constitute a violation of *hashchosas zera*. The act of *Tashmish* is completely normal *kiderech kol ho'oretz*.[100] According to *Igrot Moshe*,[101] the same is true of the use of the Pill.

95. *Igrot Moshe*, Even Ho'ezer, vol. I, end of responsum 63.

96. See *Dover Meisharim* (by Chebiner Rov), vol. I, end of no. 20. Even Maharsham, who was known to be most lenient in his decisions, did not accept this point of view. See also *Igrot Moshe* in note 95.

97. *Ahiezer* vol. III, no. 24,5.

98. *Chavazelet HaSharon*, p. 231.

99. Vol. I, no. 131. See also *Igrot Moshe* Even Ho'ezer, vol. I, no. 62.

100. The opposing minority opinion is recorded in *Mishneh Halachot*, vol. 5, pgs. 287, and 316-317.

There is no problem of *hashchosas zera* since the *Tashmish* is not affected in the least.

Use of the Pill, however, poses two additional halachic problems:[101] 1) staining will often result from the change of hormone levels in the woman's body. This will cause the woman to become a *Niddah*. Although the bleeding does not relate to a normal menstrual cycle, the halacha still considers this to be a regular din of *Niddah*, and 2) use of the pill has been ascertained to be dangerous. It should therefore be forbidden on the basis of *V'nishmartem me'od l'nafshoseichem*, the biblical command enjoining us to protect our health.[102]

As medical science improves the Pill, the above hazards may disappear or diminish; thus in the future, these considerations may become minor in arriving at a halachic determination of the permissibility of this form of contraception.[103]

The author wishes to thank Moshe Rosenberg for his assistance in the preparation of this essay.

---

101. Even Ho'ezer vol. I, no. 65.
102. Devorim (4,15). See Brochos (32b).
103. "Update on Oral Contraceptives", by E. Conneil M.D., in *Current Problems in Obstetrics and Gynecology* Vol. II no. 8, April 1979. p. 28.

   "The oral contraceptive is the most effective method of birth control ever developed. It does not satisfy all the criteria of the "ideal contraceptive" but it comes closer to it than any other technique in the history of mankind. Its use is accompanied by the development of a number of side effects, both major and minor. The precise incidence of each of these is still a matter of debate, but it appears that earlier estimates may perhaps have been too high. In addition, as more and more woman move to the lower-dose preparations, even these new estimates may again prove to be too high. Continued study has also pointed out many ancillary beneficial side effects of the pill."

Various Aspects Of Adoption

Rabbi Dr. Melech Schachter

"Whosoever rears an orphan in his own house is considered by Scripture as if he fathered the child... Whosoever teaches Torah to the son of his companion, Scripture considers him as if he begat him."[1] These statements are corroborated by quotations from Scripture. Bathiah, the daughter of Pharaoh, saved and reared Moses, and was therefore called his mother.[2] Michal, the daughter of King Saul, reared the children of her sister Merab, and was therefore considered their mother. Ruth's child was also called the son of Naomi[3] by virtue of the fact that he was reared by Naomi. For the same reason the Psalmist called the children of Jacob also the children of Joseph[4] because he fed them.

These and other similar statements may be quoted to prove that adoption, rearing, and teaching someone else's children are most meritorious virtues for which one is honored as a parent.

Horav Yosef Dov Soloveitchik has been quoted regarding the

---

1. סנהדרין יט ב
2. דברי הימים א, ד יח
3. רות ד יז
4. תהלים עז טז

---

*Member of Faculty of Yeshiva University
and Former Co-ordinator of the Beth Din
of the Rabbinical Council of America*

positive[5] aspects of raising someone else's child as one's own (e.g.
adopting), thereby partially living up to the commandment of
reproduction *(Piryah v'rivyah)*. The Rov bases it upon the word of
the Rambam that he who is seized by the desire for learning so
that there remains no room for the earthly desire of being married,
as did Ben Azai who remained a bachelor, is considered no sinner,[6]
because his Torah disciples will be considered his offspring.
Similarly, adopting a child and raising him in a Torah-true
atmosphere and giving him a Torah-true education in a traditional
yeshiva will be considered as if he partially abided by the mitzva of
reproduction. This is also the opinion of R. Shlomo Kluger.[7] The
lofty practice of rearing someone else's child with parental devotion
is moral conduct on the highest level. Consequently, the adopted
child is ethically bound to display the highest regard for his
adoptive parents and hold them in the highest esteem, possibly
even surpassing the one displayed by children towards their own
parents.[8]

However, from the viewpoint of Jewish Law, adoption does
not constitute natural relationship. Should the adopted child smite
or curse his adoptive parents, he will not be subject to the stern
punishment reserved for a child acting this way toward his natural
parents.[9] All forbidden incestual relationships apply only to
relatives by nature, not by adoption.[10] If the adoptive father is a
Kohen or a Levi it does not make the adopted child also a Kohen
or a Levi. When the adoptive parent dies, the adopted child should
obviously mourn the loss in a proper fashion, including the

5. In a lecture, "Adoption in Jewish Law," given by Rabbi Herschel Schachter,
   son of the author and Rosh HaKollel of R.I.E.T.S. of Y.U. A synopsis appeared
   in *Chavrusa*, Nissan 5742, published by Rabbinic Alumni of R.I.E.T.S.
6. רמב״ם הלכות אישות פ׳ ט״ו הלכה ג
7. חכמת שלמה, אבן העזר ס״א ס״א
8. שמות רבה פרק ד שכל הפותח פתחו לחברו חייב בכבודו יותר מאביו ואמו
9. שמות כא טו ובחולין יא ב ״דלמא לאו אביו הוא, אלא ...״ הרי שבכל מקום שכתוב
   בתורה אביו ואמו הכוונה להורים הטבעיים דוקא.
10. באבן העזר סימן טו סעיף יא: מותר אדם בבת אשת אביו שיש לה מאיש אחר ואפילו...
    הגדלה בבית בין האחין. ״הרי שאיסור עריות תלוי בלידה טבעית ולא בגידול ביחד עם
    שאר הבנים.

recitation of the kaddish.[11] But he is not subject to all the minute regulations governing the mourning of a child for his natural parents.[12] Nor does an adopted child free his adoptive mother from "chalitzah" in case his adoptive father dies without issue.[13]

When there is an established custom to have only one mourner recite the kaddish, the adopted child should not take this privilege away from one who mourns his natural parents.[14] Obviously, the same preference would apply to "davening" before the omud and leading the congregation in prayer throughout the eleven months and on the subsequent anniversaries of their demise, their yahrzeits.

In case a boy infant is adopted right after his birth, he should be circumcised on the eighth day.[15] The infant may, of course, be named after a deceased parent of any one of the adoptive parents. In case the boy infant is the first child of his natural Jewish mother, and neither one of his natural parents is a descendant of Kohanim or Levites, the adoptive parents should have a *Pidyon Haben* celebration on the 31st day after the infant's birth, irrespective of the status of the adoptive parents, whether or not they are descendants of either Kohanim or Levites. Later in this article we shall discuss this law in greater detail.

As for the question of inheritance, in the absence of a will, no one has a right to inherit the estate of an adoptive parent in preference to blood relations. However, everyone has a right to bequeath his possessions to anyone he desires. Adopting a child through a civil court may be considered equivalent to the writing of a will, bequeathing to the adopted child his entire estate or a proportionate percentage thereof.[16]

---

11. דין קדיש יתום באו״ח סי׳ קלב ט״ו בהגה, והמג״א בס״ק ב מאריך בדינים אלו ומסיק שלא רק בן הנפטר אומר קדיש אלא ״שאפשר גם להשכיר אחד לומר קדיש במקומו״. ועיין בביאור הלכה בסוף הסימן ״ואם בעה״ב מגדל בביתו...״ ועיין שדי חמד אבלות קנו שהמאומץ צריך לומר קדיש לכבוד המאמצים אותו על פי מ״ר המצוטט לעיל אות 9.

12. פתחי תשובה ביו״ד שם סק״ז

13. דברים כה ה: ״ובן אין לו״ וביבמות כב ב ״עיין עליו״. ולפיכך ״כל שיש לו בן מכל מקום״ ואפילו ממזר פוטר את אשת אחיו מן היבום״ שם במשנה בעמוד א. ״אפילו ממזר״ ובלבד שהוא בן טבעי, דבלא״ה אינו נקרא בן.

14. שו״ת חת״ס חאו״ח סי׳ קסד

15. קידושין כט א

16. עיין שדי חמד אות מ כלל לח

All this, moreover, does not in any way affect the rights of the adopted child with respect to his inheritance from his *natural* parents. Rambam[17] writes that the language of the Torah[18] "and the law of inheritance shall be unto the Children of Israel a statute of judgment" implies that this has a religious connotation and is not merely a civil matter. Consequently, his legal adoption would not diminish his religious rights as the son of his natural parents.

Knowledge of adoption should not be concealed

Should a child be told that he is adopted? For various reasons, it is wise for the child to know his true status. There is the consideration of the possible consequences should the child, when he or she grows up, wish to marry someone who halachically is forbidden. An adopted girl, who was converted, would not be permitted to marry a Kohen. If the antecedents of the child are known, he would have to avoid marrying a close natural relative; if the antecedents are not known, he would have to avoid marrying someone with a similar problem, such as another adopted child.

There is an additional factor to be kept in mind when adopting a child. The Lubavitcher Rebbe raised the problem of *yichud v'kiruv basar*. According to Jewish Law, a man and a woman, not married to each other, are forbidden to hug and kiss one another or even to be alone together except when they are closely related, e.g. mother and son, father and daughter, etc. This prohibition is especially stringent when the woman is married to another man. How do we allow the adopted son, after he matures, to embrace his adoptive mother and kiss her or even to sleep with her in the same room all alone?[19]

Rabbi Eliezer Wohldenberg, a great sage of the Holy Land, tends to be lenient in this respect if the adopted child is ignorant of the status that he is adopted. It seems that Horav Soloveitchik of Boston also tends to be lenient because in the course of all the years during which the adopted child was raised the relationship was that of mother and son or father and daughter.

---

17. ריש פ"ו מהלכות נחלות

18. במדבר כז יא: והיתה לבני ישראל לחוקת משפט

19. אוצר הפוסקים לאה"ע סוף חלק ט, עמ' קל, והערה ארוכה עמ' 263

However, the late Rabbi Joshua Ahrenberg, head of the Beth Din in Tel Aviv and author of *Dvar Yehoshua*,[20] vehemently disapproved of such a lenient attitude. The Chazon Ish[21] likewise sided with the stringent opinion.

Whether to adopt a Jewish child

For the prospective parents, a major question is whether to adopt a Jewish or non-Jewish child. There are special problems arising from either course of action. We will now proceed to examine the halachic questions aising from adoption of either type of child.

The possible illegitimacy of the adopted Jewish child

A very important aspect in connection with Jewish children offered for adoption is the problem of illegitimacy. Should the adopted child be an offspring of an adulterous relationship, i.e. the mother being married to one and having the child from another, then it is illegitimate (*mamzer*) and is biblically forbidden to intermarry with legitimate Jewish children.

Halachically, the child of an immoral woman, who still lives with her husband, is not considered a *mamzer* because we attribute the fatherhood to the one who cohabits with the mother most of the time. This decision falls into the category of "majority rules" or "majority prevails."[22]

In the case of an unmarried girl giving birth to a child, this majority principle is obviously not applicable.[23] There is reason to fear that the child is the product of an incestuous relationship which renders him a *mamzer*. (Even though the majority of men are not related to the mother of the child, yet there is the possibility of the mother making the advances and approaching the man in which case the principle of *kovua* negates the principle of majority.)

---

20. ח״ג אה״ע סימן טז
21. אוצר הפוסקים שם, פאר הדור חלק ג עמוד מ
22. אבן העזר ד כו
23. שם

In the case of a child born out of wedlock, the law prescribes a thorough investigation. If the father of the child is not a relative, then both mother and child are permitted to be married to fellow Jews. If the father turns out to be a close relative, the mother is termed a *zonah* and is not allowed to be married to a Kohen, and the child is a *mamzer* and is not allowed to be married to a legitimate child.

Most of the children offered for adoption are born to unwed mothers. If the mother refuses to cooperate in the investigation, the mother is not permitted to marry a Kohen, and the child in question is termed a *"shetuki"* — a possible *mamzer*. If the mother's identity is unknown and the question is centered exclusively on the child, the *"kovua"* principle may be ignored, and on the basis of the majority principle — most men are not related to the mother — the child is considered legitimate and permitted to marry other legitimate Jews. This is the view of Rabbi Ezekiel Landau.[24] There are, however, many scholars who differ with him because at the time when the child was born the doubtful aspect of the child's father, involving the subsequent marriageability of both the mother and the child, immediately arose. The disappearance of the mother can therefore not alter the negative decision for both of them.

Whenever a child from a Jewish mother is up for adoption all these possibilities must be taken into consideration.

Adoption of non-Jewish children

The aspects of adoption discussed hitherto are all valid if the natural mother of the adopted child is Jewish. Should the mother be non-Jewish, most of the above problems are eliminated. Yet, the adoption of non-Jewish children inescapably presents an acute problem. Non-Jewish children are adopted by Jewish couples and are raised as Jews. Some of the boys go through a bar-mitzva ceremony, and like all their Jewish friends, they declare themselves as full-fledged members of the Jewish congregation, without

---

"circumcision and immersion for the sake of conversion"[26] Sometimes these children even assume the status of Kohen and Levi. These adopted children later intermarry with children of Jewish parentage — all under the assumption that they are Jewish.

However, there is a very serious halachic problem involved — is it possible to perform a valid conversion on a Gentile infant? And if conversion cannot be valid until the child is mature, how can we assume that the child at that point will want to be Jewish?

There is one Talmudic source in favor of such practice. Rav Huna maintains that a minor can become a proselyte "in accord with the Beth Din."[27] The knowledge of the three rabbis, constituting the Beth Din, is potent enough to bestow Jewishness upon the child. One may wonder: since the responsibility of so tremendous a change, a change of faith, obviously necessitates the mature consent of the party involved — how then could a minor, a small child and at times only an infant, be converted to Judaism without his consent? The answer to this question is to be found in the basic assumption that to be a Jew is a z'chus, a privilege, and one can perform a meritorious deed in behalf of another without consulting him.[28] Hence, the minor's consent is not necessary.

It is on this basis that many rabbis, and sometimes even mohalim alone, participate in the circumcision of newly adopted non-Jewish children with the assumption that in due time proper immersion will also take place and thus consecrate them in their new faith. Such practice is to be severely criticised, because even on the basis of this Talmudic passage, there is need of immersion in the presence of a Beth Din and, unfortunately, this absolutely essential procedure hardly ever takes place. The very same rabbis or mohalim do not pursue the matter any further, and the adopted child is raised as a full-fledged Jew without further ado. This practice could perhaps be followed in a well-organized Jewish community like the Kehillas of yore. In those days, every Jew was registered as such and the status of every individual was scrutinized and carefully followed. In American Jewish life this is obviously not possible.

---

27. כתובות יא: גר קטן מטבילין על דעת בית דין

28. בכתובות שם: "מאי קמ"ל דזכות הוא לו וזכין לאדם שלא בפניו כו'"

After an analysis of conditions nowadays, we must come to
the conclusion that Rav Huna's statement is not altogether
applicable today. Many Jewish couples who adopt non-Jewish
children are non-observant themselves. These adopted children that
are officially converted to Judaism are brought up in an
atmosphere of Sabbath violation and total disregard for kashruth
and all other precepts of the Torah. Can this kind of Judaism be
considered a z'chus, a privilege, that would give us the right to
perform the conversion ceremony without their mature consent?
(We are all aware of the celebrated statement that doing a mitzva
under command is greater than doing it voluntarily, but it would
be preposterous to assume that not doing a mitzva which we were
commanded to do is greater than not doing it when not
commanded to do it.) Even when the consent of the child's natural
parents is obtained to have him adopted by Jews and reared in the
Jewish faith, the predominant view of most early Talmudic
scholars is that the Beth Din's accord is still required, and all on
the assumption that this change of faith constitutes a z'chus, a
privilege. Obviously, the way conditions are today, it is by far a
greater z'chus to remain a non-Jew than to become a Jew and
violate every commandment.

It is also important to note with reference to the concept of
Jewishness as being a z'chus, a privilege, that the Avnei Nezer
maintains that the entire privilege concept applies only when the
recipient of the benefit is aware of it. This is an additional reason
for not concealing the fact of adoption from a child. According to
the Avnei Nezer, should the non-Jewish child be raised in
ignorance of the beneficial status bestowed upon him, the entire
conversion ceremony is ineffective and in vain.[28]

One could argue that the adopted child may in due time join
the baale tshuvah movement and thus the conversion will
retroactively be a privilege. Aside from the fact that this is
unlikely, in the Responsa of Rabbi Elya Pruzhiner we find that if
the privilege aspect is not evident at the time of conversion and is
based only on the possibility thereof in the future, the conversion

---

28a. אבני נזר, אה"ע, קצד אות ד

is not valid.[29]

The question may still be raised in the case of a genuinely observant Jewish couple that wishes to adopt a non-Jewish child and have him or her immersed for the sake of conversion in the presence of a Beth Din in accord with Rav Huna's statement — are we justified to do it?

Before we answer this question there is yet another point to be considered. Rav Yosef added his remark to that of Rav Huna that when the non-Jewish minor, who was converted to Judaism in the presence of a Beth Din, matures, that is when he grows up, he can nullify the conversion ceremony and go back to his former status and remain a non-Jew.[30] There is a difference of opinion among the early scholars as to the exact interpretation of this statement. With reference to the case discussed in the Talmud of a non-Jewish girl who was converted to Judaism in the presence of a Beth Din, then married and divorced while still a minor, we do not grant her the *Kesubah* immediately, lest upon maturity she rejects Judaism and nullifies the act of conversion.[31]

How and when does this rejection take place? Some maintain: a day before her maturity, before her twelfth birthday, she begins to behave demonstratively in a non-Jewish manner; she eats *trefa* food or violates the Sabbath and so she continues to behave several days after she reaches maturity.[32] On the other hand, Tosafot and other *Rishonim* emphasize the aspect of her consent upon maturity to remain a Jewess. The *kesubah* is granted to her when she matures and demonstratively behaves like a Jewess.[33] The difference between the negative and the positive interpretations imply a difference in the concept of the conversion performed "al daas Beth Din." Does this kind of conversion in accord with the Beth Din immediately go into effect in full force, with only this

---

29. שו״ת הליכות אליהו חאה״ע סי׳ לא

30. כתובות יא א: אמר רב יוסף הגדילו יכולין למחות

31. בכתובות שם: ״יהבינן לה כתובה דאזלה ואכלה בגיותה? לכי גדלה ... כיון שהגדילה שעה אחת ולא מיחתה שוב אינה יכולה למחות.״

32. עי׳ שיטה מקוצבת: כגון שהתחילה מנהג גיות יום לפני גדלותה, וכן נהגה יום או יומים לאחר גדלותה.

33. תוספות שם ד״ה לכי: לכי גדלה ונהגה מנהג יהודית

weakness that it could be rejected upon maturity, or is this conversion conditioned upon the child's subsequent consent? The difference in halacha is obvious.

Suppose the converted child registers neither a confirmative consent nor a definite rejection, what then? If we assume that the conversion went into effect in full force and can only be nullified by a definite rejection, as long as this rejection was not forthcoming, as long as the converted child did not flagrantly and demonstratively behave in a non-Jewish manner when he or she reached maturity, the conversion stands and remains irrevocable. If, on the other hand, we are to assume that the original conversion is conditioned upon the child's subsequent consent, that is upon a positive, demonstrative Jewish behavior at the time of maturity, as long as this consent was not forthcoming the child remains non-Jewish. And so from this viewpoint, even if the child met all other requirements, namely, it went through the entire procedure of conversion in the presence of a qualified Beth Din and it has been reared in an observant atmosphere, as long as the child fails to demonstrate upon maturity a definite Jewish behavior, such as putting on t'fillin or observing the Sabbath, the original conversion remains ineffective.

In connection with Rav Huna's statement that since to be a Jew is a privilege, a non-Jewish child can be converted to Judaism in the presence of a Beth Din on the principle that the rabbis may perform a meritorious deed in behalf of the child without his mature consent — in connection with this statement there is a difference of opinion as to whether its validity is biblical or only rabbinic. If it is only rabbinically valid, then only to the extent of rabbinic laws, such as the wine touched by a non-Jew that becomes "nessech," we consider the child Jewish. But we do not permit such a minor to marry one from Jewish parentage, nor do we consider the "shechita" of such a minor valid, even if adult shochtim watch him — all because biblically the child's status is that of a non-Jew, a non "Bar Zvicha." (This is so unless we assume that the Rabbis sometimes have the power to set aside a biblical law even when active violation is in involved.[34]) If, on the

---

34. יש כח ביד חכמים לעקור דבר מה"ת אפילו בקום ועשה. עיין יבמות צב. ועי' תוס' כתו' שם ד"ה מטבילין.

other hand, Rav Huna's statement is biblically sound, we consider him a full-fledged Jew in every respect even insofar as to marry a Jewess or to slaughter in the presence of others.

It seems that the above question, as to whether the child's rejection upon maturity nullifies the conversion or his affirmation confirms it, depends upon this problem. If we assume that the conversion is biblically sound and we allow the child to marry a Jewess, apparently the conversion is not conditioned on something that is yet to happen. As to the question, how do we allow such a marriage since the child could possibly reject Judaism upon reaching maturity, the answer is that in all likelihood the child, raised in a genuinely religious atmosphere, will continue to be observant after it matures.[35] On the other hand, if we assume that the conversion is not biblically sound, it is because it depends upon the child's *positive* consent retroactively at which time we probably interrogate and warn him regarding the difficulties involved in the observance of Torah and mitzvot,[36] in the same spirit as Naomi warned Ruth. Since this procedure is rarely followed, the conversion of non-Jewish children is often of questionable validity.

Although Rabbi Moshe Feinstein is usually quite definitive in his halachic decisions, in the course of a lengthy responsum on the subject of whether to adopt a non-Jewish child, he fails to come to a conclusion. He does, however, append the following comment:

> I would add this note of advice, that there is no need
> or purpose in accepting a minor (for conversion) and
> only when an adult non-Jew himself comes for
> genuine reasons should one accept him.[37]

To recapitulate briefly the points we have outlined:

1. Civil adoption does not constitute conversion to Judaism.

2. Unless the adoptive parents are observant, there can be no conversion on the assumption of a z'chus that is in reality a great disadvantage.

---

35. בשט"מ שם: שמן הסתם כשנתחנך מקטנותו בתורת ישראל לא יסור ממנו, ומלתא דלא שכיח היא ולא חיישינן לזה אף בדאורייתא.

36. קלות וחמורות. עיין יבמות מז א ויו"ד רסח ב ועי' שט"מ בכתו' שם

37. אגרות משה יורה דעה קס"ב

3. Even if the above requirements are met, there is need for a positive consent on the part of the adopted child when it reaches maturity, without which the conversion may not be valid halachically.

4. If all the above conditions were to be met, there is yet special precaution to be taken in the case of a girl that she should not marry a Kohen.

Whose "son" is the adopted child?

In Jewish tradition a person is identified by his or her father. This is the way an infant is called at the time of naming it at the circumcision ceremony or at the synagogue, e.g. Isaac son of Abraham, Dinah daughter of Jacob. This is the way a man is called up to the Torah, and this is the way a person is identified in a *kesubah*, (the marital document read under the canopy) and also in a *Get*, the biblical divorcement paper nullifying the marital bond. An adopted child presents a problem in this area. Is the child to be known as the son or daughter of the adoptive father or of the natural father, or the "son of Abraham our ancestor" in case of non-Jewish parentage, as a convert is usually called? How can we call a person the son or daughter of Mr. B, the adoptive father, when he is really not the father?

A. When a *Get* is written

This problem is particularly acute in writing a *Get*, where the slightest deviation from the truth may invalidate the document. According to one authority, mentioning a grandfather as the father renders the *Get* ineffective, even though grandchildren are usually identified as children.[38] How much more so should the *Get* be invalidated when a totally unrelated man is ascribed as the father of the person! (Perhaps in a case like this when an adopted child grows up, marries and divorces, his father's name should be omitted altogether. Indéed, a *Get* in which a father's name is omitted is valid,[39] while a wrong name renders the *Get* invalid.)[40]

38. בית שמואל אבה"ע סי' קכט ס"ק יט

39. אה"ע קכט פתחי תשובה סק"כ

40. עי' בב"ש שם ס"ק ה. דשינוי גרע טפי

In our Responsa literature we have recorded a case when a man who divorced his wife used his adoptive father's name and then disappeared. There was no way of having him give another *Get* and the woman was faced with the bleak future of remaining an *aguna* — never to remarry again. Ri Halevi[41] validated the *Get* on the basis of the Talmudic dictum that "whosoever rears an orphan in his house is considered as if he fathered the child."[42] However, Tosafot maintains that we find nowhere in the Torah "a wife's child to be called as his child."[43] Rabbi Moshe Sofer differentiates between one who has children of his own — to which case Tosafot's statement refers — and one who has no children of his own when he could be identified as the father of the adopted child.[44]

Rabbi Aaron Gordon likewise took a lenient view and rendered a similar *Get* aceptable.[45] He added an additional source, namely the verse in Joshua XV, 17, where Caleb's father is mentioned by the name of Kenaz erroneously, to which the Talmud[46] answers that he was Kenaz's stepson.

Many Rabbinic scholars oppose this lenient view because the above statements are Aggadic in nature and there is an established principle that no halachic decisions can be made on the basis of Aggada.[47] How would it be if a devout disciple of a great scholar would indicate in his *Get* the name of his revered mentor as his father? Obviously that *Get* would not be valid notwithstanding the Aggadic statement that "whosoever teaches Torah to the son of his companion is as if he begat him."[48]

A famous controversy of a similar case is recorded in detail in *Pischei Tshuva*.[49] The author of *Avodas Hagershuni*[50] took a lenient view in a case where the woman's father's name was

41. שו״ת אמירה נעימה סי׳ קכד
42. סנהדרין יט א וכמו שמצוטט לעיל בהערה ו
43. פסחים נד.
44. שו״ת חת״ס אבן העזר ע״ו
45. בריש ספרו אבן מאיר על שמות גטין
46. תמורה טז א
47. ירושלמי פאה פ״ב ה״ו, ועיין אנציקלופדי׳ תלמודית ח״א ריש עמ׳ כב
48. סנהדרין יט ב וכמצוטט לעיל בהערה ו
49. אה״ע קכט כא
50. סימן נח

written in the *Get* erroneously. His contention was that any item, which, if omitted would not invalidate the *Get*, then an error in that item is insufficient to render the *Get* invalid.[51] However, the author of *Zemach Zedek*[52] and others point out that this assertion refers exclusively to an item which used to be included in the *Get*, namely, the birthplace of each one of the couple. If leniency could at all be applied to a false paternal name, it could perhaps be only if the husband hands the *Get* over directly to his wife. But if it is done through the medium of an agent who was ordered by the husband to hand over the *Get* to "my wife X the daughter of Y" and he hands it over to X the daughter of Z, the divorce is definitely not valid. This great scholar concluded that even if the husband hands the *Get* directly over to her she is not divorced, because the document was written by the scribe under false instructions and therefore is totally worthless. A host of other great Sages are recorded to coincide with this stringent opinion.

What follows is that no adopted child may use his adopted father's name in a *Get* unless it is indicated that he is only his adopted father, as for example, "X, called X the son of Y who raised him" or "who adopted him."[53]

B. When called up to the Torah

A man, the identity of whose father is wrapped in mystery, is to be called up to the Torah as the son of his mother's father.[54] The Taz[55] opposes this decision for fear that should he ever divorce his wife, he will use his grandfather's name as his father and thus render the *Get* invalid. He prefers the man to be called up as is a convert to Judaism, namely, "son of Abraham" since we all are descendants of Avrohom Avinu.

R. Moshe Feinstein[56] writes that a child can be called up to the Torah without any reference to his adoption - for example, simply

51. תוס' גטין פ"א ד"ה ושם
52. סימן פג
53. "פלוני דמתקרי פלוני בן פלוני המגדלו" או "המאמצו"
54. או"ח קלט ג בהגה
55. שם ס"ק א
56. אגרות משה יורה דעה קס"א

as Reuven son of Yaakov. R. Feinstein sees no reason to fear that his origins will thereby be obscured or forgotten. This is also the accepted practice of the British Beth Din, although they caution that this practice should be followed only if there are no other children of the couple, whether natural or adopted.[57]

It should be noted that in the case of a convert who divorces his wife, "the son of Abraham" will not do. It must be stipulated which Abraham is referred to — "the son of Avrohom Avinu."[58] The Taz probably meant to have the adopted son called up as "the son of Avrohom Avinu."[59]

If he prefers to be called up by his adoptive father's name, the word "hamegadlo" should be added to make sure that should he ever have to go through a divorce proceeding the Get would be valid. The additional hamegadlo (who raised him) is particularly essential if the adoptive father is a Kohen or a Levi. Without hamegadlo he will be considered a Kohen and be called up to the Torah first as is his adoptive father. Furthermore, the people may send him up to "duchan" along with his "father" or use him in the ceremony of Pidyon Haben. If the adoptive father is a Levi, he may be called up next to the Kohen, and when he marries the daughter of a Yisroel and is blessed with a son, he may be given erroneous information that there is no need for a Pidyon Haben. The same holds true of an adopted girl whose adoptive father is either a Kohen or a Levi.

Above all, "hamegadlo" will prevent the serious violation of his adoptive mother's ever remarrying without chalitza after his adoptive father's demise.

Should the family have other sons of their own and later in life should one die and his wife would need chalitza, the adopted brother is not the one to go through with this procedure. "Hamegadlo" added to his name will make sure that such a mistake shall never come to pass.

---

57. Dayon Meyer Steinberg, *Responsum on Problems of Adoption in Jewish Law*, Office of the Chief Rabbi, London, 1969, p. 12.
58. אה"ע קכט ב
59. הרב משה פינדלינג בנועם ח"ד עמ' עז

C. When the name is written in the *kesuba*

When the adopted boy or girl is getting married, the name in the *kesuba* "son or daughter of Mr.X" should also be accompanied with the word *"hamegadlo"* indicating that Mr. X is the adoptive father for the same reasons enumerated above. According to the author of the *Nachlas Shivoh*[60] the names in the *kesuba* must be written with the same care as in a *Get*, because should ever that marriage terminate in a *Get* the names of the kesuba will probably serve as guidelines. However, in order that no one should be embarrassed in public, when the *kesuba* is read at the marriage ceremony, the officiating Rabbi should not read aloud the word *hamegadlo.*[61]

D. Naming the adopted baby

When naming the adopted baby at the time of circumcision or in the synagogue, the word *"hamegadlo"* should accompany the name of the adoptive father for the above reasons. Some synagogues issue special documents in which the name of the baby is recorded. This is especially done at the time of bar-mitzva. These documents are framed and kept for future reference. Surely, the word *"hamegadlo"* should be added for subsequent purposes.

At the circumcision ceremony

"Blessed are Thou...Who...Hast commanded us to make (the son) enter into the covenant of Avrohom Avinu." This benediction is recited by the father at the time of his son's circumcision.[62] If the father is not present at the time, the benediction is recited by someone else, customarily by the *"Sandik"* - the one who holds the infant at the circumcision.[63] According to Rabbi Akiva Aiger[64] the grandfather — especially so if he is the *"Mohel"* — should be the one to recite this benediction rather than the *Sandik*, because he, like the father, is obligated to see to it that his grandchild receives a

---

60. סימן יב אות טז
61. *Responsum on Problems of Adoption in Jewish Law*, p. 20.
62. יורה דעה רסח א
63. ברמ"א בשם הטור
64. שו"ת רעק"א סימן מב

Torah-true education, the spiritual implication of ushering him into the covenant of Avrohom Avinu.

In the case of an adopted son, the adoptive father, by virtue of his obligation as such, has obligated himself to give him a Torah-true education. Consequently, preference should be given to him as far as the recitation of this benediction is concerned. Far more preferable is to have the adoptive father act as the *Sandik* and thus avoid all possible argumentation.[65]

Obviously, in the concluding prayer, naming the child, it is reasonable to omit the words *"beyotzei chalotzov"* and *"befree vitno"* and amend the text thus: *"...preserve this child to his adoptive father and mother, and let his name be called in Israel — the son of — hamegadlo. Let the adoptive father rejoice and the let the adoptive mother be glad..."*[66]

At the *Pidyon Haben*

There are two alternatives in the redemption of a first-born son: First and foremost the father is obligated to redeem his son from the Kohen. Secondly, if the father fails to abide by this commandment, then the boy, when he grows into maturity, redeems himself from the Kohen.[67]

In the case of an adopted Jewish child the question begs itself as to whether the adoptive father could perform this redemption. Rabbi Moshe Isserles (Ramo)[68] maintains that, unlike circumcision, no one can act as an agent of the natural father, nor does the Beth Din redeem him without his father. Rabbi Sabbattai Cohen (Shach)[69] differs, maintaining that the principle of agency is applicable to this mitzva as well. Some scholars differentiate between an agent directly ordered by the natural father to represent him at the *Pidyon Haben*, which is valid, and when no such demand was made by the natural father and the adoptive father

---

65. הרב פינדלינג שם בנועם עמ' פח

66. קיים את הילד הזה להמגדלים אותו, ויקרא שמו בישראל פלוני בן פלוני המגדלו. ישמח האב המגדלו ותגל אמו המגדלתו...

67. יו"ד סי' שה סעיפים א וטו

68. יו"ד שם סעיף י

69. ש"ך שם ס"ק יא

wishes to act in his behalf voluntarily, which is not valid. Still others claim that one can voluntarily act in behalf of the natural father as his agent, only that he is not obligated to do so unless he so chooses.[70] The British Beth Din expressed a novel thought on this subject:[71]

> With regard to an adoption case... it could be argued that the adoptive father is able to redeem his adopted son because he is his legal guardian. Proof for this can be adduced from Mamonides [משנה תורה הלכות נחלות יא:י] who states that all affirmative commandments may be performed by the legal guardian on behalf of the child. In this respect, an adoptive father who accepts the responsibility for educating and rearing the child is a legal guardian [מלמד להועיל, יורה דעה, צז, צח]. Rabbi D. Hoffman mentions the case of a Jewish woman who gave birth to a first-born son where the father was non-Jewish. He decides that the Jewish legal guardian may redeem the child without reciting the benediction. [אגרות שרידי אש II, צז] Rabbi Weinberg [משה, יו"ד קצח] considers the case of a Jewish unmarried mother who gives birth to a child and raises doubts as to whether it is the duty of the Beth Din to redeem the child. He quotes authorities who give varying views on this point. [בנין ציון, קד, קה, מנחת אליעזר IV, כד]
>
> It is recommended that the redemption should take place without the usual benediction being recited. Where, however, the Beth Din definitely established that the adopted child is a first-born, without the doubts referred to above, then the adoptive father may recite the usual benediction and should conclude with the words על פדיין הבכור instead of על פדיון הבן.

Because of these different opinions it would be advisable to have the adoptive father perform the *Pidyon Haben* without the recitation of the benedictions — since the validity of any mitzva is

---

70. צדה לדרך והג׳ צבי לצדיק ביו"ד שם
71. *Responsum on Problems of Adoption in Jewish Law*, pp. 25,26.

not affected by the omission of the *brocha*. When the boy grows up, he should redeem himself again, lest the original redemption was not valid on account of the natural father's not ordering anyone to represent him. Obviously, the benediction should again be omitted lest the first redemption was valid. (However, the opinion of the author of the *Aruch Hashulchan*[72] coincides with the *Shach*, to have the *Pidyon Haben* with the benedictions take place on the thirty-first day, and "this seems to be the prevalent custom.")

Parenthetically, in case the natural father of the child dies before the thirty-first day when the ceremony of *Pidyon Haben* is due, there is ample reason to doubt the above procedure of two redemptions. According to the Taz,[73] no one can act as the agent of the infant because the concept of agency is inapplicable to minors.[74] Therefore, he must wait until he matures and redeem himself. While the Shach[75] offers a method to circumvent the problem of agency, a host of scholars agree with the Taz, including the Chazon Ish.[76] In such a case, some tangible sign should be made to serve as a reminder to the child to redeem himself when he grows up. In *Shulchan Aruch*[77] it is suggested to have a silver amulet suspended from his neck to serve as a reminder. If this is impractical, some other method should be undertaken to assure that the child will be aware of the obligation of *Pidyon*.

At Bar Mitzva

Rabbi Elazar's opinion is quoted in the Midrash[78] to the effect that until the son attains the age of thirteen, the father must busy himself with guiding him in the right direction. Henceforth, the father proclaims: "Blessed be He Who Hath freed me from the responsibility for this (child)."[79]

---

72. סימן שח סעיף יד

73. שם ס"ק יא

74. אין שליחות לקטן היכי שיש קצת חוב כבנידון דידן שיקיים המצוה בגופו כשיגדיל

75. נקודות הכסף שם

76. בהוצאה חדשה חאבה"ע דף רפה ע"ב

77. סימן שה סעיף טו

78. בראשית רבה סג יד

79. ברוך שפטרני מענשו של זה

Ramo quotes the custom of having the father of a bar mitzva recite this benediction, usually at the time the son is called up to the Torah.[80] Since this benediction is not mentioned in the Talmud, the name of G-d and His all-pervasive Kingdom[81] are omitted.[82] According to Rabbi Mordecai Jaffe the meaning of the benediction is the exact opposite of the above explanation. It is the bar-mitzva boy who recites this benediction, because according to an Aggadic statement minor children die on account of their parents' sins.[83] Once he reaches bar-mitzva, he is relieved of this responsibility.[84]

Whether this benediction should be recited when the adopted son reaches his bar-mitzva depends upon these two opinions. Assuming the adoptive father has accepted all responsibility for his minor adopted son's misbehavior and that he adopted him on this condition, he could very well recite it when the "son" reaches his bar mitzva. If, however, the adopted son is to recite it, then certainly there is no place for him to say it, because he was never held responsible for his adoptive parents' misdeeds.

As long as the name of G-d and His Kingdom is omitted, there is no reason for a possible violation of a wrong benediction and the adoptive father could recite it without hesitation.

Mutual obligations and rights

Whether or not the acquisitions of the adopted child, either by sheer luck (found treasures) or by the dint of labor (earnings), rightfully belong to the adoptive parents is a matter of serious debate. From a strictly halachic view, raising someone else's child implies one-sided obligations from the adoptive parents to the child but not the other way around.[85] This is so because as a minor, the child cannot be subjected to responsibility and obligations. Yet, these mutual obligations are of supreme importance for the normal

---

80. או"ח רכה ב

81. השם אלוקינו מלך העולם

82. עין בערוך השלחן רכה ד. דנוטה לומר הברכה בשם ומלכות

83. ספרי דברים כד טז: איש בחטאו יומתו. גדולים מתים בעון עצמם; קטנים מתים בעון אבותם.

84. מגן אברהם שם ס"ק ח

85. אבה"ע קיד ב, ורמ"א בחו"מ סי' עב ס"ב

and psychological development of the child as an integrated member of the family unit. Consequently, we have to resort to another legal principle, namely, the Beth Din has a right to declare someone's possession ownerless,[86] because of which the adoptive parents may appropriate the child's earnings since they are considered ownerless.[87]

Sitting in judgment or rendering testimony

Persons related to one another are disqualified from sitting in judgment or rendering testimony for one another.[88] The disqualification of a relative from rendering testimony is considered a biblical law not necessarily rational, because the testimony is rejected under all circumstances whether rendered in favor or disfavor of the relative. Furthermore, even relatives are not suspected to lie and distort the facts.[89] However, disqualifying a relative from sitting in judgment is quite rational. It is assumed that relationship subconsciously motivates the judge to interpret the law one-sidedly. It is for this reason that one should disqualify himself from acting as a judge in a case in which he may have a far-fetched interest in the outcome.[90]

Insofar as adoptive parents and their adopted child are concerned, it stands to reason that neither may act as judge for the other, but may render testimony to establish the facts the way they occurred.[91]

Marrying an adopted brother or sister

Rav, the founder of the Sura Academy, was Rabbi Chiya's nephew from both sides of his family — both his father and his mother were the brother and sister of Rabbi Chiya. Rav's father was Rabbi Chiya's half-brother on his father's side; and Rav's mother was Rabbi Chiya's half-sister on her mother's side.[92] To be

---

86. חו"מ ריש סי' ב הפקר ב"ד הפקר

87. שער עוזיאל ח"ב דף קפד; הרב פינדלינג בנועם שם

88. חו"מ סי' ז סעיף ט, וסי' לג סעיפים ב-ט

89. חו"מ שם סעיף י

90. חו"מ ז-ז

91. הרב פינדלינג שם

92. סנהדרין ח סוף ע"א

more explicit, when Rabbi Chiya's parents married each other, they each had a son and a daughter, respectively, from previous marriages. Those two children were allowed to marry each other since they were not related at all. [93] They were later blessed with a son who turned out to be the famous Rav. Whether Rav's parents were raised in the same home after their parents married (for the second time) is not known. However, it is assumed that even when they are raised together there is no reason to fear that they would be considered brother and sister.[94]

Is an adopted son allowed to marry the natural daughter of his adoptive parents? From a strict biblical viewpoint it is permissible, as is evident from Rav's parents. This seems to be the opinion of the celebrated Rabbi Moshe Sofer,[95] "the Hungarian Groh."[96] The reason he gives is that the two step-children, parents of Rav, were known not to be natural brother and sister. However, on this basis we should not allow the adopted son, who bears the family name of his adoptive parents and is always identified with them, to marry their natural daughter because it is generally not known that they are not natural brother and sister. Furthermore, according to Rabbi Yehuda Hachosid, even two step-children should not marry each other for fear of being identified as brother and sister, the story of Rav's parents notwithstanding.[97] As a matter of fact there is even a Tannaitic opinion to this effect. [98] Consequently, an adopted son should not marry his adoptive parents' natural daughter.[99]

* * *

An additional consideration is the treatment of adopted children by their parents and teachers. Reb Herschel Schachter points to the fact that an adopted child, forsaken by his natural

93. עיין אה"ע טו יא
94. עיין שו"ע שם
95. שו"ת חת"ס אה"ע ח"ב סי' קכה
96. כידוע מה שהגר"א הי' לבני ישראל מליטא הי' החת"ס לבני ישראל מארץ הגר
97. צוואת רבי יהודה החסיד אות כט
98. ראב"י בסוטה מג סוף ע"ב
99. ככה דעת הרב הרב יצחק וייס בהערותיו לספר ליקוטי מאיר של הרב מאיר הלוי שטיינברערג. אמנם לדעת הרב משה פינדלינג בנועם ח"ד עמ' צ יש לב"ד לפרסם הדבר שאינם אח ואחות כדי לבטל המראית עין שבזה.

parents or orphaned by them, is usually more sensitive than children under normal conditions. There is a special biblical command not to vex a widow or an orphan[100] or anyone who feels inferior to others and is therefore very sensitive to the slightest derogatory remark. "One must be careful with orphans and widows because their souls are downcast and their spirits low, even if they be wealthy...one must speak to them kindly and respect them...He, by Whose Words the World was called into existence made a covenant with them, their prayers will be answered. For it is said:...'If he cries unto Me, I shall hearken unto his cry.'[101]

"All this applies to a case where he afflicts them for his own advantage, but when he afflicts them for the purpose of teaching them the Torah or a trade, or to lead them upon the right path, it is permitted. Nevertheless, one must...lead them with kindness, great mercy and with respect as it is said: 'The L-d will plead their cause'..."[102]

Reb Herschel concludes: "When parents or teacher scold an adopted child or stepchild for purposes of *chinuch*, they must be very careful not to be harsh with them as they would naturally be with other children."[103]

---

100. שמות כב כא
101. שם כב
102. רמב״ם הל׳ דעות פ״ו ה״י
103. Chavrusa, Nissan 5742.

Natural Childbirth: May The Husband Attend?

By Dr. Avrahom Steinberg

A. Introduction

Throughout history, women have suffered the pangs of childbirth, almost as a law of nature. The Torah teaches that this was Eve's punishment for eating from the forbidden fruit: בעצב תלדי בנים, "You will bear children in pain."[1] The Catholic church regarded this dictum as an imperative, so that human beings were not allowed to change it under any circumstances. Rabbi I. Jakobovitz quotes a historic fact that "before the discovery of anesthesia, a woman in France was detected in an attempt to ease the pain of childbirth with the help of another woman. This was construed as a blasphemous attempt to thwart the curse which G-d had laid upon Eve and both women were burnt to death."[2] It was not, in fact, until 1949 that the Holy Office announced papal sanction for painless births.

---

1. בראשית, ג', ט"ז.
2. I. Jakobovits, Jewish Medical Ethics, 2nd Ed., New York, 1975, p. 104.

Director, The Dr. Falk Schlesinger Institute for Medical-Halachic Research; Editor, "Assia", a quarterly in matters of Halacha and Medicine; Department of Pediatrics, Sha'are Zedek Medical Center, Jerusalem, Israel

Among Jewish scholars this problem is never raised. The reference regarding Eve never presented any difficulty, as she was *cursed*, not commanded, to suffer birth pains. Zimmels[3] remarks that the prohibition of analgesics for pangs of birth would, in fact, contradict Jewish ideology, since the ways of Torah "are ways of pleasantness and all her paths are peace"[4].

Since pain of labor and delivery is so great, one would not be surprised to find — from time immemorial — various attempts to reduce and alleviate this suffering. We encounter in all cultures and throughout human history the usage of medical-anesthetic devices as well as psychological attempts to relieve the pain of birth and encourage the woman at her difficult time of parturition (labor and delivery). In all but one of 150 cultures studied by anthropologists, a family member or friend, usually a female, remained with a mother during labor and delivery.[5] In Jewish tradition the onlookers at labor used to encourage her, saying: "The L-rd who answered your mother in her time of need, will also answer you in your time of need"[6].

Several scientific articles have been published recently, pointing out the importance of human companionship during birth. One of these studies[7] proved that when there was a companion to the woman during her labor, the length of time from admission to the hospital until delivery was shortened. Furthermore, mothers who had a companion present during labor were more awake after delivery, smiled and talked to their babies and were more alert and active compared to control mothers without companions. The frequency of development of certain problems that require intervention during labor and delivery was lower for mothers who had a supportive companion. This — and other previous studies — suggest that there may be a major perinatal benefit of constant human support during labor.

3. H.J. Zimmels, Magicians, Theologicians and Doctors, London, 1952, p. 7.
4. ‏משלי, ג׳, י״ז‎.
5. R. Rosa et. al., New Engl. J. Med., 303: 597-600, 1980.
6. ‏מדרש תהילים, כ׳, ד׳‎.
7. R. Rosa et al, *loc. cit.*

In the past three decades, an extended birth psychoprophylaxis has developed. This is a psychologic method of
preparation during pregnancy designed to prevent — or at least to
minimize — pain and difficulty during labor. The pregnant woman
is taught in various modes to use her natural brain processes to her
advantage. The basic principles and methods of psychoprophylaxis were developed by Russian obstetricians. In 1951, Dr.
Lamaze, a French obstetrician, visited Russia and saw women
trained in psychoprophylaxis deliver without pain. Upon his return
to Paris, Dr. Lamaze adapted this method for use in the Western
world. This technique — as well as some other variants — have
spread to many countries all over the world.

Most of these methods include training programs during
pregnancy together with a companion — usually the husband —
who continues to accompany the woman at labor and delivery,
encouraging and reminding her to use the psychotherapy and
relaxation exercises learned and practiced during pregnancy. These
include learning how to relax the muscles via various breathing
exercises. The husband is also trained to ease his wife's pain by
applying pressure to painful areas, mopping her brow, and
massaging or rubbing her as needed to relieve tension.

B. The Halachic Problems

From the halachic viewpoint, there are two aspects to the issue
of the husband's participation at parturition. On the one hand a
woman in labor and delivery is considered a Nidah, and therefore
the husband is prohibited to touch her and to look at certain parts
of her body. On the other hand a woman giving birth is considered
a dangerously sick person for whom many prohibitions are
permitted. The question now is — which halachic definition should
be operative? May he try to alleviate her distress by implementing
the Lamaze techniques, or is he forbidden to touch her as she is
Nidah?

(a) The Status of Nidah

In Shulchan Aruch we find the following *Din*[8]:

> יולדת, אפילו לא ראתה דם, טמאה כנדה, בין ילדה חי בין
> ילדה מת ואפילו נפל.

"A woman giving birth, even if she did not see any blood, is 'unclean' as a *Nidah*, whether she bore a live child or a dead child, or even had a miscarriage." According to this halachic definition, all laws of *Nidah* are applicable to a woman in parturition. The definitions of various stages of labor were discussed by *Chazal* in reference to the woman's status as a dangerously sick person — see further in section (b). These definitions are valid to her *Nidah* state as well. As soon as regular contractions commence, she should be regarded as "*safek Nidah*" (possibly a *Nidah*)[9], unless it is proven that those were false contractions. Of special relevance to our discussion are two *Dinim*: (1) The prohibition to look at certain parts of one's wife's body during her period of *Nidah*; (2) The prohibition to touch her at that time.

(1) Regarding observation — the following *Psak* is cited in Shulchan Aruch[10]:

> „מותר לאדם להביט באשתו, אע״פ שהיא נידה והיא ערוה
> לו, אע״פ שיש לו הנאה בראייתה, הואל והיא מותרת לו
> לאחר זמן אינו בא בזה לידי מכשול, אבל לא ישחוק ולא
> יקל ראש עמה.“

"It is permitted for a man to look at his wife, even if she is a Nidah and is (sexually) forbidden to

---

8. ‏שו״ע, יו״ד, קצ״ד, א׳.

9. ‏סד״ט, קצ״ד, סק״ה; שו״ת אגרות משה יורה דעה ב שאלה ע״ה.

10. ‏שו״ע, אה״ע, כא׳, ד׳.

him, and even if he derives pleasure from seeing her,
for since she will be permitted to him later on, he will
not (by looking at her) come to do a sin. However, he
should not joke around or be light-headed with her."

Although according to this statement, one might argue that it
is permitted to look at all parts of a *Nidah*-wife, elsewhere the
Shulchan Aruch limited this permission[11], and subsequent *Poskim*
have followed this ruling[12]. Some have forbidden looking at genital
organs, whereas others have expanded the prohibition to all parts
of the woman's body which are ordinarily covered[13]. Therefore the
husband is forbidden to look at the actual delivery — whether
directly or through a mirror; nor may he take pictures or movies of
the delivery, etc.

(2) Regarding touching the *Nidah* — The *Rishonim* are in
dispute whether this prohibition is Biblical[14] or Rabbinic. The
leading *Posek* who rules that the prohibition to touch a *Nidah* is
mi'd'oratha (Biblical) is the Rambam[15]:

„כל הבא על ערוה מן העריות, או שחיבק ונישק דרך תאוה
ונהנה בקירוב בשר — הרי זה לוקה מן התורה, שנאמר, לא
תקרבו לגלות ערוה, כלומר לא תקרבו לדברים המביאים
לידי גילוי ערוה."

"Whoever has relations with a woman prohibited
to him, or embraces or kisses her in an affectionate
manner and derives pleasure from the closeness of
flesh — he is punishable according to the Torah, since
it is written 'you shall not come near to uncover

---

11. ‏יורה דעה ק"צה ס"ק ז: „לא יסתכל במקומות המכוסים שבה"‏.
12. Based on the following: ‏„כל המסתכל בעקבה של אשה, הויין לו‏
      ‏בנים שאינם מהוגנים, אמר רב יוסף, ובאשתו נדה" — נדרים, כ', א'‏.
13. See in detail — ‏אוצה"פ, אה"ע, סי' כא', סקל"ב‏.
14. This is based on the verse: ‏„איש איש אל כל שאר בשרו לא‏
      ‏תקרבו לגלות ערוה" — ויקרא, יח', ו'‏.
15. ‏רמב"ם, איסורי ביאה, כא', א'‏.

nakedness', meaning do not come close to those things which lead to forbidden relations.

Most *Rishonim* are in agreement with the Rambam. The leading representative of the opinion that the prohibition of touching a *Nidah* is only Rabbinic, is the Ramban[16], and some of the Rishonim agree with him[17]. Most *Acharonim* confirm the halacha to be in accordance with the Rambam[18].

However, another problem pertinent to the prohibition of touching a *Nidah* is whether it is only contact in a way of affection and passion which is proscribed (דרך תאוה,, in Rambam's language), or even when the touch is for the wife's immediate need. Some *Poskim* forbid the husband to touch his *Nidah*-wife even when she is sick and needs his help to get out of bed[19]. Others maintain that when there is no one else to assist her in the above-mentioned circumstances, then the husband is allowed to touch her for her sake and need, even if she is not dangerously ill. The Ramo adds[20]: "And this is the custom when she needs it very much." Of similar relevance is the halachic dispute whether a physician is allowed to palpate the pulse of his sick wife when she is *Nidah*.[21-22]

---

16. רמב"ן, ספר המצוות, מצות ל"ת, שנ"ג.

17. See summary of these opinions: אנציקלופדיה, אות א', סק"ה, כ' סי' אוה"ע, אוצה"פ,
תלמודית ערך גלוי עריות, כרך י', עמ' קי"א-קי"ב.

18. See note 17. Also שדי חמד, כללים, מערכת קו"ף, כלל ז'; ובאספת דינים, מערכת
חתן וכלה, אות יב'; תורה תמימה, ויקרא, י"ח, אות כ'.

19. המחבר, שו"ע, יו"ד, קצה', טז'.

20. רמ"א, שם, וראה רדב"ז בפת"ש, שם, סקט"ו.

21. מחלוקת המחבר והרמ"א, שם, סעיף יז'. וראה בהרחבה אוצה"פ,
סי' כ', סק"ג, אות א'; אנציקלופדיה תלמודית, ערך חולה, עמ' רפ"ב
— ובמקורות שצויינו שם.

22. See שדי חמד note 17.
Others relate this same logic to the question of shaking hands with a woman. It should be pointed out that all opinions agree that touching another woman is forbidden; the argument is only whether it is דרבנן or אסור דאורייתא. In our case, we are following the opinion that touching a woman is an *issur derabbanan* only, and since she is sick, it would be permitted. In order to permit shaking hands with a woman, it would be necessary to find a similar justification for abrogating the issur *derabbanan*.

Nevertheless, in the context of our discussion, I would tend to
define the husband's touch of his wife in labor closer to "affection
and passion", since it cannot seriously be stated that such a touch
is of immediate medical need and help.[23] Therefore, the husband is
forbidden to hold the hands of his wife during labor and delivery,
to support her head, or to touch any other part of her body.

(b) The Definition of Parturition as a Dangerous Condition

The Shulchan Aruch gives us the following Din[24]:

„היולדת היא כחולה שיש בו סכנה ומחללין עליה את
השבת לכל מה שצריכה."

> "A woman in labor and childbirth is like a person
> who is dangerously sick, and we transgress the
> Sabbath for her for whatever she needs."

Regardless of whether medical opinion is in agreement with
the above assessment, the halachic status of a woman in labor is
that she is dangerously ill (חולה שיש בו סכנה). When a person is in
mortal danger, we are commanded to do virtually anything which
is required to save his life, without giving thought even to
desecration of Shabbat. Generally, one need not even seek a Gentile
to drive that sick person to the hospital, but should himself
immediately do so, and personally perform any other required
service. Thus we see that the needs of a dangerously ill person set
aside almost all the laws of the Torah.

However, since parturition is a natural occurrence and the

---

23. From the Mishna אהלות, ז, ד one cannot deduct the assumption that a woman in
    labor was carried in a prohibited way — since most likely this was done by
    girlfriends, as we find a similar expression in שבת, קכ"ט, א׳ — "At at time when
    her girlfriends carry her under her armpits."
24. שו"ע, או"ח, ש"ל, א׳.

great majority of women in this situation do not die, our Rabbis found it necessary to set more stringent regulations regarding her care than in other dangerous conditions. They recommend that every action needed for the woman in labor on Shabbat be performed in a manner somewhat different from the usual (שינוי). (If activity forbidden on Shabbat is done differently (בשינוי), it is not considered as a Biblical transgression but rather as disregarding a Rabbinic law, which is less severe). Nevertheless, this recommendation holds true only if no delay in the treatment is anticipated due to the deviation. Otherwise, one is encouraged to do everything necessary in mode and manner to save her life.[25]

Our Rabbis have defined three manifestations of labor, from which time on the woman is considered "dangerously sick":[26]

משתשב על המשבר או משעה שהדם שותת ויורד, או
משעה שחברותיה נושאות אותה בזרועותיה שאין בה כח
להלוך."

From the time when she sits on the birthing stool or from the time that blood comes forth, or from the time that her friends have to support her arms and hold her up since she cannot walk.

Although for most purposes these stages define the status of labor, there are some actions which are permitted on Shabbat even beore the onset of one of the above-mentioned signs.[27]

---

25. מגן אברהם ס' ש"ל אות ג.
26. שו"ע, או"ח, ש"ל, ג' — עפ"י שבת, קכ"ט, א'.

These 3 stages can be defined in modern situation as follows: (a) Sitting on the birthstool — coming into the delivery room; (b) Blood running down — would probably include the stage of rupture of the membranes; (c) Friends carrying her — is probably very close to delivery.

The meaning of משבר is discussed by J. Preuss, Biblical and Talmud Medicine, trans. by F. Rosner, 1978, pp. 395-396.

27. משנה ברורה, ש"ל, סק"ט. ראה גם: שו"ת צפנת פענח, (ח"ב), סי' רל"ג,
שו"ת אגרות משה, חאו"ח, סי' קל"ב.

(c) Peace of Mind as a Reason for Concession

Since a woman in labor is considered a dangerously sick person, all laws of *pikuach nefesh* (a life-or-death situation) are
applicable. Any action necessary for immediate treatment is
permitted, even if it is a desecration of the Shabbat under ordinary
conditions. But is one permitted to perform an action on Shabbat
which is done only for the peace of mind of the patient, even if
medically it is unnecessary? In other words, the action is done for
the sole aim of preventing the patient from "losing his mind"
(טירוף הדעת) if things will not be performed according to his
wishes.

If טירוף הדעת is a viable basis for Sabbath desecration, might
it also be considered as sufficient grounds for permitting a husband
to comfort his wife in labor by touching her? Although his touch is
obviously not medically essential, if *she feels* it is necessary, would
the halacha permit it so as to prevent טירוף הדעת?

We find several examples in which the patient's psychologic
state of mind was taken into consideration to enact a lenient *Psak*:
(1) If a person is on his death bed (שכיב מרע), certain otherwise
forbidden acts may be done for him, so that he should not become
upset and perhaps die more rapidly due to his distress.[28] One such
ruling refers to his giving a Get (religious divorce) on Shabbat. If
he wishes to divorce his wife on Shabbat before he dies, so that she
will not become a Yevama*, he is allowed to do so.[29]

---

* A Yevama is a woman whose husband died childless. According to the Torah, she
must marry her dead husband's brother, or else obtain a release from him prior to
marrying anyone else. However, if she were divorced, she would not be his widow
(yevama) and would thus be free of any restrictions in remarrying.

---

28. בבא בתרא, קנ"ו, ב'.
29. שו"ע, או"ח, של"ט, ד'.

„ואין מגרשין [בשבת] אלא אם כן הוא גט שכיב מרע דתקיף
ליה עלמא.".

"A divorce may not be issued (on the Sabbath) except
in the case of a deathly-ill person." The Mishna
Brura appends the following:[30]

„כדי שלא תיטרף דעתו עליו אם לא יעשו כרצונו.".

"...so that he will not become upset if they do not do
as he wishes."

(2) A further example regarding peace of mind and hilchot
Shabbat is the following:[31]

„חולה דתקיף ליה עלמא ואמר שישלחו בעד קרוביו —
ודאי שרי.".

"A sick person who is failing rapidly and requests
that his relatives be sent for — it is certainly
permissible." This is to say that one is permitted (or
even obliged[32]) to hire a Gentile who will travel
beyond the limit of Shabbat (תחום שבת) in order to
inform the relatives of the sick man's condition. This
is done only for the purpose of keeping the patient
calm and reassured.

(3) The above examples indicate the extent to which Rabbinic

---

30. משנה ברורה, שם, סק"ט.
    The situation is such that the Get was written prior to Shabbat, and the
    שכיב מרע wants to hand it to his wife on Shabbat, which involves a prohibition
    דאורייתא but not דרבנן.
31. שו"ע, או"ח, שו', ט'.
32. ערוך השולחן, או"ח, שו', כ'.

prohibitions may be lifted as a concession to the peace of mind of a dangerously sick person. But we also find indications that even a Biblical prohibition can be set aside to assure the peace of mind of the dangerously ill.[33-34] Of special relevance to our discussion is the classic example of this principle, as recorded in Tractate Shabbat:[35]

ומילדין את האשה בשבת ... ומחללין עליה את השבת ... לאתויי הא דתנו רבנן, אם היתה צריכה לנר חבירתא מדלקת לה את הנר ... פשיטא, לא צריכה בסומא, מהו דתימא כיון דלא חזיא — אסור, קא משמע לן איתובי מיתבא דעתא, סברא אי איכא מידי חזיא חבירתא ועבדה לי.

We assist a woman to give birth on Shabbat ... and for her sake we desecrate Shabbat ... as our Rabbis taught: If she required a light, her friend may kindle a light for her ... Now it is obvious that a blind woman in labor does not need light, and we might think that since she cannot see, it would be forbidden to kindle a light for her (on Shabbat) — this passage comes to inform us that we set her mind at ease, for she believes that if there is anything required, my friend will see it and do it for me.

In Mishna Brura, it is stressed that the major consideration here is not the *medical* efficacy of the act, but its psychological impact.[36]

ואע״פ דהדלקת הנר עיקרה אינה לרפואה, אעפ״כ מחללין, דקים להו לרבנן דייתובי דעתא דיולדת הוא מילתא דמיסתכנא בה בלאו הכי.

---

33. רמב״ם, עבודה זרה, יא׳, יא׳.

34. שו״ת הרשב״א, חד׳, סי׳ רמ״ה; מנחת חינוך, מ׳ תקי״ב; נפש חיה על או״ח, סי׳ רע״ח.

35. שבת, קכ״ח, ב׳. וכן הלכה: רמב״ם, שבת, ב׳ יא׳, טושו״ע, או״ח, של׳, א׳.

36. משנה ברורה, ש״ל, אות ד.

> And even though kindling the light is not
> primarily for therapeutic reasons, nevertheless we
> desecrate the Sabbath since the Rabbis considered
> that setting the woman's mind at ease during
> childbirth is something which, if it is lacking, could
> be a dangerous matter.

This clear-cut permission to violate even a prohibition
d'oraitha for the peace of mind of a woman in labor is expanded
by some *Rishonim* to include all dangerously sick patients, the
woman in parturition being only an example of this type of
patient.[37]

It is somewhat surprising to find that some of our
contemporary Rabbis try to differentiate between various conditions
of danger and apply limiting and more strict ruling towards
different types of patients.

For example, Rabbi Neuwirth[38] distinguishes between patients
who ask for certain actions which have no direct implication on
their condition — for which only a prohibition *derabbanan* may be
violated — as opposed to a patient whose chances of improving
depend on his psychological strength — for which even a
prohibition *d'oraitha* is permitted.[39]

Rabbi Y. Henkin[40] (grandson of Rabbi Eliyahu Henkin ל"ז)
distinguished between the "טירוף הדעת„ of a woman in labor and

---

37. הרמב"ן, תורת האדם; מסוגיא דיולדת קמ"ל יתובי דעתא **דחולה בעלמא מחללין שבתא**
במידי דמסתכנא"; שו"ת התשב"ץ, תא' סי' נ"ד: „שאפילו מפני ישוב דעתו של חולה,
ואפילו אינו צריך לרפואותו אלא ישוב דעתו, מדליקים את הנר אע"פ שהוא סומא ואינו
נהנה מן האור, וה"ה לשאר מלאכות שהחולה מתיישב בהן שעושין אותן בשבת." וע"ע
בשו"ת הרדב"ז, ח"ד, סי' סו'; פמ"ג, סי' ש"ו בא"א סקי"ח; שו"ת חלקת יעקב, ח"א, סי'
ס"ד.

38. שמירת שבת כהלכתה, מהדורה חדשה, תשל"ב, פל"ב, סכ"ה-סכ"ו.

39. The implication from the blind woman in labor who wants a light seems to
contradict this distinction. Also, Rabbi Neuwirth's remark (in note 82) against
חלקת יעקב is unjustified according to the תשב"ץ (see note 37 above).

40. הרב י.ה. הנקין אסיא י"ט תשל"ח ע"מ 44-52.

that of other dangerously sick persons. The woman has to be
active during her labor — to expel and deliver her baby. Therefore
her peace of mind is an important component of her "cure".
However, another sick person has only to be passive and quiet —
for which maximum peace of mind is not of such importance.

In my opinion one cannot formulate rigid rules regarding the
importance of the peace of mind of a dangerously sick person, but
rather judge and evaluate each patient and situation individually,
and ask Rabbinic advice accordingly.

This was best summarized by Rabbi Weiss[41] who concluded
that "הכל לפי העניין", it depends on each situation.

Moreover, I would like to stress a responsum of Rabbi
Feinstein, which is of great importance in defining and applying
the concept of טירוף הדעת. Rabbi Feinstein was asked whether a
husband is allowed to accompany his wife in labor in a taxi on
Shabbat. His answer was positive, for the reason of keeping the
wife's mind at ease. Although there might be different types of
fear, Rabbi Feinstein disregarded these variations and concluded:[42]

> „אבל מכל מקום לדינא, כיון שמצינו ביולדת שעלולה
> להסתכן מחמת פחד, מי **הוא שיכל לסמוך על חילוקים**
> **בחשש פיקוח נפש**. ולכן אם היא אומרת שהיא מתפחדת אף
> אחרי שמסבירין לה שאין מה לפחד ליסע בעצמה — יש
> בזה חשש פקוח נפש וצריך הבעל או האם ליסע עמה. ואף
> אם נוסעת להאספיטאל כשעדיין אינה צועקת בחבליה, אם
> הוא במקום רחוק יש לו גם כן ליסע עמה, דאף שעתה לא
> תסתכן, אבל הא אפשר באמצע הדרך יתווספו לה החבלי
> לידה עד השיעור שתצעק בחבליה שאז יש לחוש שמא
> תסתכן מחמת פחדותה."

But in any case, according to the law since we
have found regarding a woman giving birth that she

---

41. שו"ת מנחת יצחק ח"ד ס' ח.
42. שו"ת אגרות משה או"ח ס' קל"ב.
    Other Poskim also stress the importance of escorting the wife in labor to the
    hospital on Shabbat. The Chazon Ish (אגרות החזו"א, ח"א, אגרת קמ"א) wrote:
    „בענין נסיעת יולדת בשבת — הדבר בהיפוך, מזרז אני שיסעו עמה."

may be endangered due to fear, who can rely on
minute differentiations when there is a possibility of
danger to life? Therefore, if she says that she is
afraid, even after they explain to her that there is
nothing to fear in riding by herself — there is here a
possibility of a life-threatening situation, and the
husband or the mother must ride with her. And even
if she has to go to the hospital while she is not yet
crying from her pains, if it is far, then he should
likewise go with her, for although at this point she is
not in danger, but since it is possible that during the
trip the pains will progress to the extent that she will
cry out due to her pangs, since then one must be
concerned that she might be endangered due to her
panic.

In the above discussion, we have shown how seriously the
Poskim considered the possibility that a fearful psychological state
might endanger the welfare of the patient. Despite this, it does not
appear that in the case of a woman giving birth we would
generally allow apprehension for her peace of mind to outweigh
the prohibitions concerning physical contact between a Nidah and
her husband. This is evidenced by the following short and concise
responsum of Rabbi Moshe Feinstein:[43]

ובאם הבעל יכול להיות שמה [בעת הלידה] להשגיח
שתעשה הדבר בסדר הנכון, וגם לחזק אותה ולאמץ לבה
הנה אם יש צורך איני רואה איסור ואף בלא צורך איני
רואה איסור, אבל אסור לו להסתכל ביציאת הולד ממש.
אך כשיזהר שלא להסתכל ליכא איסור.

And if the husband can be there at the time of
the birth to supervise that everything is being done

---

43. שו״ת אגרות משה יורה דעה ב שאלה ע״ה.

properly, and also to strengthen her and encourage her — If there is a need for this, I cannot see any prohibition, and even if there is no need for him to be there, I do not see any prohibition in his being there, but it is forbidden to watch when the baby emerges. But if he is careful not to look, then there is no prohibition.

Conclusion להלכה – לא למעשה

1. A woman in labor is considered a *Nidah*.
2. The husband is not allowed to touch his wife in parturition; he is not permitted to look at parts of her body which ordinarily have to be covered.
3. The fear, anxiety and apprehension of a woman in labor is a significant factor — scientifically and halachically.[44]
4. For alleviation of this fear and in order to keep her mind at peace, one may be permitted to violate some prohibitions *d'oraitha*, but each case must be judged individually.
5. A private companion to the woman in labor and delivery is of significant importance.
6. The preference is for this companion to be a woman, who can be effective and who involves no halachic problems.
7. If the woman in labor insists that her husband should stay with her to alleviate her fears and encourage her — he is obliged to do so.
8. The husband should be taught and warned not to touch his wife

---

44. Rabbi Weiss in שו״ת מנחת יצחק ח״ה סכ״ז makes the following statement: נשים דעתן קלות ויש לחוש שמבקשין כן [היינו נוכחות הבעל] משום קלות הדעת ולא משום טירוף הדעת.
Similarly, Rabbi Halberstam (in Assia 21:5738, p. 18) makes the following statement: טענות אלו הנשים שרוצות שבעליהן ישארו בנימוק של פחד נובע בעקרו מתוך בקשת נוחות יתירה.
These statements are in dispute with the scientifically proven evidence cited in note 5. Also relevant to the halacha, note Rabbi Feinstein's statement and definition (note 42 above).

during labor and delivery (unless needed medically) and not to look at parts of her body which usually have to be covered.[45]

---

45. Rabbi Halberstam (in Assia) objects to the husband's participation in parturition, lest he touch his wife or look at forbidden parts of her body. In my opinion, this can be explained to the husband, and one should not assume that in spite of the explanation he would violate these prohibitions. People who care enough to ask a Shailah do not have to be suspected of violating a halachic ruling אטו ברשיע עסקינן. On the other hand, to formulate a new law to forbid an act which is permitted, lest one perform another act which is forbidden, is a procedure which we do not have the power to enact nowadays. See שו״ת יחוה דעת ח״ג ס׳ כ and particularly in Talmudic Encyclopaedia, ע׳ גזרה.

Child Custody: Halacha and the Secular Approach

Sylvan Schaffer

The emotional pain experienced by divorcing couples is a source of great communal concern. Of equal importance is the effect of divorce on the innocent children in these families.

While most Jews realize that one component of the divorce, the *get*, is governed by halacha, not as many realize that this is also true for issues of child custody and support.

As with almost any halachic topic, the issues of child custody and support are subject to many different opinions in the *Rishonim* and *Aharonim*. It is not the purpose of this paper to review (and certainly not resolve) all of these positions. Our goal is to identify and analyze the common thread running through the child custody halachic literature and also to compare it with the approaches of civil law.

Before analyzing the halachic sources, it would be useful to survey briefly the evolution of the civil law in this area as well as some of the psychological aspects of child custody.

The author wishes to thank Dr. Marcy Schaffer, without whose invaluable assistance this paper could not have been written.

Attorney, family therapist and Visiting Scholar in Law and Psychology at Hastings Institute for Bioethics.

Historical overview of child custody under civil law

The civil law related to the child custody issue has been characterized by an evolutionary process that has resulted in an almost complete reversal of the standards used to determine custody.

In ancient Rome, Persia, Egypt, Greece and Gaul, the father had absolute power over minor children, including the permit to sell his children and even put them to death. However these powers were vested only in the father and not the mother.[1]

Under English law the right of the parent was viewed in the context of the power of the king or feudal lords. The king (through his courts) could intervene between parent and child based on the need of the king to protect his subjects.[2]

Under French civil law the father had exclusive authority over his children until they reached the age of twenty-one. The mother only had power over the children if the father died before the children reached majority.[3]

A gradual change affected the preference for the father shown by the British and American legal systems. The most dramatic change was the British Act of 1839 which directed that children under the age of seven years be put in the mother's custody. This preference for the mother evolved into the "tender years doctrine" which is a presumption favoring the mother for the custody of young children.

Some states based custody on the success of the parties in the divorce action. Thus the party which was found to be "at fault" often lost on the custody issue.[4] Other states, such as Kansas, Oregon, and Pennsylvania, gave equal custody rights to both parents.[5]

---

1. A. Roth, Tender Years Presumption 15, Journal of Family Law 423 (1976-77). W. Forsyth, A Treatise on the Law Relating to the Custody of Infants in Cases of Differences Between Parents or Guardians. 7-9 (1850) [hereinafter, Forsyth.]
2. A. Story, Commentaries on Equity Jurisprudence 557-62 (§§ 1327-30) see also Cardozo in *Finlay* v *Finlay* 240 N.Y. 429, 433-34 (1925)
3. G. Abbott, The Child and the State (1949)
4. La. Cio. Code Ann. Art 157 (West Supp. 1976); Ga. Code Ann. title 30 §127 (1969)
5. See Abbott above

In 1970, the National Conference of Commissioners on Uniform State Laws approved the Uniform Marriage and Divorce Act. The Act adopted a test based on the best interests of the child. Several states have adopted the Act.[6]

Recently the "tender years doctrine" which gave preference to the mother was weakened by both state statutes and judicial decisions. In states such as New York, statutes were enacted stating that neither parent had any prima facie right to the custody of the child.[7] In addition, the United States Supreme Court ruled in *Orr v. Orr*[8] that a state statute which gave preference to women in regard to alimony was unconstitutional since it violated equal protection. This may also then be true for a rule which gives women preference in custody cases.

Another recent alternative which has been implemented in a number of cases is 'joint' or shared custody.[9]

Many of these developments reflect changing societal perceptions with respect to interpersonal relationships.

Halachic approach:

The sources which provide a Jewish Court (Beth Din) with the basis for custody decisions are in part explicit rabbinic statements concerning child custody as well as other statements concerning the responsibility for child support from which custody rules are inferred.

A caveat is crucial at the outset of this section: none of the rules hereinafter cited should be used in their skeletal form as rules of *psak* (decision), but should be viewed in context of the explanations of the *Rishonim* and *Aharonim* who clarify the appropriate application of the rules in the light of the specific facts in each case.

Responsibility for support:

In the eyes of the halacha, the most basic rule of child support

---

6. 9 U.L.A. 455 (1970); Ariz. Rev. Stat. Ann. §25-311 to 25-339
7. N.Y. Domestic Relations Law §240.
8. 99 Sup. Ct. 1102 (1979).
9. *Braiman* v. *Braiman* 407 N.Y.S. 2d 449, 450 (1978)

is that the burden of support rests solely on the father and not on the mother.[10]

א. כשם שאדם חייב במזונות אשתו, כך הוא חייב במזונות
   בניו ובנותיו הקטנים...

ב. ואם לא רצתה האם שיהיו בניה אצלה אחר שגמלתן
   אחד זכרים ואחד נקבות הרשות בידה ונותנת אותן
   לאביהן או משלכת אותן לקהל אם אין להן אב והן
   מטפלין בהן.

a. The same way that a person is obligated to support his wife, so too is he obligated to maintain his young children.

b. If after weaning her sons or daughters, the mother does not want to keep them with her, she does not have to, and she may give them to their father or cast them upon the community for support if they have no father.

This rule applies to claim for support by the children. For example, it is possible that in a situation in which the mother and father entered into an agreement which stated that the mother would provide a portion of the child support, the children have no claim against the mother for such support. Their claim would be limited to the father who bears the responsibility for their upkeep. However, the father could turn to the mother and enforce his claim against her based on their agreement.[12]

There is some controversy about the source of the father's responsibility for child support: Some sources[13] say that the duty to support the children is part of the husband's duty to support his wife, their mother. Other sources[14] say that the father's duty is

---

10. רמב"ם הלכות אישות פי"ב הל' י"ד

11. רמב"ם הל' אישות פכ"א הל' י"ח

12. שרשבסקי **דיני משפחה** 334 n.2

13. כתובות ע"ה:: ר"ן שם: רש"י שם ד"ה יוצא
    בעירוב אמו; רמב"ם אישות י"ב הל י"ד

14. שו"ת הרא"ש כלל י"ז סימן ז'; שו"ת הריב"ש מ"א

based on a direct, independent obligation to the children and is not dependent on the duty to the wife.

Two important differences result from the outcome of this controversy: if the responsibility of the father is based on his duty to the mother then a) the amount of his obligation would be based on *his* customary living stadard as is his obligation to his wife; b) his duty to the children would not exist in a situation in which the duty to the mother did not exist, i.e. if the child were born out of wedlock or when the mother were no longer the father's wife (after divorce or her death). However, according to those who hold that the responsibility is directly to the children, then a) the father's obligation is measured by the needs of the *children* and not his means and b) the obligation exists even for a child born out of wedlock. The second approach seems to be the more widely accepted.[15]

Whereas there is general agreement that the duty to support children falls on the father, the age until when such a duty exists and the nature of that duty is not as clearcut, i.e. after the child is six years old the duty may arise as a component of charity. Therefore, in order to avoid any problems which might be detrimental to the children, in Israel the Chief Rabbinate has instituted the practice that the father is responsible for support until the children reach the age of fifteen.[16]

Custody

The general rules of child custody which emerge from halachic research are:

1. Until the age of six years, both boys and girls are usually in the custody of the mother even if after the divorce she remarries another.[17]

---

15. שו"ע פ"ב ז'; משנה למלך אישות י"ב, י"ד פסקי דיני הרבנות (פדר) 22 ,16 ,551 :42 ,01 :7.
פלדער נחלת צבי 283;

פסקי דיני הרבנות (פדר) 1:55,61,62; פד"ר 7:10,24

16. פריימן: התקנות החדשות של הרבנות הראשית לא"י בדיני אישות, "סיני" כרך י"ד, רנ"א-
רנ"ח שרשבסקי 340

17. כתובות ס"ה:; רש"י שם ד"ה יוצא בעירוב אמו; רמב"ם אישות כ"א י"ז; מגיד משנה שם.
טור והב"י פ"ב; שו"ע פ"ב ז'

2. After the age of six years, boys generally are in the custody of
their fathers and the girls are in the custody of their mothers.[18]

At this point it is important to explain how these basic rules
are applied. Although the rules serve as substantive guidelines for
the Beth Din, the application of the rules is subject to the general
principle of the best interests of the child which the *dayanim*
weigh in light of the specific facts of each case.[19] In fact, according
to many *poskim* the topic of child custody actually refers primarily
to the rights of the children to be appropriately placed and cared
for, and not to the "right" of the parent to have custody of the
child.[20] Although it is possible to debate whether the halachic
approach is founded on a duty-based system or on a right-based
system[21], the emphasis should nevertheless be on the
implementation of the substantive rules in a manner beneficial to
the children.

The first rule cited above indicates that until age six, both
boys and girls should be with their mother. However, since the
mother is not obligated to support her children she is also not
obligated to accept custody. Her right to refuse exists even in the
case of a child so young that he is still being suckled. The mother
has the right to turn the children over to the father.[22] However, if
the child who is being suckled is capable of recognizing his mother,
she must continue to feed him (and will be compensated by the
father) because failure to do so could prove dangerous to the
child.[23] At this point if the father claims that since he is already
paying the mother to feed the child therefore he may as well hire a

---

18. כתובות ק"ב: -ק"ג.; רא"ש שם; תשובות הרא"ש כלל פ"ב ב'; רמב"ם אישות כ"א י"ח;
מגיד משנה, שם. שו"ת המבי"ט חלק ב' סימן ס"ב.

19. תשובות הרשב"א המיוחסות להרמב"ן סימן ל"ח, פדר א', 61; שו"ת הרדב"ז חלק א' קב"ג.
שו"ע פ"ב פ"ת ז' שרשבסקי 343, נחלת צבי 283.

20. פד"ר א' 145, 147
Warburg 14 Israel Law Review 480 1979.

21. Warburg op. cit.

22. רמב"ם אישות כ"א י"ח; אבל כנראה הרמב"ם סותר דבריו באותו הפרק, וצ"ע, מגיד
משנה, שם; טור, פ"ב; שו"ע פ"ב ח'; נחלת צבי, 284.

23. רמב"ם אישות כ"א ט"ז; אבן העזר פ"ב ה'.

wetnurse, the Beth Din will not allow this since it is in the child's best interest to be fed by his mother.[24]

An interesting situation arises when a boy reaches the age of six years and custody should normally be transferred to the father according to halachic custody rules.

According to Rambam[25]

ואחר שש שנים יש לאב לומר אם הוא אצלי אתן לו מזונות
ואם הוא אצל אמו לא אתן לו מזונות.

After the child is six years old, the father can say "If the child stays with me, I will support him but if he stays with his mother, I will not pay for his support."

There are three different interpretations of the Rambam's position on the enforced transfer of custody in such a situation:

1. The father cannot remove the son from the mother against her will, but if the son remains with the mother then the father is absolved from his duty to support him.[26]

2. The son can be removed against the will of the mother, but not against his will.[27]

3. The son can be removed until the age of thirteen.[28]

It is important to point out that according to the first approach, the exemption of the father from child support is only in a case in which the son, due to his own volition, decides to stay with his mother. However, if the Beth Din decides that it is the best interest of the child to remain with the mother after age six, then the father is still obligated to support the boy.[29]

The halachic rules for child custody indicate the presence of other concerns in addition to the best interests of the child.

---

24. מהרשד״ם אבן העזר קצ״ג.

25. רמב״ם אישות כ״א י״ז.

26. מהר״ם אלשיך שאלה ל״ח; מהר״י אבן לב ח״א כלל י״ב שאלה ע״ב.

27. חלקת מחוקק שו״ע שק״ט, מגיד משנה, שם.

28. מביט על הרמב״ם, שם.

29. פד״ר ז׳ 10 א׳ 55, 61, שרשבסקי 349

First, although the father has considerable control, he is not granted absolute power and discretion over his children; the interest and needs of the children are seriously taken into account. In fact, until the age of six, the father has most of the obligations and few of the custodial benefits. Second, the halacha incorporates principles into the process for assigning custody which evidence an understanding that the needs of very young chidren differ from those of older children. In addition there is an awareness that as the child gets older, i.e. after age six, boys and girls benefit from same-sex role models.[30]

Finally, the halacha demonstates a flexibility in child placement. Exceptions to the usual custody rules, for example when a son wishes to remain with the mother after age six, are dealt with in great detail (see discussion above).

Best interests of the child:

The central importance of "the best interests of the child" principle has been stated unequivocally:[31]

> היסוד לכל פסק בעניינים אלה הוא הכלל שהניח הרמב״ן
> בתשובות המיוחסות סימן ל״ח בדבריו בענין הבן והבת אצל
> מי: דאע״ג דמצד הדין... לעולם צריך לדקדק בדברים אלו
> אחר מה שיראה בעיני בית דין בכל מקום ומקום שיש ב־ׄ
> יותר תיקון.. לחזור אחרי תיקונן.
>
> וביאר דבריו בתשובות דרכי נועם שאלה כ״ו:
> „כי חכמי התלמוד אמרו על הסתם, דסתם מילתא הבת
> אצל האם והבן ג״כ בקטנותו ואחר כך עם האב... שכל זה
> תיקון הילד על הסתם, ואם ראו ב־ׄד שאין בזה תיקון אלא
> אדרבא קלקול, מחזירין אחר תקנתן כפי ראות עיני הדיינים.
> וכל הפוסקים הסכימו לזה שהכל תלוי כפי ראות עיני ב״ד
> מה שהוא תיקון לולד."
>
> היינו שאין כלל יציב בדבר מקום ילדים אלא רק כלל
> של „סתמא," אם אין הכרעה אחרת.

---

30. אוצר הגאונים כתובות חלק התשובות סימן תל״ד.
31. פד״ר א' 55, 61

The basic rule of thumb to be followed in these matters is the general principle laid down by the Ramban in Paragraph No. 38, wherein he discusses with whom the son or daughter ought to be:... Each Beth Din must ponder at great length which way will be best to proceed and which is the most beneficial.."

The opinion of Ramban is further elaborated by *Darkei Noam* 26:

"Speaking generally, the Rabbis of the talmud felt that it was usually best that a girl remain with her mother and that a young boy also should remain with his mother and thereafter be with the father ... If however for some reason the Court feels that it would not be beneficial or might even be detrimental, then they may amend the decision in any way they feel best for the child. And all the Rabbis agree that the prevailing principle is that the Court must rule as it considers best for the good of the child."

Thus, there is no firm rule regarding placement of the children, only a general guideline if there is no contraindication.

It is clear from these statements that the halacha does not apply the custody rules in an impersonal, rote manner, i.e. all boys must be with the father after age six with no exceptions. Rather, a review of actual *piskei halacha* indicate that rules are often taken only as presumptions[32] and their application is subject to the general prinicple of the child's best interests, which serves as the foundation for the specific rules.[33]

By seeking recourse to the underlying prinicple, the child's best interests, the Beth Din is able to resolve conflicts between specific rules. A classic demonstration of the use of this approach involved the question of whether a custodial father could leave Israel with his 2½ year old son for about six months. The father

---

32. פד"ר א' 61,59 Warburg above
33. Warburg at 495

had custody of the son as result of an agreement with the mother (see discussion on custody agreements below). The wife claimed that if the father left the country, custody should be transferred to her since otherwise she would be denied her visitation rights.

The Beth Din weighed several issues in its decision making process. First, the child should not be leaving Israel:

„הכל מעלין לארץ ישראל ואין הכל מוציאין..."

A person can be forced to come up to the Land of Israel, but no one can be forced to leave ...[34]

The court also considered the role of the mother and father in raising the child until that point. Finally, the court said that the issue had to be resolved from the child's perspective and to his advantage. Although it is better for a child to remain in Israel, it is still more important for the child to remain with his father. The court found that although the child was under six years old, the primary caretaker was the father and a transfer of custody, even on a temporary basis, could be psychologically harmful. It found that the father was, in a sense, the 'psychological parent'. Thus we see how the court weighed the various rules and found that the visitation rights of the mother and the requirement to stay in Israel were both subject to the doctrine of the best interests of the child.

The best interests principle also governs private agreements made between the father and mother concerning custody, support, or any other matter affecting the children. For example, if the wife agrees to free the father of all support obligations in exchange for a *get*, she can later renounce the agreement since it is not in the best interest of the children who lose out monetarily, and:

„אין חבין לאדם שלא בפניו"

A person cannot be caused damage in his absence.[35]

---

34. כתובות קי: פד"ר 175, 1:173
35. כתובות י"א א'

Also, if the agreement embodies a custody arrangement which does not follow the usual halachic rules, i.e. the daughter is placed with the father, the daughter is not bound by such an agreement unless it is shown that it is in her best interest.[36] The burden in such a situation is on the parent who seeks to vary the usual rules.[37] Finally, if a custody agreement is made by the parents and approved by the Beth Din, the other parent will not be estopped from requesting at a future time that custody be transferred, as long as such transfer is in the best interest of the child, since the approval which was given was based on the facts at the time of the decision and is subject to change as needed to implement the interests of the child.[38]

Given the central role that the child plays in these custody deliberations, it is appropriate to consider the child's preference if the child seems capable of making an informed choice which is not merely the result of undue influence by the parent. However, if the Beth Din feels that it is not in the child's best interest to honor his choice, it is not bound to do so.[39] In doing so, however, one must be very cautious since forcing a child to choose between parents can be very stressful. Therefore when the judge or *dayan* is interested in the child's preference, he will often elicit it indirectly.

Since the custody rules are designed to help the children, they are generally not to be used to punish a parent for wrongful acts committed during the marriage. Such behavior is not held against the parent when the custody decision is made unless such behavior would have a negative impact on the child.[40]

Visitation:

The rules of visitation for the non-custodial parent are also based on the needs of the children. There is a privilege of visitation designed for the benefit of the child so that the bond with the non-

---

36. שרשבסקי 348
37. נחלת צבי 286
38. שרשבסקי, 348
39. שרשבסקי, 348‎-9
40. שרשבסקי, 346; פד"ר 2:3,5,8

custodial parent should be maintained.⁴¹ The visitation privilege is
not a proprietary right of the parent.⁴² If the Beth Din determines
that such visits are harmful to the child, the visits may be
curtailed. Another purpose of the visitation rules is to enable the
father to provide חינוך (education) for a son living with the mother.
Considerations of visitation and חינוך also affect the right of the
custodial parent to travel with the child to another city.⁴³

Conclusion:

While the placement of children has posed a difficult problem
to judges since Solomon, the halachic approach has long attempted
to minimize the trauma to the children by emphasizing their
interests as central to the custody process. Unlike the various civil
law systems, which, until quite recently emphasized the parental
right to custody, the halacha has given primacy to the doctrine of
the best interests of the child.

The halacha does seem to differ from American law in that it
does still seem to apply the tender years doctrine, favoring the
placement of very young children with the mother. However, the
halacha applies this rule based on the premise that such placement
is in the best interest of the child, and not because of a
discriminatory policy against fathers. Should the Beth Din
determine that placement of a child with the father would be
advantageous for that child, it would do so. Unlike the American
system, which has begun to apply equal protection rules to gender
discrimination, the halacha recognizes differences between the sexes
and will follow a gender-related presumption if such a presumption
will help the child.

The current emphasis in the psychological literature on the
father as role model for boys is not in conflict with the halachic
approach. Although halacha favors the placement of very young

---

41. ‏347, שרשבסקי; י"ז. הל' פכ"א אישות הלכות משנה מגיד
42. ‏1:158 ,176 פד"ר
43. ‏תלמוד הלכות רמב"ם שם מ"ב, הרא"ש, קידושין כ"ט עמוד ב; 342, שרשבסקי, פד"ר 7:10,
תורה א' ג', שו"ע יורה דעה רמ"ה.

children with the mother, it recognizes the importance of contact between the father and son even during that period.

In contemporary American society, we find an increasing sensitivity for the many factors which ought to be considered in settling a child custody issue. While this bespeaks a growing awareness of the complexities of the problem, the halacha has always taken cognizance of the many factors which must be weighed in arriving at a decision bearing momentous consequences.

THE COMMUNITY

"Dina De'malchusa Dina":
Secular Law As a Religious Obligation

Rabbi Herchel Schachter

Normative Judaism is concerned not only with religious ritual; a major area of concern is the relationship of the individual to the society in which he lives, and to others in that polity. A familiar exemplification of this principle is evident in the Ten Commandments, wherein the first five speak of the man-G-d relationship, and the second tablet teach the proper attitudes in the man-man relationship.

When the Jewish people lived in their own political and social milieu, the laws of the Torah governed their environment. However, in the centuries of our Diaspora, one of the most difficult areas of adjustment has been in finding the proper mode of accommodating the rules of a secular or Christian society to a Torah *weltanschauung*. The Torah-true Jew does not lose sight of Torah ideals, even while subject to the discipline of another system. The topic which we will discuss herein, is to what extent the laws of the Torah are superseded or ignored or adapted—or perhaps *not* superseded or ignored—by the realities of existence in a non-Torah framework.

So, for example, we have to consider the committed Jew in his role as American citizen, tax-payer, businessman, professional. To what extent does being a "good Jew" require a person also to be a "good American"? How about cutting corners on one's income tax—is it prohibited by the religion? Do American ceremonies of marriage and divorce have validity in the eyes of halacha? Should two Jews who enter a business partnership be guided by American law or by the Shulchan Aruch—or both? What if there is a conflict?

The basis of any accommodation of Torah principles to secular law lies in the Talmudic dictum, "Dina de'malchusa dina". In several places, the Gemara quotes[1] the principle of the teacher Shmuel, that the laws of the government are binding on Jews, even when they differ from the laws of the Torah. The main application of this principle is the collection of taxes. The government officials are permitted to collect taxes, and the cash or property they collect in taxes are considered as legally belonging to the government, and not considered as stolen property in their hands.

The right of the government to levy taxes is restricted only to a bona fide government, and does not apply to any pirate who decided on his own to rob the masses in an organized fashion.[2] Even when it is the official government levying the taxes, if the system of taxation is unjust, as for example—if one segment of the population is discriminated against and is taxed more than another—then, too, this principle does not apply. Shmuel formulated his principle by stating "Dina de'malchusa dina," "The law of the government is binding", but not "Gazlanusa de'malchusa," "The robbery of the government".[3]

Before proceeding with an analysis of the specifics of the principle "Dina de'malchusa dina," we ought to point out that

---

1. Bava Kama 113a; Bava Bathra 54b; Nedarim 28a; Gittin 10b.
2. Rambam Hilchot G'zeloh V'avedah, end of Chapter 5, section 18.
3. Ibid, section 14; Magid Mishnah to section 13; Choshen Mishpot 369, section 8 in Ramo.

this is a much more narrow concept than is often imagined. "Dina de'malchusa dina" cannot be interpreted to mean that the law of the land is the law, period. Were this so, it would mean that wherever the law of the land is different from the law of the Torah, it is the law of the land which we are to follow. This is absurd, for it would reduce Judaism to a practice of rituals alone, and would effectively nullify about half of the Shulchan Aruch.

Rather, we take the principle "Dina de'malchusa dina" to indicate that in certain *areas* and under certain, specific *circumstances*, the halacha requires that we be governed by the dictates of the sovereign state in which we live rather than by the teachings of the Torah alone. We will now consider some of those areas.

The Mishna in Nedarim[4] tells us that in order to avoid paying taxes, one may even swear what *might seem to be* a false oath, which under normal circumstances would not be allowed. In commenting on this Mishna, the Gemara asks, but why should we allow this even for the purpose of avoiding paying taxes, if the government is legally entitled to collect their taxes? Why consider this a case of "sha'as hadechak" and "oness", to permit what seems like a false oath? To this the Gemara answers that the Mishna is obviously referring to a case where "Dina de'malchusa" does not apply: a) either the tax-collector was not authorized by the government, but is merely collecting for a pirate; or b) the government sold the right to collect taxes to a private individual, who is unjustly holding up the public to pay much more than the government needs in order that he himself should gain a tremendous profit; in such a case we no longer are dealing with a "dina de'malchusa," but rather a "chamsonusa" or a "gazlanusa

---

4. 28a.

de'malchusa," an unfair tax, which the government has no right to levy.

What is the halachically-binding force of the taxes levied by the government? Why isn't the money collected by the government—without the consent of the individual taxpayer—considered as stolen property? The Mei'ri[5] and the Vilna Gaon[6] both maintain that this is based on the "Parshas Melech": In the Book of Shmuel I (Chap. 8), the prophet Shmuel warns the Jewish people against the evils of a King; among other things, Shmuel warns that he will tax the people heavily. In the Talmud[7] there is a dispute as to the understanding of "Parshas Melech", this chapter dealing with "the evils of the King". Was the prophet Shmuel warning the nation by exaggerating the limits of royal authority, and mentioning things that the King was not really legally authorized to do; or was Shmuel portraying accurately the rights and privileges of the King? The halacha has accepted the second understanding of that Parsha, that "Kol ho'omur beparshas melech", everything spoken of in that section of the Book of Shmuel, "melech mutar bo", the King is legally entitled to do. Since levying taxes is mentioned among the various warnings of Shmuel Ha'novi, we can clearly derive from this section in the Novi the right of the government to tax the people.

This suggestion of the Mei'ri and the Vilna Gaon is, of course, assuming that the Parshas Melech applies to all kings, both Jewish kings in Eretz Yisroel, and non-Jewish governments ruling over other countries. Tosafot in their comments on that discussion in Gemara Sanhedrin[8] limit the Parshas

---

5. Commentary to Nedarim.
6. Commentary, Choshen Mishpot 369, sub section 34.
7. Sanhedrin 20b.
8. Ibid, section beginning "Melech..."

Melech only to a *Jewish* king ruling over *all* of Eretz Israel. This is obviously in contradiction to the opinion of the Mei'ri and the Vilna Gaon. Other objections were raised against the suggestion of the Mei'ri and the Gaon by the D'var Avrohom.[9]

This dispute between Rabbinic authorities is not just a hair-splitting technicality. Upon the resolution hinges the major question of whether a Jew living under a non-Jewish government has to consider the laws of the land as legitimately binding upon him or not. For example, would the government of the United States, whether through the President or the Congress, have the status of a "King" (i.e., the legitimate ruler), or not; and if so, what are the limits of the ruler's power?

It is not necessary at this point to follow through to the end of the technical dispute; suffice it to record that practical halacha generally accepts that the ruler does have certain legitimate powers over the individuals under his control, and that to some extent, as part of keeping the Torah, Jews must accept these restrictions or guidelines. We will now proceed to examine the nature of that power.

According to the Ramban,[10] the rights of the government to tax are very limited. Only such taxes that had already existed in the past may be continued. The king has no right to institute any *new* taxes, even if they are just and fair. The Ramban seems to have understood the basis of "Dina de'malchusa" for the purposes of taxation as being based on the principle of "hischaivus mi'daas," one's own personal acceptance of an obligation. The fact that the people have been paying taxes in the past is taken as an indication of their willingness and their

---

9. Volume I, page 14, in footnote.
10. Quoted by Magid Mishnah, Hilchot G'zelah, Chapter 5, section 13.

agreement to continue to pay them; and anyone who accepts upon himself any monetary obligation, is obliged to pay that debt.[11]

This view of the Ramban was not shared by the majority of the Rishonim. In their view, the king may even institute new taxes, and they too will be legally binding, provided they are fair and just and do not discriminate. Where then is the Biblical source for the principle of "Dina de'malchusa dina"? If one

---

11. Whatever is commonly practiced (minhag ha'medinah) is considered as if all the people had expressly accepted upon themselves to follow. In the Talmud we find this principle regarding cases where all that is needed is a T'nai (condition) to regulate an already existing legally-binding agreement. (Yerushalmi, Bava Metziah, beginning with Chapter 7). The Ramo, Choshen Mishpat (Chapter 46, section 4) quoting the Terumas Hadeshen, has extended this principle to apply even to cases where no previous binding agreement (hischaivut) had been enacted, and this understood and assumed agreement to follow the minhag ha'medinah is what actually serves to create the obligation.

Usually, a monetary obligation does not become legally binding until an act of Kinyan is done. (For example: a shtar—a document—is handed over to the one who is acquiring the obligation; or a Kinyan suddar is made.) This is required only where the obligation is towards a private individual. If, however, one is obligating himself to the public, or to the government, no formal "act of acquisition" (maaseh Kinyan) is needed. See Hadorom, Nisson 5740, pp. 29-30, Chazon Ish, Orlah, (I,15) Comments of Rabbi Akiva Eiger to Choshen Mishpot, Chapter 333, section 2.

Therefore, according to the view of the Ramban, all that is needed is that the minhag ha'medinah should establish the individual's implicit agreement to pay his taxes to the government; and although there is no formal maaseh Kinyan, the obligation in this case would be legally binding.

See D'var Avrohom (Vol. I, p. 13a), and Chazon Ish, end of volume on Choshen Mishpot, collection of essays on miscellaneous topics (16,9), who gave different interpretations to the view of the Ramban.

does not accept the opinion of the Vilna Gaon, should this lead us to assume that this principle of "Dina de'malchusa" is only of Rabbinic origin?

That was indeed the view of the Bais Shmuel,[12] one of the major commentaries on the Shulchan Aruch, that "Dina de'malchusa dina", is only "Miderabanan," (of Rabbinic origin). However, most Poskim following him have not accepted his view, and have assumed that the principle of Shmuel is of Biblical origin—Midoraisa.[13]

At first, it may seem to matter little whether the authority of the ruler to make regulations rests upon a Biblical or Rabbinic basis; in either case, the regulations would be binding upon the Jew. Actually, however, the resolution could have quite far-reaching consequences. For example, if the Torah accepts government regulation as binding, then transactions conducted in accordance with the law of the land would have the same force as those executed in accordance with Torah stipulations. Thus, the sale of chometz before Pesach could be effected by a simple bill of sale, which would be legal under secular law; there would be no need for the various forms of kinyan and transferral of property which the Rabbis undertake.

* * * * * * *

A new approach to the issue of the halachic legitimacy of secular law was developed by the last Rabbi of Kovno, Rabbi

---

12. Commentary to Even Haezer, Chapter 28, sub-section 3.
13. Avnei Miluim, Even Haezer; Tshuvot Chasam Sofer, Yoreh Deah responsum 314, D'var Avrohom, Volume I, p. 9.

Avraham Dov Ber Cahana Shapiro, in his classic work, Dvar
Avrohom:[14] The Talmud shows[15] from various verses that
"hefker Bes Din hefker", that the Rabbinic Court has the
authority to take away someone's property, and to declare it
ownerless (hefker); and even to declare that it should be considered as if that property belongs from now on to someone
else, despite the fact that the other person made no "kinyan" or
formal "act of acquisition."[16] This ability of the Bes Din to
declare as hefker someone else's property, is not due to the
"authority of Torah" they possess, for here they are *not* following the laws of the Torah, but rather due to "governmental
authority" possessed by the Bes Din. Therefore, the Biblical
passages which indicate to us the power of the Bes Din to make
something hefker apply also to non-Jewish jurisdiction, and

---

14. Volume I, p. 12a.

15. Gittin 36b.

16. Rashba, Gittin. There is a major dispute between the Kzos Hachoshen
    and the Nesivos to Choshen Mishpot, Chapter 235, section 7, regarding
    this principle of Hefker Bes Din. Do the Psukim indicate that Min
    Hatorah (Biblically) Bes Din only has the ability to declare someone's
    property as Hefker, and their authority to declare that it belongs to
    somebody else is not Mid'oraitho; or should we assume that even the
    ability of the Bes Din to declare that someone's property should belong to
    another person is also Biblical in origin? The major difference in this issue
    would be whether something acquired through a Kinyan D'rabonon
    belongs to the person only Mid'rabonon or even Mid'oraitho. Could one
    use a Lulav and Esrog which he acquired merely by having picked it up
    (Hagboho) without having paid for it (payment constituting the Kinyon
    Mid'oraitho, and Hagboho being only a Kinyan Mid'rabonon) on the first
    day of Succos, where the mitzvoh d'oraitho requires that it must belong to
    me? See Divrei Yichezkiel by Rabbi Yechezkiel Burstein, Chapter 56,
    where he shows that this Machlokes between the Kzos and the Nesivos is
    rooted in a much earlier disagreement amongst the Rishonim.

are actually the source of the principle of "dina de'malchusa".[17]
It is interesting to note that the famous Chassidic Rebbe of
Sochochov, Rabbi Avrohom Friedman, in his classic work
"Avnei Nezer," a contemporary of the "Dvar Avrohom",
developed a very similar notion in his fascinating responsum[18]
dealing with the case of a son-in-law interested in inheriting his
father-in-law's rabbinical position.

Assuming that the government has the legal right to levy
taxes, and that the citizens are obligated to pay these taxes, like
any other debt that any individual owes to someone else, the
question now arises, what would be the status of one who does
not pay his taxes; or does not pay the full amount that he
should legally be paying? If an individual owes money to
someone else and fails to pay, he violates the aveirah of "lo

---

17. According to the view of the Nesivos (in note 16), that Biblically the Bes
Din only has the ability to declare someone's property as ownerless, Rab
bi David Rappaport explains in his work Zemach Dovid (pp. 110-111)
that the basis of this principle runs as follows: the Bes Din (and hence,
the government as well) has the authority to act as if they were the true
owners of the property. Therefore, just as the owner himself could
declare his property as Hefker (ownerless) without any need for any additional action (maaseh Kinyan), so too the Bes Din can declare it as
ownerless without the need for any act of Kinyan. But regarding declaring someone else as the owner, just as the true owner himself was unable
to transfer ownership of his property to someone else without a formal
act of Kinyan, so too the ability of the Bes Din to declare someone else as
the owner would only be Mid'rabonon in nature, and not Min Hatorah.
    With respect to accepting upon oneself a monetary obligation
towards the government, just as the individual could have accomplished
this without the need for any formal act of Kinyan (see above note 11), so
too the government has the ability—Min Hatorah—to levy taxes upon individuals, and the obligation to pay those taxes would be the same as in
the case where the person himself had accepted that debt.
18. Yoreh Deah, Responsum 312, sections 46-52.

sa'ashok" and possibly also the aveirah of "lo sigzol".[19] If someone should refrain from paying the taxes due to a Jewish government, these two violations will apply.

[This raises an interesting incidental question—is there any *religious* restriction against changing American dollars into Israeli currency on the famous black market in Israel? Since this is a Jewish government, would it be a violation of these two prohibitions? It would seem that technically these particular issurim would not apply; in changing money for a higher rate, one is not actually stealing anything, nor is he failing to pay the government a legitimate tax. I do not mean to imply that other issurim might not be applicable.[20]]

If however it is a non-Jewish government to which one owes taxes, the following question arises: The Talmud clearly forbids "gezel akum" stealing from a nochri, but "hafka'as halva'oso" is allowed.[20a] That is to say that although theft from a nochri is forbidden, *not paying back* a debt which one owes to a nochri is not considered an act of gezel (theft). If this be the case, then the non-Jewish government has all the legal right to

---

19. According to the Talmud (Bava Metziah 61a and 111a) one who fails to pay his debts violates both the Laws of "Lo Sigzol" and "Lo Saashok". The Rambam (at the very beginning of Hilchot G'zeloh V'avedah) clearly distinguishes between these two violations; Lo Sigzol only applies when a person takes away someone else's property. If someone fails to pay his debts, he violates only Lo Saashok. The commentary Maggid Mishnah attempts to discover a source in the Talmud for the Rambam's view.

20. Any government regulations imposed for the purpose of protecting the consumers or for enhancing the economy, etc., are halchically binding based on another aspect of the principle of "Dina de'malchusa". One of the major functions of any king (or government) is to keep law and order in his country. "The king preserves his country by insisting on mishpot" (Proverbs 29,4). See Avnei Nezer in note 18. This aspect of "Dina de'malchusa" will be covered later in our discussion of "makin ve'onshin shelo min hadin".

20a. Bava Kamma 113b.

levy just and fair taxes; still, what is to forbid the individual from failure to pay his taxes on the grounds that "hafka'as halva'oso" (non-payment of a debt) of a nochri is allowed?

If one fills out a tax form with false information in such a way that he pays less than he really owes the government, this involves a violation of "sheker," dealing falsely with others.[21] The question remains however, is it ossur if one simply never fills out any tax form at all, or does not pay sales tax, where there is no problem of "sheker", but is merely a situation of one's not paying his debts to a nochri? This question has practical immediacy, with the proliferation of myriads of little business enterprises which are not registered with the government. The private basement businesses neither collect nor pay sales tax. Is it "muttar" for an observant Jew to maintain such a store? Furthermore, may one *buy* from such a store? And would it even be permissible to report to the pertinent government agencies the existence of this illegal business? Does the principle of "Dina de'malchusa dina" apply in such a case?

To the question of whether it is permissible to operate a store and not collect or not pay sales tax, we find a mixed response. In the view of the Vilna Gaon[22] and other Poskim,[23] not paying the secular government that which it is owed is permitted. But if one might possibly create a situation of "chilul hashem" by not paying his taxes, there is no doubt that the

---

21. See Vayikro 19-11, that one is forbidden to falsify in money matters. If one signs a false oath, according to many Poskim this is a violation of Shvuas Sheker. (See Teshuvos Rabbi Akiva Eiger 30-32.) Even if one has not violated either of these injunctions, the Talmud (Kiddushin 45b) points to the Biblical passage in the book of Tzefaniah that the Jewish people must be especially outstanding in the area of honesty and truthfulness, and must never lie or falsify, even when there is no monetary issue involved.
22. Choshen Mishpot 369, sub-section 23.
23. Kesef Mishneh to Hilchot G'zeloh V'avedah, Chapter 5, section 11.

"heter" of "hafka'as halva'ah" of akum does not apply. In the *rare instance* where (a) there is no question of signing a false statement, and (b) there is no possibility of causing a chilul hashem, this group of poskim does not consider it forbidden.

However, the Ramo[24] in his comments to the Shulchan Aruch, as well as the Baal HaTanya (R. Schneuer Zalman of Liady), have both rejected this view. They feel that although "hafka'as halva'ah" of a private individual and nochri may be permissible, this principle has no application with respect to paying of one's taxes to the government. The reasoning for this distinction is as follows: The government not only imposes the tax, but in this instance also requires that the individual send the taxes to it.[25] The principle "Dina de'malchusa dina" cannot only create an obligation of a debt, but it can also obligate one to do specific actions—such as paying the debt. Therefore, although considering the Biblical law alone, one would not be required to pay one's debts to the non-Jewish government (following the principle that hafka'as halva'ah of a nochri is muttar), yet, based on the rule "Dina de'malchusa dina", he would

---

24. Choshen Mishpot 369, section 6, in Ramo.

25. See Mishneh Lemelech, end of Chapter 5, Hilchot Gezelah Veavedah. According to the view of the Kzos (mentioned above in note 16), the Bes Din (and therefore also the government) has the authority both to declare ownership and non-ownership, but does not necessarily have the power to otherwise act as if they themselves were the Baalim. Following the opinion of the Nesivos, however, (mentioned above in notes 16 and 17) that the Bes Din acts as if they were the Baalim, we can understand quite well how they are able to impose upon an individual an obligation to do a specific action (as, for example, to fill out his tax form and pay his taxes) and not just to create the Chiuv Momon (the debt). Just as the individual could have accepted upon himself as a Poel (a worker) the obligation to do a specific job, so too the Bes Din (or the government) can impose such an obligation upon him, as if he himself had agreed to it.

still be required to pay his taxes just as if he had accepted the obligation of payment willingly by himself.[26]

If we accept the latter argument prohibiting maintaining a business without paying sales tax for the merchandise sold, what is the status of a prospective customer? May he buy in such an establishment? Rabbi J.B. Soloveitchik has said that it is forbidden to buy there, because of the Biblical prohibition "lifnei ivair" (one may not tempt or make it attractive for someone else to commit a transgression). However, as far as reporting the illegal shopkeeper to the authorities, this would be forbidden, as we will show later in our discussion.

- - - - - - -

The first area of "Dina de'malchusa dina", as we have seen, is in the taxation function of government. A second area is minting coins and establishing the value of the currency. According to the Shach in his commentary on the Shulchan

---

26. There is yet another significant view amongst the Rishonim regarding the right of the government to levy taxes. According to the opinion of some Baalei Tosafot, (see Ran to Nedarim 28a beginning B'Muchas), just as a landlord is entitled to charge rent for the use of his apartment, so too the government owns the land of its country and is entitled to charge rent (in the form of taxes) for the individual's right to stay in that country. Following this view, the Israeli government would not have the power to levy any taxes upon Jewish people living in that country, for all Jews are entitled to live there rent-free. Although some claim in the name of the Chazon Ish that he felt one could rely on this opinion, it would seem to me that this view was not shared by the majority of the Poskim.

In addition it should be noted that even to this opinion, only the first aspect of "Dina d'malchusa" would be excluded in Eretz Yisroel, namely, regarding the government's right to levy taxes. With respect to the other three areas of "Dina D'malchusa Dina", all Rishonim would agree that they apply even in Eretz Yisroel.

In this essay I have followed the D'var Avrohom (Vol. I, p. 14, in note) in dividing the topic into four parts: (1) taxation; (2) minting of currency; (3) keeping law and order and punishing criminals; and (4) introducing a legal system.

Aruch,[27] this is a specific function of government. If the government should suddenly change the monetary system, and declare new coins as legal tender, even if the new coins are intrinsically of much lesser value than the older ones, the principle of "Dina de'malchusa" definitely will apply.[28]

- - - - - - -

27. Yoreh Deah 165, sub-section 8.
28. This point is most relevant with respect to two areas of Halacha: (1) the law is that Maaser Sheini (the second tithe on vegetation grown in Eretz Yisroel) may only be eaten if it is first redeemed into cash. Although one may redeem Hekdesh, or redeem a first-born son using "Shoveh Kesef" (commodities), the pidyon or redemption of Maaser Sheini requires "Kesef sh'yesh olov Zurah". (Talmud B'choros 51a). This would imply that in America, one who happens to have some Maaser Sheini could only redeem it in American coins; and one in France could only redeem his Maaser Sheini into French currency. Those groups who do not recognize the present Israeli government, and consider the Zionists as pirates who took over Palestine from the Arabs illegally, would not be able to redeem their Maaser Sheini in Israel using Israeli currency.

(2) Regarding the prohibition against collection of interest on debts: If a loan of English money were made in the United States, and at the time the debt were due the American currency had gone down due to inflation, one would not be permitted to repay the full amount of English money he had borrowed but only the amount it was worth in American money at the time of the loan. (See Bris Yehuda, end of Chapter 18.) If however one had borrowed cash of the local currency, and the value of the money had increased by the time the debt was due, he would be permitted, and indeed obligated to pay in full the entire amount of money he had borrowed. The Halacha declares that cash always retains the same value, and only commodities fluctuate in their value. See Igrot Moshe, Yoreh Deah, Volume II, Responsum 114.

Some view money as an evil of society, and feel that a more perfect society would prevail if it were eliminated. The Chazon Ish has pointed out (Yoreh Deah 72:2) that in his opinion this can not be true. Since the Torah requires that for the redemption of Maaser Sheini only cash may be used and not commodities, apparently currency is an essential component of the ideal Torah-oriented government. Wherever Jews are in control of a government, it would be proper for them to see that their country should have a system of currency.

A third, and most significant area of application of "Dina de'malchusa" is the right of any government, Jewish or non-Jewish, to punish criminals as they see fit, for the purpose of keeping law and order.[29] The Gemara states[30] that there was a tradition that "the Bes Din may issue corporal punishment or monetary fines even when not warranted by the Torah". The Ran commenting on that Gemara points out that this permission not only applies to a Jewish religious Bes Din, but even to a secular or non-Jewish government. Proof to this is shown by Ritva from the Talmudic story[31] of Rabbi Eliezer ben Rabbi Shimon who was by profession a policeman for the Roman government, and would arrest Jewish criminals and have them punished based on circumstantial evidence. His contemporary Rabbi Yehoshua ben Korcha was angry at him for "giving over" fellow-Jews to the Roman government to be punished by death. Rabbi Eliezer answered that he was "cleaning out the Jewish vineyard of its thorns," whereupon Rabbi Yehoshua ben Korcha replied, "let the master of the vineyard (G-d) clean out his own vineyard."

Similarly, Rabbi Yishmael ben Rabbi Yosi was also appointed by the government as a policeman for the purpose of identifying Jewish criminals who were to get the death penalty. The prophet Eliyahu appeared to him, and recommended that he give up his position. And the if the Roman government would not allow him to resign, Eliyahu urged him that if need be, he should leave the country, just in order not to have to hand over the Jewish criminals. The Ritva points out that neither Rabbi Yehoshua ben Korcha nor Eliyahu ha'Novi said it was *forbidden* to be in such a position. They merely argued that it was *not proper* for these prominent rabbis to do that type of work.

---

29. See Avnei Nezer in note 18, and note 20.
30. Sanhedrin 46a.
31. Bava Metziah 83b-84a.

◆§ Mesirah

The above case is unrelated to the prohibition against "mesirah". A "mossur" is one who aids a pirate, or a crooked government official, or a tyrant-king to obtain money illegally from his fellow Jew. Even if the Jew has actually done something wrong, but if the secular government or the ruler would exact a punishment far beyond that which the crime should require, then it is likewise forbidden to report him. If, however, the government is entitled to its taxes, or is permitted to punish criminals as offenders, there is no problem of "mesirah" in informing goverment officials of the information needed for them to collect their taxes or to apprehend their man.

One critical point should however be added: There is no problem of "mesirah" in informing the government of a Jewish criminal, even if they penalize the criminal with a punishment more severe than the Torah requires, because even a non-Jewish government is authorized to punish and penalize above and beyond the law, "shelo min hadin", for the purpose of maintaining law and order. However, this only applies in the situation when the Jewish offender or criminal has at least violated *some* Torah law. But if he did absolutely nothing wrong in the eyes of the Torah, then giving him over to the government would constitute a violation of "mesirah."

The Shulchan Aruch points out, however, that in most cases, "mesirah" is still not allowed, for a different reason: This is the rule regarding "aveidas akum", property lost by a nochri. "Aveidas akum" may only be returned in a case of chilul hashem. Under ordinary circumstances, a Jew should not return something lost. Now, in our case, the non-Jewish government is searching, so to speak, for its missing man or its missing money, and one is not permitted to help them.[32] If, however, it is known that the only ones who can testify on the government case against a Jewish criminal are Jewish people, and by not testifying it will become clear and evident that Jews are covering up for other Jews who are guilty of crimes, then "Mishum Chilul Hashem", the Shulchan Aruch explicitly requires[33] the Jews to testify in the non-Jewish court of law even though this will lead to the prosecution of his fellow-Jew.

How could Rabbi Eliezer ben Rabbi Shimon and Rabbi Yishmael ben Rabbi Yosi have undertaken to act as policemen? Doesn't the Shulchan Aruch indicate that it is forbidden to hand over a criminal unless there is·a possibility of desecration, chilul hashem, involved? But these two were salaried officials acting in the line of duty! Their informing on fellow-Jews was not done merely as a favor to the Roman government (which would be forbidden as "aveidas akum"). Rather, they were being paid to hand over the criminals; they were not returning the lost "article" to the government but were rather engaging in actions for which they were being paid. If a non-Jew hires a Jew and pays him as a worker, and his job is to look for lost articles, this will not fall under the category of "aveidas akum". The Jew who is returning the lost article is doing so as a "job" and not as an act of hashovas aveidah. The same is true of the Jewish investigator for the non-Jewish government. But even in this job, which is permitted, there is a limitation as we have noted previously—if the Jew did absolutely nothing wrong in the eyes of the Torah, then it is forbidden to hand him over.

32. Sanhedrin 76b.

33. Choshen Mishpot, Chapter 28, section 3.

⋑ Harboring a Criminal

A problem related to this situation is that of harboring a criminal. The Talmud[34] tells about such a situation which proved a vexing dilemma for the Rabbis: There were some people from Galilee who were accused of murder, and were running away from the government to avoid prosecution. They came to Rabbi Tarfon and asked if he would hide them in his house. Whereupon the Rabbi told them: "If I will not hide you, the government officials will apprehend you and punish you. But on the other hand, if I should choose to hide you—maybe I am not allowed to! Our Rabbis have said that although one may not *believe* "loshon horah" (slander) told about others, still one *must be cautious* and act as if the story might be true. In that case, I am not allowed to hide you. Therefore, I recommend that you go and hide on your own."

What does this anecdote teach about the actual halacha of abetting an alleged criminal? Rashi comments that if it were true that the fugitives had really killed, it would not be permissible to hide them, for one may not help a murderer hide from the police. Tosafot, however, quotes the Sheiltot, who had a different way to understand Rabbi Tarfon's comment: "If it is true that you are guilty, and I hide you, then I too will be punished by the government for harboring a criminal. Therefore, for the sake of protecting myself, I do not want to hide you." From this Tosafot we might infer that they disagree with Rashi—i.e., that Tosafot feels that one *may* hide a criminal from the hands of a non-Jewish court, and that the only reason Rabbi Tarfon was reluctant was that he was fearful that then the government would punish him.

---

34. Nidah 61a.

But the Maharshal in his commentary[35] points out that we would be incorrect in making such an inference from the Tosafot. Tosafot agrees wholly with Rashi that one may not obstruct justice by actively hiding a criminal from the hands of the court. Just as this applies to the Jewish court, so too it applies to a non-Jewish court. And although the Temple does not stand, and the Jewish court may not administer the death penalty today,[36] the non-Jewish courts are not so restricted, and one *may not* assist the criminal in escaping from the law. There is a specific sin in harboring a criminal, even from the secular courts. This is the commandment of "u-beearto horo mikirbecho",[37] to eradicate the evil from our midst. According to Rashi, this is what Rabbi Tarfon was afraid of neglecting, and therefore was loathe to hide them. The reason why Tosafot and the Sheiltot did not interpret Rabbi Tarfon's comment the same way Rashi did, is because of another factor: Rabbi Tarfon had not yet ascertained the guilt of the people who had come to him, and he should have assumed that they were innocent and therefore aided them in hiding from the police, were it not for the fact that (according to Tosafot) if he were caught, he himself might be punished for harboring the criminals.

This discussion leads us to another very perplexing modern problem—how can an observant Jewish lawyer act in good conscience to help a defendant escape the consequences of his misdeeds? Although this is not the context in which to discuss the full implications of the principle, we may state briefly that if a lawyer knows that his client has committed a crime, it is *forbidden* for him to help the criminal escape the consequences of his act, by relying on some technical legal

---

35. Ibid.
36. Sanhedrin 52b.
37. See comments of Ramban to Sefer Hamitzvot, end of Shoresh 14; and Megillat Esther there, note 3.

points or other devices. The lawyer, just as any Jew, is directed by the Torah to "eradicate the evil from our midst", and may not actively assist someone to avoid his punishment.[38]

- - - - - - -

A major issue with respect to "Dina de'malchusa" is, to what extent do we follow the secular law of the land, as opposed to the laws of the Torah.

In the area of issur ve'heter (religious laws) there is no doubt at all that "Dina de'malchusa" has no application.[39] Just because the American law does not forbid working on Shabbos, or remarrying without a religious "get" (divorce), we cannot say that "Dina de'malchusa dina". This principle is certainly only to be applied in the area of dinei momonot (money matters). The reason for this is simple enough to understand. The basis of "Dina de'malchusa" is identical with the principle of "hefker Bes Din", which only has application in that area.

---

38. Mishna Halochos by Rabbi Menashe Klein, Volume 7, p. 366b.
39. See S'dei Chemed (Grossman edition, N.Y.) Vol. II, p. 70. Reform groups have erroneously distinguished between marriage and divorce requiring a religious marriage ceremony, while not requiring a religious Get. Their reason for this distinction is that while we recite Brochos (blessings) at the Jewish marriage, no Brochos are recited at the time of a Get. This would seem to indicate that having a Jewish marriage is a Mitzvah whereas obtaining a Jewish Get is not a Mitzvah but merely a Jewish law. The government's laws are able to substitute for the Jewish laws, but not for the Jewish Mitzvos.

It is questionable as to whether this is the true reason for the lack of a Brocha at the time of a Get. (See essay of Rabbi Yosef Ibn Palat on the topic of reciting blessings on various Mitzvos, printed in the beginning of the sefer Avudraham.)

But even if this point were to be accepted, that giving of a Jewish Get does not constitute a Mitzvah, the conclusion that the secular law of the land may be followed in the area of divorce is definitely an error. Anything outside of the area of Dinei Momonot, cannot be covered by the principle of "Dina d'malchusa dina".

In addition, Rabbenu Yona notes[40] that even within the area of dinei momonot, the laws of the secular courts only apply when the case in question involves a Jew and a non-Jew, or when both parties are non-Jews. Any case between two parties both of whom are Jewish, is only subject to the Torah laws of jurisprudence as set forth in the Shulchan Aruch Choshen Mishpat. The Chazon Ish wrote in his essay[41] on "Dina de'malchusa", that in his opinion none of the Rishonim (earlier commentaries) disagreed with this view of Rabbi Yona.

The Shach, however, points out[42] two exceptions to this rule: 1) Whenever the halacha is such that if a t'nai (a condition) were stipulated, then the Torah laws would be altered, then we assume that although the laws of the secular courts do not apply where both litigants in the case are Jewish, still we say that the fact that the common practice in that area (where non-Jews are involved) is in accordance with the laws of the secular courts, there is an understood agreement of a t'nai (condition), that secular law be followed.[43] For example: If someone

---

40. Quoted by Rashba, Gittin 10b.

If, however, the secular government enacts laws of price control or rent control, it would seem that even if both the landlord and the tenant were Jewish, these laws would apply to them as well. The only area Rabbenu Yona applied his principle (that "Dina d'malchusa" only applies when only one Jew is involved) is this fourth area of introducing a legal system. Establishing price controls is a function of government (Bava Bathra 89a) belonging to the third area of keeping law and order. It should therefore apply even in a situation where no non-Jews are involved at all. (See "Dina D'malchusa Dina," Shmuel Shiloh, pp. 175-176.)

41. End of volume on Choshen Mishpot, essay 16 on miscellaneous topics, section 1.

42. Choshen Mishpot, Chapter 73, sub-section 39.

43. In this type of case, we are not really following "Dina de'malchusa", but rather our own law, Dina D'Dan (see Chazon Ish mentioned above in note 41), which does allow one to alter the laws by adding on a Tnai. See Bava Metziah 94a.

leaves his watch with a jeweler to be repaired, according to the
law of Torah as explained by the Talmud,[44] that jeweler would
be responsible for the watch, even in the event of a burglary in
the jewelery shop, where the jeweler was not at fault, and suffered a great loss himself. If, however, the jeweler would have
stipulated a condition at the very outset, and specified that he
does not accept any responsibility for any burglary, then he
would not have to pay. If the *secular law* relieves the jeweler of
any responsibility in such a case, then even if both the jeweler
and the customer are Jewish, and no explicit stipulation of such
a condition were made, nevertheless we would assume that established secular law would be considered like the "minhag
ha'medina" (the local custom), and therefore we would also assume that this condition was obvious and understood,
although it was never formally verbalized.[45]

2) A second exception would be where the halacha has no
explicit law pertaining to the case at hand, so that the secular
law of the courts is not in *contradiction* to the Torah-law. In
this case, according to the opinion of the Shach, the "Dina
de'malchusa" is binding even in cases where both parties involved are Jewish. For example: in any case involving corporations, or buying futures, where the Talmud and the Shulchan
Aruch have nothing to say on the matter, the secular laws
would be binding even between two Jews.

The Chazon Ish[46] took strong issue with this second point
of the Shach—he said there are no blank areas where the
halacha has nothing to say. Of course, the Talmud has no dis-
cussions of corporate law or futures, but *based on* the Talmudic

---

44. Bava Metziah 80b.
45. See above note 11.
46. Mentioned above, in note 41.

law we can figure out what the halacha should be in any given area. Therefore, there is no area of secular law outside the purview of the halacha, and secular law may not be followed.

Even in a case between a Jew and a non-Jew, the halacha is not all that clear that secular law should be followed. The Mishna in Gittin[47] states that all deeds completed by the secular non-Jewish courts are valid and acceptable, except for a "get" (a religious bill of divorce), which must be written "lishma", and signed by religious Jews. The Talmud questions the scope of the statement of the Mishna, that all documents and deeds in the area of dinei momonot (monetary matters, as opposed to religious matters) are valid. The Talmud seeks to determine whether the document is a "shtar rayah" (a proof), indicating that one party owes another party money, or that one party has already sold his property to another party; or whether the document of the non-Jewish court is a "shtar kinyan", (a bill of sale), namely, that is serves as the vehicle for the *transfer* of the property, or as the vehicle *to create* the indebtedness. In the first instance, where the document serves merely the purpose of "rayah" (proof), we can understand why the deed of the non-Jewish court should be accepted, because we know that the courts are reliable and would not issue a false document. Hence, we consider it as acceptable evidence that the one party really owes the money to the other, or that the one party really transferred ownership of his property to the other party. But in the case of a "shtar kinyan", where the document is serving as the vehicle whereby the legal transaction *should take effect*, or with which the indebtedness *is initiated*, how can we say that the deed of the non-Jewish court is to be accepted; the transaction never took place in a legal fashion (according to Jewish law) and the indebtedness never was effected in a halachically legal manner.

---

47. 10b.

In response to this question the Talmud offers two suggestions: a) Based on the principle of "Dina de'malchusa dina", the secular non-Jewish courts are empowered to effect and create a "kinyan" (a transfer of property) or a "hitchayvut" (an indebtedness), according to the laws that they themselves set down.

b) Perhaps the Mishna only declares as acceptable documents of "rayah", but not those serving the purpose of "kinyan", which the Mishna would declare as invalid.

The Rishonim are puzzled with the need for the second suggestion of the Gemara. Isn't the principle of "Dina de'malchusa dina" universally accepted? Why shouldn't a transaction between a Jew and a non-Jew, effected according to the laws of the secular courts, be legally binding?

Because of this difficulty, some Baalei Tosafot[48] were led to understand that the second suggestion of the Gemara, (which is accepted as the final decision and the more authoratative view among the Amoraim), is of the opinion that "Dina de'malchusa dina" is limited to the government's right to collect taxes and the like, where the law is *for the benefit of the government.* This they take to mean is the *literal* translation of "Dina de'malchusa"—the laws *on behalf* of the government—such as laws of taxation and the like. But the legal system enacted by the government would not be included in the scope of "Dina de'malchusa dina".

The Ramban[49] attacks this view as totally unacceptable. Although the Ramoh in his additions to the Shulchan Aruch quotes the above Tosafot in one place[50], he himself makes it clear in another place[51] that this is *not* the accepted view.

48. Quoted by Magid Mishnah Hilchot Malveh Veloveh, beginning of Chapter 27, and by Shach, Yoreh Deah, Chapter 165, sub-section 8.
49. Quoted by Shach, loc. cit.
50. Choshen Mishpot, end of Chapter 74 and end of Chapter 369.
51. See Shach in note 48, and Shach to Choshen Mishpot, end of Chapter 74.

As to the difficulty in the Gemara—why there was a need at all for the second suggestion, since "Dina de'malchusa dina" is universally accepted even in this type of case—the other Rishonim explain[52] that the Talmud wanted to cover even a case where the court was a private institution and was not authorized by the government. But the legal system of a court of law, which is under the auspices of the government, *would be* binding in cases involving a Jew and a non-Jew, even though that legal system does not correspond to the Torah law.

* * *

The Chazon Ish pointed out the Gemara[53] which states that when a Jew and a non-Jew appear before a Jewish Bes Din, in a case where there is a discrepancy between Jewish law and the secular law, then if the Bes Din can acquit the Jew based on the secular law, they should do so, and tell the litigants that they have followed the secular law; but if by following the Jewish law, rather than secular law, the Jew will be acquitted, then they should render their decision based on Jewish law, and tell the parties that they have followed Jewish law. The Chazon Ish writes that one could have understood the Talmud to be saying that this is really the law—that the Jew is entitled to whatever benefits he can possibly get from following *either* system of law, since both systems apply to his case against the non-Jew, as far as he is concerned. However, we see that the Rambam[54] did not understand the Gemara in this fashion. Basically, whenever a non-Jew is involved in the case, *only* the secular laws are binding—to the exclusion of the Torah laws. And if the Jew's opponent in the case is a "Ger Toshav" (a non-Jew who has formally accepted upon himself the seven

---

52. See commentaries of Rashba and Ran to Gittin.
53. Bava Kamma 113a.
54. Hilchot Melochim, end of Chapter 10.

Noachite mitzvot, and is therefore assumed to be a decent religious and observant person), then only the secular law must be followed. Only if the Jew's opponent in the case presented to the Bes Din is a non-Jew of the lower class, then the Rabbis *penalize* the heathen to have the judges favor the Jew by following either Talmudic law or the secular law, depending upon which is better for the Jew.

It is still unclear from the Talmud, as well as from the Rambam, as to the exact nature of this penalty. Does this mean that if the case between the Jew and the heathen were brought up to a Bes Din, then they should issue such a decision? Or does it mean that even *before* the case comes up, as soon as the *situation presents itself*, this penalty is already in effect; and even if the non-Jew converts to Judaism (or becomes a Ger Toshav) before coming to the Bes Din, the judges must apply this Talmudic penalty? The Chazon Ish dwells at length upon the exact details of this point in his essay on "Dina de'malchusa".[55]

- - - - - - -

We have noted previously that the principle "Dina de'malchusa dina" is generally operative in the area of monetary matters. Thus, it would be logical to assume that if a Jew dies, leaving only a secular will, it would be considered valid. However, this is not the case, for two reasons: a) if the din-Torah is between the rightful heirs, and other Jews or Jewish organizations designated in the will, then "Dina de'malchusa" does not apply. This principle applies only when

---

55. Mentioned above, in note 41, section 8.

at least one of the litigants is not Jewish; b) according to Rambam,[56] issues of inheritance are not only labeled as monetary matters (dinei momonot), but also, at the same time, as a matter of religious law (issur veheter). The Torah refers to the laws of inheritance as "chukas mishpat". Although "mishpat" has the meaning of "a monetary law", "chok" has the connotation of "a religious law." Since the will, then, can be considered a religious instrument and not only a financial transaction, it must conform to the requirements of Torah law.

Although the topic requires a great deal of discussion and explanation, which is not possible here, it would be correct to state that, in many circumstances, a secular will executed by a Jew is *not* valid.[57]

In the Torah,[58] the laws of inheritance are noted. And although the Torah does give a person the right to make a will,[59] it is only under the following two conditions: (1) The will is only valid if it is instructed when the testator is sick, and in the state of a "schechiv mira".[60] (2) The will can only choose from among the relatives who are directly in line to inherit,[61] to change the amounts of their respective yerusha (inheritance). For example, if a man dies leaving sons, daughters, and a wife, strictly speaking according to the halacha, only the sons get the

56. Hilchot Ishut, Chapter 12, section 9; Hilchot Nachalot, beginning of Chapter 6. The Rambam's view is shared also by Tosafot, Ktubot 50b, beginning Umai Aliyah.

See also Rabbi Yosef Rosen, Tzofnas Paaneach, (Tshuvot, New York,) no. 313.
57. See essay by Rabbi Mordechai Willig on the "Halacha of Wills" in "Chavrusa," (publication of Rabbinic Alumni of Yeshiva University,) Kislev, 5740.
58. Bamidbar, Chapter 27.
59. Bava Bathra 130a.
60. Choshen Mishpot, Chapter 281, section I.
61. As above, in note 59.

yerusha, which they divide evenly among themselves. If the father makes a tzavaah (will) when he is sick, he can see to it that not all the sons get an even share. He cannot, however, accomplish, even with a will, that his wife or his daughters should get any yerusha. He also cannot accomplish, even with leaving a will, that the first-born son should not get his "pi shnayim" (double share).[62]

For that purpose, one of two methods is required: a) the halacha has a principle of "mitzvah lekayeim divrei hames".[63] Rabbinically, the desires of the deceased person must be honored, at least with respect to where his money should go.[64] This principle applies only in the case where the person has handed over that amount of money to someone else during his lifetime specifically for the purpose of seeing to it, after his death, that it reaches the hands of the desired recipients.[65] Rabbi Chaim Ozer Grodzenski of Vilna[66] entertained the thought that handing over a will to a lawyer might possibly substitute for the handing over of the amount of money itself, but he later rejected that notion. Only in the case of a will to leave the

---

62. Bava Bathra 126b.
63. Gittin 14b.
64. See Torah Shleima (by Rabbi Mendel Kasher) to Breishis, Parshas Vayechi, (47-30), note 126, regarding the applicability of this principle to other wishes of the deceased, outside of the area of distributing his wealth.
65. Tosafot, Gittin 13a, beginning V'ho; Choshen Mishpot, Chapter 252, section 2.
66. Teshuvot Achiezer, Vol. III, responsum 34.
    Rabbi Yaakov Ettlinger in his responsa work "Binyan Zion", Vol. II, 24, maintains that the Shulchan Aruch has not really accepted the view of the Tosafot that Hushlash Mitchila Lekach is needed. His arguement is not that convincing, and obviously was not accepted by Rabbi Chaim Ozer, who often quoted and relied on decisions of the Binyan Zion; in this instance he did not even quote his view.

money to charity did he feel that the will should be binding Rabbinically, despite the lack of "hushlash mitchillah lekach" (having been handed over specifically for that purpose). b) The Ramo in Shulchan Aruch[67] refers to a second method of apportioning one's inheritance, which would not require having the money put away in escrow. For example, if a man feels that at the time he will die, he will leave over *less* than a hundred thousand dollars, and he would like to leave half of his inheritance to his wife, he should legally obligate himself as of today to his wife (by having someone else give him a "suddar", a handkerchief, or any other k'li, representing the wife,[68]) to the amount of fifty thousand dollars, collectible only on the day he dies,[69] on the condition that his rightful heirs have the option of invalidating his debt by paying off his widow with half of their inheritance. Or, if he would like to leave *all* of his money to his wife, he should obligate himself towards his wife in a debt (by someone giving over a handkerchief or any other useful object,

---

67. Choshen Mishpot, Chapter 281, section 7.
68. See Tosafot, Kiddushin 26b, beginning Hochi Garsinon.
69. If the obligation would take effect immediately, the recipient of the grant could insist on collecting right away. The testator was not interested in giving away all his money yet. If the obligation were made in such a way that it could not be collected until after death, the entire Kinyan would not be legally binding at all. One cannot enact obligations set to take effect only after his death. If the Kinyan Sudar were to be made now, and it would be stipulated that no obligation at all should take effect until the day before he dies, it would also not be legally valid for two reasons: 1) since at the time the obligation is supposed to begin to go into effect, the action of the Kinyan Sudar is completed already, and this would constitute a case of Kolsa Kinyono. (Only according to the Rambam is there no problem of Kolsa Kinyono with a Kinyan Sudar done now to take effect at a later time. See Ran to Nedarim 27b, beginning V'ho, and Kesef Mishnah to Hilchot Mechira, Chapter 11, end of section 13.)

   2) If something is to take effect at a time which cannot be determined until later, we are not able to declare that we have determined retroactively (huvrar hadovor lemafreia) that the matter took effect at the earlier

for that purpose) in an amount in excess of the amount of money he expects to leave over at the time of his death. The debt should be said to take effect immediately, and should be collectible on the day of his death.

To cover the possibility of divorce, in which case he would *not* be interested in leaving his present wife any or all of his inheritance, he can make this "kinyan suddar" for the purpose of creating the hischayvus (indebtedness) towards his wife on the condition ("all hatnai") that "he does not change his mind before he dies." In this way, he has left himself the possibility to change his will, if that turns out to be necessary.

---

time. This is the meaning of the principle Ain Breira regarding issues which are d'oraitho.

It is because of all of these above considerations that it must be specified that the Kinyan Sudar is to effect the actual obligation of the debt immediately, and only the right of the recipient to collect is delayed till the later time.

We still seem, however, to be faced with a problem of Breira. Regarding the actual date that the recipient acquires the rights of collection of the debt, this can only be determined retroactively after the death of the testator. Shouldn't this still pose a problem of using Breira? An answer to this point can be found in the commentary of the Ran to Nedarim 45b.

Whenever the key part of the Chalos (that which is being effected) is not involved in any problems of retroactive determination, even though regarding some of the minor details of the case we must rely on Breira, this does not bother us.

The Sale of a Synagogue

By Rabbi Israel Poleyeff

Introduction

Changes that have occurred in the demographic make-up of Jewish communities, often with unexpected suddenness, have transformed a question that was in the past more often than not discussed only in theory into a vexing and difficult problem very common in our day. The departure of Jewish populations from once proud and vibrant Jewish communities has left these communities with once thriving institutions standing empty. Investments of millions of dollars are in danger of being lost, and in many cases have already been lost.

Synagogue buildings, the centers of religious life in their respective communities, present an even greater problem, for as *devarim she-bekedusha* (articles of inherent sanctity) the simple solution of selling these buildings to the highest bidder for whatever purposes the buyer wanted to make of them, could not so easily be implemented, if at all. What then shall be done with these old, yet functional, synagogue buildings? Left alone and abandoned, they would represent a massive financial loss. Does *halacha* permit their sale? If so, in what way? And for what uses?

In generations past, movement of Jewish communities was in no way as rapid as it is today. Children tended to remain in the

---

Rabbi, Cong. Ahavath Achim; Instructor of Talmud, Hebrew Academy of the Five Towns and Rockaway

towns in which they were born and raised. If they did leave their
birthplace for marriage or to earn a living, quite often it was to
relocate in a nearby town not far from their original home. Jewish
communities tended to remain in their same locations, often for
centuries. When their populations did in fact depart, it was
invariably a precipitous flight resulting from persecutions and
expulsions. Under these circumstances there was little thought
given to the possibility of salvaging anything from the physical
structure of the synagogue. The synagogue buildings were lost, and
that was it.

But in America, movement of Jewish populations is primarily
by choice. Community pressures and changes that may contribute
to this choice do not, however, force the Jews into a precipitous
departure leaving all behind. Sometimes these changes begin to
take shape even while the synagogue is in the process of being
built! Nonetheless, the possibility of recouping much of the losses
from these abandoned synagogues by their sale does in fact exist.
Can it be done?

The Sanctity of a Synagogue

Whether and under what circumstances a synagogue may be
sold falls under the broader question regarding the permissibility of
selling any article of special, inherent holiness (דברים שבקדושה).
Though it appears obvious that a synagogue is a *davar
shebekedusha*, the *gemara* nonetheless makes this abundantly clear
when, for example, in regard to the possible sale of a "public"
synagogue (של רבים) for use as a "private" synagogue (של יחיד),
the question involves the fact that מורידין אותו מקדושתו,[1] there is a
decrease in the synagogue's sanctity by virtue of its diminished
use.

What the source of this *kedusha* may be is a matter of
dispute. Many suggest that this *kedusha* is biblical in origin.[2] They

---

1. מגילה דף כ"ז ע"ב.
2. רמב"ם מנין המצוות ל"ת ס"ה ועיין שו"ת מהרש"ם שנתברר כל השיטות בעורך.

point out, among other comments, that the passage in *Vayikra*[3] which reads ומקדשי תיראו ("and you shall revere my sanctuary") refers to the sanctity not only of the *beth-hamikdosh*, the holy Temple, but of every *beth-medrash* (study hall) and *beth-knesses* (synagogue) as well. Others,[4] however, maintain that a synagogue's sanctity is only rabbinic in nature and results from the fact that it is a place where declarations of the holiness of G-d are made on a regular basis. Still others[5] equate the sanctity of a synagogue to that of any other of the many תשמישי מצוה, articles of sanctity, such as a *lulav* or a *succah*. This might be described as a קדושה של כבוד, a sanctity deriving from an inherent respect we have for all religious articles, and does not equal either of the previous two levels of *kedusha*.

These differing opinions in regard to the source of a synagogue's sanctity will have a crucial effect on the *halacha* of its sale. Obviously, only extremely cogent reasons would have to be present to permit this sale if the *kedusha* is biblical in origin. If it is rabbinic, then the *chachomim* could build into their *halacha* any conditions, lenient or otherwise, they deem necessary and appropriate. If, further, it is merely a קדושה של כבוד, no different from any other *tashmishei kedusha*, then its sanctity would automatically terminate with the completion of its use.

The question before us is, in reality, a two-fold one. Firstly, may a synagogue be sold only for use as another synagogue (or *beth-medrash*) by its new owners, or may the purchaser use the property for whatever he chooses? Secondly, does any sanctity attach to the money realized from the sale? Perhaps a third question may be added: when sale of a synagogue *is* permitted, are there any requirements as to the manner of the sale, or can it be accomplished in the same manner as any other business transaction?

---

3. ויקרא פרק י"ט פסוק ל'.

4. ר"ן מגילה כ"ו ע"ב ד"ה ומאן, פרי מגדים על אורח חיים משבצות זהב סי' קנ"ג סק"א.

5. רמב"ן הובא בר"ן מגילה דף כ"ו ע"ב ד"ה ומאן.

Talmudic Background

The first *mishna* in the fourth chapter of the *gemara* Megillah, dealing with the conditions under which a *davar shebekedusha* may be sold, reads:

> If the people of a town have sold its town square (or open space) they may purchase a synagogue with the proceeds thereof; a synagogue, they may purchase an Ark; an Ark, they may purchase mantles; mantles, they may purchase books; books, they may purchase a scroll of the Law. But if they sold a scroll of the Law they may not buy books; books, they may not buy mantles; mantles, they may not buy an Ark; an Ark, they may not buy a synagogue; a synagogue, they may not purchase a town square.[6]

Clearly, the underlying principle in this *mishna* is that the money realized from the sale of any article of *kedusha* be used only for the purchase of another article of greater *kedusha*. Thus for example, a *taivah* (an *aron kodesh*) may be sold only if the funds will be used to purchase coverings for the Torah, *neviim* in scroll form (what the *mishna* calls *seforim* - books), or a *sefer* Torah itself, but not the reverse. In this *mishna* a synagogue has a degree of sanctity between the street of a city, where occasional prayers were offered, such as on fast days — equivalent, perhaps, to what in Eastern Europe was called the "Shul hoif" - and an *aron kodesh*. Thus a synagogue may be sold to purchase an *aron kodesh*, but not the street. The well-known rule of מעלין בקודש ולא מורידין, in matters of sanctity we reach towards higher plateaus and not lower levels, is clearly applicable throughout the *mishna*.[7]

But what of the sale of an article for the purpose of

---

6. מגילה דף כ"ה ע"ב.

7. רמב"ם הלכות תפלה פרק י"א הלכה י"ד. A well-known application of this rule is the decision of the rabbis to accept Hillel's opinion to light one candle on the first night of Chanukah and increase the number to eight on the last night, rather than Shamai's view of beginning with eight and decreasing the number daily until one.

purchasing an article of *equal* sanctity? There are those of the opinion that such a sale is inappropriate since there is no increase in sanctity as required by the *mishna*.[8] Others maintain that our *mishna* is concerned only lest there be a *decrease* in *kedusha*, therefore sale of an article with the intent of using the funds to acquire another article of equal *kedusha* is permissible.[9]

These limitations regarding the use of funds realized from the sale of a *davar shebekedusha* apply only when the sale is made without the approval of the seven most distinguished personalities of the town in a convocation of the community's citizens, שבעה טובי העיר במעמד אנשי העיר. If such approval *is* forthcoming, however, then the funds may be used for any purpose whatsoever, even for the drinking of beer.[10]

Actually there are additional purposes for which articles of *kedusha* may be sold that are not recorded in this *mishna* and which do not require approval of either the community's leaders or citizens. The Orach Chaim, drawing on a responsum of the Rosh, states that a synagogue, and so too any article of *kedusha* including even a *sefer* Torah, may be sold for the purpose of supporting students learning Torah or to assist orphans in finding an appropriate mate for marriage.[11] Still another valid purpose for the sale of articles of *kedusha*, is to use the funds to ransom Jewish prisoners.[12] The reason for this latter purpose is the overwhelming sacredness of Jewish life and thus the extreme importance of rescuing Jews from the hands of their captors, who too often had no hesitation to putting their Jewish prisoners to death. Yet in spite of this, the Yoreh Deah declares that a synagogue is not sold for the purpose of ransoming prisoners, unless it is sold for use by

---

8. אורח חיים סי' קנ"ג סעיף ד'.

9. טור הובא במג"א או"ח סי' קנ"ג סעיף ד' סק"ד. Based on a deduction on the statement that one cannot *lower* its sanctity, implying that where equal sanctity is involved, the sale is permitted. Also Rambam, Hilchos Tefila, perek 11, halacha 17. The Chofetz Chaim in Mishna Brura maintains that this is only בדיעבד, after the fact, ex post facto.

10. מגילה דף כ"ו, ע"א וע"ב.

11. או"ח סימן קנ"ג סעיף ו'.

12. מג"א שם סק"ט.

others as a synagogue so that there is no change in its level of sanctity.[13]

All this assumes the permissibility of a synagogue's sale. Yet a number of factors must be seriously considered before the proposed sale of a synagogue may take place, even if the funds will be used for the purpose of erecting another synagogue. The first concern is expressed in the term איכא למיחש לפשיעותא, the possibility that between the time of the sale of the first synagogue and the purchase or building of the second, something unexpected may occur that may prevent the acquisition of the second synagogue, leaving the community without an appropriate place for *tefila*.[14] When such a possibility does not exist, such as if the second synagogue has already been built, then the opinions just mentioned would apply. Where the possibility of leaving a community bereft of a place of *tefila* does in fact exist, then the original synagogue may not be sold or torn down. In our day, this possibility is usually of no concern to us since members of a Jewish community invariably leave an area to become part of other communities long before the contemplated sale. The sale of the synagogue usually marks the final act in the history of that community, with the money from the projected sale earmarked for various charities and institutions, but not for the relocation of the original synagogue.[15]

The *gemara* sets another general restriction upon the sale of a synagogue, even for something of greater *kedusha* and, therefore, obviously even for something of equal *kedusha*. This restriction relates to the extent of the original use of the synagogue. If it is

---

13. יו"ד סי' רנ"ב סעיף א' על פי פירוש הש"ך.
14. מגילה דף כ"ו ע"ב.
15. Some communities have used their funds to sponsor synagogues in towns and *kibbutzim* in Israel, sometimes on the condition that the original synagogue's name be maintained, an admirable practice. On the other hand, a practice severely condemned by Rabbi Elyahu Henkin (Hapardes, Iyar 5722) was one where proceeds from a synagogue's sale were divided amongst its members. He ruled that the money should be returned and distributed according to halachic principles.

של כפרים, located in small towns with limited use of its synagogue facilities, then it may be sold according to the rules already stated in the *mishna*. If, however, it is של כרכים, located in cities with a large Jewish population, then the sale is prohibited.[16]

The *gemara* offers the explanation that since worshippers come from far and wide, the synagogue "belongs to the masses" (דהוה ליה דרבים). This is understood to mean that even Jews who may live far from the town have a share in the synagogue's ownership, either by virtue of their participation in *tefila*[17] or by their contributions,[18] and it would be virtually impossible to gain the agreement of the entire *rabim* (masses) for the contemplated sale. In addition, sale of a "public" synagogue, built for the use of Jews both within and without the immediate community, no matter where they may live, would deprive them of a place of prayer in that community.[19]

What standards, however, are to be applied in determining whether a synagogue is indeed של כפרים, a village shul, or של כרכים, the synagogue of a metropolis? Merely the fact that large numbers of individuals from different areas often travel to the town does not automatically designate it as של כרכים. The *gemara*[20] offers the statement of Rav Ashi who declared that the synagogue of Masa Mechasya is not של כרכים, since the public travels to this town only because of Rav Ashi, to be in his presence and to learn Torah from this scholarly giant, and not because of the town itself. Apparently the designation of a synagogue as של כרכים must result from the inherent popularity of the town itself and not because of a distinguished individual who may live there. Yet notwithstanding this *gemara*, the Mogen Avraham declares that if large numbers are attracted to a *chacham* of whom they have great need, then the

---

16. מגילה דף כ"ו ע"א.

17. תוס' שם ד"ה כיון.

18. Ibid. Based on this explanation, if it is clearly known that no contributions at all were accepted from outside the community then it has the status of של כפרים (או"ז ח"ב סי' שפ"ה).

19. רמב"ם הלכות תפלה פרק י"א הלכה ט"ז.

20. מגילה דף כ"ו ע"א.

synagogue of that town shall be considered של
כרכים.²¹ Albeit the Mogen Avraham declares that those "masses"
must come to the town with regularity and not on an occasional
basis.²²

Nor does the physical size of a community affect its status as
either של כרכים or של כפרים. The rules of של כפרים would apply
also to a synagogue in a large city if it happens to be a rather small
place of prayer. Such was the case of the synagogue of the
Tarsians (or bronze workers, according to Rashi) that was located
in no less a city than Jerusalem, yet because of its small size was
considered של כפרים.²³ This concept has great significance for our
discussion, for most of the abandoned synagogues being considered
for sale are located in large cities, but each served its own limited
community.

From what we have seen so far, the *mishna* and *gemara*
require certain prior conditions to be considered, each of which
limits the possibilities of the sale of a synagogue: the availability of
another place or prayer after the sale, its prior designation as של
כפרים, and proper disposition of the funds realized from the sale.

There is yet another consideration with which prospective
sellers must be concerned: the synagogue building itself. May it be
sold to a buyer who will make use of the property in a manner that
would not be considered honorable for a synagogue? Does any
sanctity still attach to synagogue property after its sale?

It is to this that the third *mishna* in this same chapter of
Megillah directs its comments:

> A synagogue may not be sold except with the
> stipulation that it may be bought back (by the sellers)
> whenever they desire. So R. Meir. The *chachamim*,
> however, say that it may be sold in perpetuity except
> for four purposes: for a bath, for a tannery, for a

---

21. מג"א או"ח סימן קנ"ג ס"ק י"ז.
22. שם.
23. מגילה דף כ"ו ע"א.

> *mikveh*, or for a laundry. R. Yehuda says it may be
> sold as a courtyard, and the purchaser may do as he
> likes with it.[24]

The four activities listed are evidently too degrading for a building that once housed a place of prayer.[25] Nonetheless, R. Yehuda is of the opinion that no pre-conditions whatsoever can be made, and the purchaser may make use of the property in any way he wishes. The explanation offered for R. Yehuda's view is that once the synagogue is sold as a courtyard the sanctity of the synagogue effectively ends, and thus it may subsequently be used for any purpose whatsoever.

The *halacha* as codified in the Rambam[26] and in the Orach Chaim[27] follows the views of the *chachamim*. But what of the שבעה טובי העיר במעמד אנשי העיר, the town's seven chief scholars with the consent of its citizens? Does *halacha* permit them to change this basic stipulation as to the use of the property, as they were empowered to do in regards to the use of the funds? The Rambam adds that they do indeed have this power: accordingly, if they wish, they may add a proviso giving the purchaser the right to use the property even for the four restricted activities mentioned in the *mishna*.[28] The Oruch Ha-shulchan goes one step further and declares in no uncertain terms that with the sale of a synagogue, the sanctity of the building and of the funds received for the sale effectively ends (פקע הקדושה לגמרי). Both buildings and money may be used for whatever purposes the people involved choose.[29] However, the Chofetz Chaim forbids any such sale on the grounds that it would be a *bizayon*, an act of disgrace, to a place of sanctity.[30]

---

24. מגילה דף כ"ז ע"ב.
25. משנה ברורה על אורח חיים סי' קנ"ג ס"ק נ"ה, adding that these restrictions apply
    even if the synagogue were reduced to rubble.
26. רמב"ם הלכות תפלה פרק י"א הלכה י"ז.
27. אורח חיים סי' קנ"ג סעיף ט', ורא"ש על מגילה פרק ד' סק"א, ועוד.
28. רמב"ם הלכות תפלה פרק י"א הלכה י"ז.
29. ערוך השלחן סימן קנ"ג סעיף כ"ז.
30. ביאור הלכה על אורח חיים סי' קנ"ג סעיף ט'.

There is one set of circumstances worth noting where even the consent of the community's citizens and leaders is not specifically required for a synagogue's sale. The statement above of Rav Ashi concerning the synagogue in Masa Mechasya, not only informs us that this synagogue was to be treated as של כפרים, but also tells us that it may be sold at the discretion of Rav Ashi alone. Since the community built the synagogue solely because of him, they implicitly agreed that Rav Ashi would have complete control over the synagogue and that he might sell it without any further consultation with the community's leaders.[31] This would be true even if the synagogue had the status of של כרכים,[32] unless contributions were accepted from outside the community.[33]

Modern Implications

The weight of halachic literature appears to lean towards the permissibility of the sale of a synagogue, as long as two fundamental requirements are fulfilled: 1) the synagogue must be determined to be של כפרים, and 2) the sale must be approved by the ז' טובי העיר with the consent of its citizens, במעמד אנשי העיר. In regard to the former requirements the preponderance of opinion considers almost all our modern day synagogues as של כפרים. In addition to reasons already offered, a number of other reasons have been suggested. One rather unusual reason is that synagogues in the time of the Talmud, even those של כפרים, served a broader Jewish population than any of their modern counterparts, even those located in large centers![34] Moreover, if each member of a synagogue has his own reserved seat, a very common practice, then the synagogue's status is again that of של כפרים.[35] Rabbi Gedalia Felder adds that the של כפרים status is achieved when a synagogue is built exclusively by members of a particular congregation, who

---

31. מגילה דף כ"ו ע"א, רמב"ם הלכות תפלה פרק י"א הלכה י"ט, אורח חיים סי' קנ"ג סעיף ז'.

32. אורח חיים סימן קנ"ג סעיף ז'.

33. משנה ברורה על או"ח סי' קנ"ג סעיף ז' ס"ק ל"ה.

34. שו"ת מהר"ח או"ז סי' ס"ה.

35. מאירי ריש פרק ג' מגילה, ריטב"א על מגילה דף כ"ו ע"א.

raise all the funds necessary for its construction[36] This, too, is a very common practice today.

R. Yitzhak Liebes suggests that synagogues in large cities like New York are not כרכים של even if they *did* raise money from people outside the community. He reasons that those who make their contributions do so with the implicit understanding that the synagogue membership may do what they wish with the money (and therefore the synagogue) and that they thus relinquish any rights they may have in this matter.[37]

If a synagogue was at one time classed as being של כרכים, it can lose that status under the weight of certain major demographic shifts. R. Moshe Feinstein[38] maintains that the של כרכים status is lost when a synagogue is no longer used for prayer,[39] or even if it *is* still so used, if by less than a *minyan* with no hope of regeneration: and even if it is used by more than a *minyan*, if its members can no longer maintain it with the care it properly deserves. Synagogues considered for sale today almost always fit into one of these categories, and thus would be של כפרים.

Even if the synagogue retained its של כרכים status, it is the opinion of R. Yehiel Weinberg that the synagogue may still be sold when it can no longer be maintained in a proper manner. The problem of של כרכים, as we stated earlier, is that all contributors have a share in the synagogue's ownership, and it would be virtually impossible to gain their total agreement to the sale. However, R. Weinberg argues, their explicit consent is not necessary since they would certainly not stand in the way of such a sale when the synagogue stands virtually empty.[40]

R. Weinberg nonetheless suggests that to satisfy the requirements of all scholarly opinions the membership should contribute some of the money realized from the sale for the

---

36. הדרום אלול תשי"ח דף 59.
37. שו"ת בית אבי, חלק ג', סימן ל"ג.
38. איגרות משה (ניו יורק, תשי"ט) אורח חיים סימן נ'.
39. Based on מג"א אורח חיים סי' קנ"ג סק"יב.
40. שו"ת שרידי אש, סימן ט"ז.

purpose of repairing a *sefer* Torah, assisting in the marriage of a poor orphan, or for any other activity for which sale of a synagogue is permitted.[41]

An interesting question was once directed at R. Yechezkel Landau (Nodah Biyehuda), regarding the status of a synagogue in a small European town which periodically conducted a *"yerid"*, regularly scheduled market days. On those days numerous farmers converged on the town from outlying districts to present their wares for sale to an even larger number of buyers who also came to the town from far-flung areas. The town on those days gave the appearance of being a large, bustling commercial center. The local synogogue, nonetheless, was declared to be כפרים של, since these visitors did not travel to the town for the specific purpose of using its synagogue for prayer.[42] This concept is also a significant factor in our discussion. In a city like New York, for example, although a synagogue may have many visitors from outside the synagogue's immediate community, these visitors come for business or other purposes, but not specifically to attend services at the local synagogue, however distinguished its *rov* may be.

But what of the second requirement? The consent of the שבעה טובי העיר, the seven distinguished persons; who are they today? And what of the מעמד אנשי העיר, the convocation of the citizens, how do we achieve that? Modern *poskim* seem to agree that, taking into account the administrative structure of our synagogues today, duly-elected synagogue officers are the שבעה טובי העיר and a properly convened membership meeting the מעמד אנשי העיר. Considering that the requirement of the שבעה טובי העיר is based on their superior knowledge and expertise in analyzing the needs of the synagogue entrusted to their case, and considering that the function of the מעמד אנשי העיר is to assure that any proposal will get the widest possible public notice,[43] the administrative body of today's synagogue does in fact perform these functions. Thus,

41. שם.

42. נודע ביהודה תניינא אורח חיים סי' י"ט.

43. שו"ת מהר"ח או"ז סי' ס"ה.

when the proposed sale is presented for a vote to the membership, the requirement of שבעה טובי העיר במעמד אנשי העיר is properly fulfilled.[44]

There are rare occasions when the requirement of במעמד אנשי העיר is not specifically needed. One such situation, presented for decision to the author of the *Mishpat Shmuel*,[45] dealt with a synagogue that was completely destroyed. The community wanted to know if they were permitted to sell the land on which the synagogue stood in order to build another synagogue from the funds realized. No other funds were available. The decision rendered was that they could, which probably elicits little surprise. Most instructive, however, was the reason: all those individuals who contributed to the construction and maintenance of the original synagogue and who therefore must be consulted, would undoubtedly agree to this move, and thus their consent can be assumed. This would be true even if the synagogue were של כרכים.[46] It is a significant statement because this reasoning is used by several *poskim* (such as R. Yechiel Weinberg mentioned earlier) in arriving at a decision regarding today's abandoned and ravaged synagogues.

The larger problem facing those who must make the decision on the sale of a synagogue is the fact that in most cases the buyer is an organization that wishes to convert the building into a church. Often this group is either the only buyer or the only one willing to pay a fair-value price for the building. The four activities listed in the *mishna* as being of a degrading nature cannot compare in their unpleasantness to this one activity that is the absolute antithesis of the cardinal principle of the Torah, the oneness of

44. אגרות משה (ניו יורק, תשכ״ד) אורח חיים סי׳ מ״ה.
45. משפט שמואל סימן י״ד הובא בשדי חמד מערכת בית־הכנסת סי׳ ט׳.
46. Not directly related to our discussion is the case of an individual who wanted to sell his house, one room of which was used as a place of public prayer. Two reasons to allow its sale are offered in שו״ת מנחת יצחק חלק א׳ סי׳ ק״כ. Firstly, at best it is a "private" synagogue, thus under the complete control of its owner. Secondly, it is only a temporary synagogue and therefore has no lasting *kedusha*. The latter reason is based on או״ח סימן קנ״ד סעיף ב׳.

G-d. Perhaps procedures may exist to permit the sale of synagogue property for use as a tannery or any of the other three degrading activities. But can halachic consent be found for its sale as a church?

The *mishna* in Talmud Avoda Zara[47] reads:

> One may not rent houses to them (idol-worshippers) in the land of Israel ... in Suria one may rent them houses ... outside the land of Israel one may even sell them houses ... This is the opinion of R. Meir. R. Yose says: in the land of Israel one may rent them houses ... in Suria one may sell them houses ... outside the land of Israel one may sell both (houses and fields). However, even in such a place where the renting of a house is permitted, it is not meant for the purpose of a residence, since he will bring idol worship into it ...

The Rambam[48] formulates the *halacha* in accordance with the views of R. Yose, as does the Yoreh Deah.[49] The Ramo, however, adds a very significant comment when he declares that "today our practice is to rent (to the non-Jew) even for the purpose of a dwelling since there no longer exists the practice of bringing into their houses any form of idol worship."[50]

It should be pointed out that the *mishna* and the early *poskim* speak only of the prohibition of *renting* one's house. Doing so runs the risk of violating the Torah's injunction "thou shalt not bring any form of abomination into your house,"[51] for the new owner might introduce idol worship into the house, which, by virtue of the fact of rental, still belongs to the Jew. It follows that this prohibition ought not to apply should the house be *sold* to a non-Jew, since the house no longer is owned by the Jew.

---

47. עבודה זרה דף כ׳ ע״ב.
48. רמב״ם הלכות עבודת כוכבים פרק י׳ הלכה ג׳.
49. יורה דעה סימן קנ״א סעיף ח׳ וי׳.
50. רמ״א שם.
51. לא תביא תועבה אל ביתך (דברים פרק ז׳, פסוק כ״ו).

Nonetheless, the restriction is extended even to the sale of a house.[52]

Considering that these restrictions deal with the sale of a house to a non-Jew on the *possibility* that he may introduce idol worship into the house, how much more so should we be concerned when we sell a *synagogue* for the *specific* purpose of introducing into it a foreign mode of worship! Indeed, the author of the Minchas Yitzchak[53] follows this exact line of reasoning. Nonetheless, he declares, it seems that the majority opinion allows such a sale if agreement is forthcoming from the leaders and citizens of the community. Perhaps their reasoning is based upon the view that Christian practices and services are not similar to ancient pagan practices and therefore cannot be classified as idol worship.[54] Therefore, the sale of a synagogue for a church, from a halachic point of view, is the same as if it were sold for one of the four prohibited activities enumerated in the mishna. As was explained previously, even the sale for these uses is permitted as long as the community's leaders and citizens are in agreement.

Prospective sellers of a synagogue for use as a church would do well, however, to be guided by the directions of R. Moshe Feinstein. In a responsum on the question of the sale of a synagogue to a Seventh Day Adventist group,[55] R. Feinstein points out that in most cases a bank holds a mortgage on the synagogue. It would be advisable, therefore, that the *bank* actually effectuate the sale. The officials of the synagogue are nonetheless permitted to give full cooperation and offer timely advice to the bank so that the community may realize the greatest financial return on its property. If this is not possible, then the sale should be arranged through a *sirsur*, (a third party) preferably a non-Jewish broker.[56]

---

52. תוס' ע"ז דף כ"א ע"א ד"ה אף, שהביא מדבר הרא"ש שחולק, עיין שו"ת מנחת יצחק חלק א' סי' ק"כ.

53. שו"ת מנחת יצחק חלק א' סי' ק"כ.

54. מאירי על עבודה זרה דף י"א ע"ב, באר הגולה חו"מ סימן תכ"ה סעיף ה' ס"ק ש' עיין נודע ביהודה סי' קמ"ח יורה דעה דיינא.

55. איגרות משה (ניו יורק, תשי"ט) אורח חיים סימן נ'.

56. אגרות משה אורח חיים סימן כ"ח.

This should not be understood to imply that blanket permission exists for the sale of every synagogue for use as a church, and that there is no dissent from this opinion. R. Yitzhak Liebes, in the strongest of terms, prohibits the sale of a synagogue for use as a church. No suggestion is even offered to use the bank or some individual as a go-between.[57]

In a recent celebrated case, the famous Pike Street Shul on the East Side of New York was sold to a church organization. This sale was later successfully challenged both legally and halachically. Perhaps the fact that the synagogue was still being used regularly and that the *mispallelim* were able to maintain it, albeit minimally, were factors in the halachic decision against its sale.[58]

Even R. Moshe Feinstein himself, in another responsum on this subject,[58] writes, "In regard to the sale of a synagogue for use as a church, I see no grounds to permit it ... even through the use of a third party". Because the questioner sought advice on a secondary issue relating to our subject, we are not told in this responsum the circumstances of the question which led to the negative decision.

What this responsum does tell us, however, is that there is no one clear *psak* that applies to every situation, and that all the facts of each case must be presented to a *gadol* for his advice, guidance and halachic decision before any action is undertaken.

---

57. שו"ת בית אבי, חלק ג', סימן ל"ג.
58. Unfortunately, the author does not have a copy of the *psak* at this time.
59. איגרות משה (ניו יורק תשכ"ד) או"ח סימן מ"ה.

The Laws of Eruvin - An Overview

Rabbi Hershel Schachter

The Rabbi's Obligation

The Gemara in *Eruvin*[1] relates an incident concerning a *Brit Milah* performed on Shabbat in the city of the sages Abaye and Rabba. On that occasion, the hot water needed for the baby could not be obtained without violating the prohibition against carrying on Shabbat, and the Gemara discusses whether one may ask a non-Jew to perform the necessary carrying for the purpose of the *Milah*. After the episode, Abaye is asked why, in a city of two great *Amoraim*, had neither he nor Rabba seen to the making of an *Eruv*. He answers that it is beneath Rabba's dignity to go collecting the requisite matzot from door to door, and that he, Abaye, is so absorbed in his learning that he has no time to supervise the *Eruv* of the city. The two Rabbis were therefore excused from their duty. The Mordechai[2] infers from this Gemara that under normal circumstances, when the Rabbi of an area is not similarly exempted, he has an obligation to make an *Eruvei Chatzerot* for the community, even as he must prepare an *Eruv Tavshilin* to enable those who forgot to make their own to cook on a Friday Yom Tov for the Shabbat to follow.[3]

---

1. *Eruvin* 67b-68a
2. *Eruvin*, no. 515
3. See *Beitzah* 16b

This article was transcribed and arranged by Rabbi Moshe Rosenberg, based on a lecture delivered by Rabbi Schachter

Following this reasoning, Rabbeinu Asher (Rosh), in a famous responsum,[4] sharply critizes the leadership of a city whose official policy it was *not* to make an *Eruv*, despite the halachic permissibility of doing so. In this area, writes the Rosh, if the *Tannaim* and *Amoraim* saw fit to be lenient, it is sheer nonsense to be strict; unnecessary strictness can only lead to profanation of the Sabbath by people who carry in a city with no *Eruv*.

Establishing an *Eruv* is then not only permissible but obligatory, with the obligation devolving upon the Rabbi. First, though, the Rabbi must determine whether, under the prevailing conditions, it is possible to make an *Eruv* in his community. In this respect, every case is unique, and must be decided based upon principles developed in the Gemara. This essay will outline those principles and briefly discuss the related halachic issues which must be dealt with in the planning of any potential *Eruv*.

Reshut Hayachid

The biblical prohibition against carrying on Shabbat includes only the transporting from one domain to another — from public domain *(Reshut harabim)* to private domain *(Reshut hayachid)* or vice versa — and the moving of an object four cubits *(Amot)* in a *Reshut harabim*. Rabbinically the prohibiton was extended to forbid carying four *amot* in a *carmelit*,[5] carrying from a *carmelit* to a *Reshut harabim*, etc. Only carrying in a *Reshut hayachid* remained permissible.[6] Thus, a primary concern in the planning of an *Eruv* is the determination that the area under question is, indeed, a *Reshut hayachid*.

Roughly defined, a *Reshut hayachid* is an area of certain

---

4. *She'elot Utshuvot HaRosh, Klal 21 Siman* 8. See also *Tshuvot Chatam Sofer, Orach Chaim*, 89. Rabbi Joseph Moskowitz (Admor of Shotz) developed at *mechitza* is not a disqualifying factor, at least on a biblical level. לענין הדין sefer *Kuntres Tikunei Eruvin of Manhattan*. (New York, 5719).

5. A *carmelit*, for our purposes, may be understood as a place which is neither a *Reshut hayachid* nor a *Reshut harabim* halachically.

6. Even such carrying will require first the setting aside of a box of matzot, etc., to blend together all the co-users of one *Reshut hayachid*, but that aspect is not the focus of the present essay.

dimensions (minimum of four by five *tefachim*) enclosed by walls called *mechitzot*. These *mechitzot* can take on different forms. The *Chacham Tzvi*[7] categorizes three types of *mechitzot*: 1. An actual wall ten handspans (*tefachim*) high. Such a *mechitza* is subject to various rules concerning the presence of breaches, their size and location. 2) A mound or other elevated area measuring at least ten *tefachim* tall (four *tefachim* in length and width) and located in a *Reshut harabim*. In this case, the *mechitzot* are the walls of the mound, and, by virtue of their being said to extend halachically to the sky, they succeed in enclosing the top of the mound, thus making it a *Reshut hayachid*. 3) A canal, surrounding a piece of land. Here, the *mechitzot* are formed by the drop below ground level, and are said to extend to the sky, thereby granting the enclosed area the status of *Reshut hayachid*.

It is the existence of this third form of *mechitza* which leads the Gemara to ask why all the continents may not be classified as *Reshut hayachid*, dropping as they do at least ten *tefachim* off their coasts, to form the continental shelf.

Tosafot[9] provides a somewhat cryptic explanation of the Gemara's answer why this cannot be. The *Chazon Ish*[10] understands Tosafot to be stating that if three conditions are simultaneously fulfilled, then the otherwise acceptable *mechitzot* are disqualified. If the *mechitzot* 1)are the product of natural phenomena, rather than man-made, 2)enclose a very large area (here the *Chazon Ish* cites the *Knesset Yechezkel* as setting 100 x 50 *amot* to be the cut-off point), and 3)do not hinder maritime

7. *Tshuvot Chacham Tzvi*, 5. The *Chacham Tzvi* was very involved in his day in the practical aspects of *Eruvin*, having been consulted about building an *Eruv* around The Hague, in Hamburg, Furth, and in England.

8. *Eruvin* 22b. From this discussion, we see that the presence of water covering the *mechitza* is not a disqualifying factor, at least on a biblical level. לענין הדין מדרבנן עין תוס' פ"ק דעירובין יב: ד"ה הבא.

9. Ibid.

10. *Orach Chaim* 108:11. The *Chazon Ish's* analysis is borne out by a later-discovered manuscript of the *Tosafot HaRosh*. In general, it is amazing how many of the *Chazon Ish's* original explanations of cryptic passages have been similarly proven correct.

11. This measurement, called a *Beit Satayim*, was the size of the Mishkan, and was

traffic, but instead allow the passage of ships above the point of the sudden drop forming the continental shelf,[12] then such demarcations are not considered valid *mechitzot* for *Eruvin* purposes.

According to this Tosafot, only the natural walls of the continent would be considered invalid, but if one would erect *mechitzot* around an entire continent, it would be converted into a *Reshut hayachid.*

The Ramban, however, is quoted by the Ritva[13] as ruling out this possibility. In his opinion, the reason for invalidating the natural *mechitzot* at the point of the continental shelf would apply as well to invalidate the *mechitza* status of walls erected around an entire continent. Once an area is so vast that, even when it is enclosed by *mechitzot*, the people inside have no sense of being in an enclosed area, then the *mechitzot* are not effective.[14]

The *Mishnah Brurah*,[15] however, writes that he saw the actual words of the Ramban[16] and that in fact his statement was limited to naturally-occuring *mechitzot* and would not apply to *mechitzot* put up by man.

But it is a fourth kind of *mechitza* which has the most practical application to the construction of an *Eruv.*[17]

---

later designated as the size of a *Karpef*, a large enclosed area in which it is rabbinically forbidden to carry. From this Tosafot as explained by the *Chazon Ish*, we then see that the rabbinic enactment of *Karpef* was not a new idea, but rather a *Ki'ein d'oraitha*, an extension of the biblical prohibition of carrying in such an area when all three conditions are fulfilled.

12. This condition, too, can be seen as the biblical source for the rabbinic rule that traffic negates a *mechitza (Atu rabim umevatli mechitzta)*. According to Rambam, this opinion is of rabbinic origin.
13. To *Eruvim* 22b.
14. The *Chayei Adam* (in *Nishmat Adam* 49, no. 2) suggests, based on a Mishnah in *Bechorot* (54b), that the maximum size for an enclosure according to the Ritva should be sixteen mils. The Maharsham, in his responsa (vol. 4, no. 1), accepts this suggestion. According to *Iggerot Moshe* (*Orach Chaim* vol. 1, pg 241), this means that the distance from the center of the enclosure to any one of the *mechitzot* should not exceed sixteen mils, i.e., the length of the enclosure should not exceed 32 mils.
15. סי' שמ"ו ס"ג בה"ל ד"ה קרפף
16. חי' הרמב"ן לעירובין
17. Constructing an *Eruv* is only a colloquialism; in fact, the *Eruv* itself refers to

Tzurat Hapetach

The Gemara in *Eruvin* (11b) is the source of the *mechitza* which is formed to resemble the frame of a door and is called *Tzurat hapetach*. The rationale behind this type of *mechitza* is as follows: since a house is most certainly a *Reshut hayachid*, even with its door(s) wide open, and even when it has several such doors, why shouldn't an enclosure surrounded totally by doorways (even when the doors are missing and only the doorframes remain) be considered a *Reshut hayachid* as well? All that is needed for such a doorframe *mechitza* is "a pole on one side, a pole on the other side, and a pole running across the two from above."[18] Strictly speaking, there is no limit to the number of such *Tzurot hapetach* which may be employed.[19]

Possible Limitations

Some authorities, however, severely limit the practical use of the *Tzurat hapetach*. The *Pri Megadim*[20] claims that this form of *mechitza* is a rabbinic enactment, geared merely to remind a person of where an enclosed area ends, and, as such, can only be used to permit carrying in areas whose original prohibition was rabbinic in

---

the matzot later set aside. In Yiddish, however, the *Tzurat hapetach* is referred to as an *Eruv*.

18. Actually, whether several doorframes, one next to the other, may be used is a matter of dispute between the *Sha'arei Teshuva (Orach Chaim* 363:9 quoting the responsa of *Ohel Ya'akov)* and R. Shlomo Kluger

(טוב טעם ודעת, עמוד קיז, סימן ב' בהשמטות השניות בטוף וזלק א').

The *Ohel Ya'akov* argues that according to the Gemara (*Eruvin* 11), *mechitzot* are valid only if they are made in the same fashion in which people normally erect walls, and people do not normally construct several consecutive doorways. R. Shlomo Kluger counters this argument by saying that, in determining the viability of *Tzurot hapetach*, we only examine each doorframe individually and not in relation to its neighbors. People *do* normally construct single doorframes, and we need not consider the fact that one doorframe is placed next to another. It should be noted, however, that even according to R. Shlomo Kluger, it is still essential that each individual frame be a viable structure for a door, able to sustain a very light door for at least ten *tefachim* from the ground up.

19. The various rules concerning the exact construction, which are found in *Eruvin*, are not our present concern.

20. Quoted in *Mishnah Brurah* to 362:10.

nature. Thus, *Tzurot hapetach* would allow one to carry in a *carmelit*, but not in a *Reshut harabim*.[21]

The *Chazon Ish* opposes this school of thought,[22] and insists that the *Tzurat hapetach* works on a biblical level, and not only on a rabbinic one. As proof, he cites a case from the Gemara[23] concerning the biblical prohibition of *Kil'ayim* (forbidden crossbreeding) in Eretz Yisrael. In order to avoid the *Issur d'oraitha* of *Kil'ayim* one must either leave four *amot* of spaces between his wheat and grape seeds or erect a fence between the two types of seeds. The Gemara states explicitly that the "fence" may be a *Tzurat hapetach*. In this way, says the *Chazon Ish*, the *Tzurat hapetach* functions on the *d'oraitha* level, to remove the biblical prohibition of *Kil'ayim*. Several *Acharonim*[24] who sided with the *Pri Megadim* anticipated this proof and refuted it by distinguishing between the types of *mechitzot* needed for *Kil'ayim* and for *Eruvin*. While for *Kil'ayim* purposes a *mechitza* need only *separate*, for Shabbat purposes it must *enclose* as well. The proof of the *Chazon Ish* shows only that a *Tzurat hapetach* is a *mechitza hamafseket*, a *mechitza* which separates, but does not prove it to be a *mechitza hamakefet*, one which encloses an area. Despite the refutation of his proof, it is the opinion of the *Chazon Ish* which is widely accepted today.

Atu Rabim

But leaving aside the *Pri Megadim*, there is yet another reason why the *Tzurat hapetach* may only permit one to carry in a *carmelit*, but not in a *Reshut harabim*. The Gemara[25] raises the problem that when traffic passes constantly through a *mechitza*,

---

21. Based on this calculation the *Pri Megadim* claims that although we allow the lintel of the doorframe not to touch the two doorposts, nevertheless, if it is more than twenty *amot* high, it disqualifies the *mechitza*, because, as we find in *Hilchot Sukkah*, anything above twenty *amot* can no longer serve as a *Heker*, a reminder. See *Orach Chaim* 630: *Eshel Avraham* ב"סק.
22. *Orach Chaim* 70:13
23. *Eruvin* 110.
24. See *Minchat Yisrael* to *Eruvin* 110.
25. *Eruvin* 22a.

we sometimes say *"Atu rabim umevatli mechitzta"* — the public comes and nullifies the *mechitza*. This principle would not do away with the entire *mechitza*, but would effectively negate it in those places where it is pierced by the traffic. Whether or not we apply this constricting rule depends upon two factors. First, Tosafot explains[26] that if the whole need for the *mechitza* is rabbinic, as in the case where there are already three other *mechitzot*, then we do not apply *Atu rabim* to the fourth *mechitza*. Furthermore, the Ritva points out based on the Gemara in *Eruvin* 21a, if the *mechitzot* are especially strong *(mechitzot briot)*, we likewise do not say *Atu rabim*. *Tzurot hapetach*, however, are generally assumed to be *mechitzot gru'ot* — weak *mechitzot*.[27]

For practical purposes, Tosafot's lenient provisions do not often help us, for we don't normally have cases where only the fourth wall needs to be made as a *Tzurat hapetach*. Here, though, it is the Maharam Rotenburg who comes to our aid. Quoted by the Mordechai,[28] the Maharam Rotenberg extends Tosafot's leniency, and rules that even if there are no previously existing *mechitzot*, if the area under question is not considered a *Reshut harabim d'oraitha*, we do not say *Atu rabim*. In other words, one must merely find some reason to declare an area not to be a biblical *Reshut harabim* in order to remove the problem of *Atu rabim*, and create a situation where *Tzurot hapetach* can be ereted to make the area a *Reshut hayachid*. It remains to be seen, however, what precisely are the conditions required to constitute a *Reshut harabim d'oraitha* and which of these factors, if any, can be the basis of leniency today.

Reshut Harabim

There are, at most, six conditions which must be met for an area to be declared a *Reshut harabim d'oraitha*.

---

26. Ibid, ד"ה קשיא.

27. This is the opinion of the Rashba, and is subscribed to by the *Chazon Ish*. The Ritva disagrees, labeling *Tzurot hapetach* as *mechitzot briot*. The *Chavatzelet HaSharon* (ח"ג כי' י"א) explains the lenient opinion at length, saying that doorframes are *made* to be traversed, unlike regular walls. Therefore the passage of traffic through it does not render the *Tzurot hapetach* a *mechitza gruah*.

28. רמ"א דרכי משה או"ח שס"ד סק"א, quoted by ר"פ הדר, סי' תקט.

a) The area must be owned by the public, and may not be the private property of any individual.[29]

b) It may not have a ceiling.[30]

c) It must be at least sixteen *amot* wide.[31]

d) If we are discussing a city, the street must go straight through the entire city, without a detour. *(Mefulash misha'ar lisha'ar b'li shoom ikum klal.''*[32]

e) It must be accessible to the public twenty-four hours a day. The Gemara states[33] that Jerusalem would have been considered a *Reshut harabim d'oraitha* were it not for the fact that the doors to the city were locked every night. Consequently, even during the day Yerusalayim lacked *Reshut harabim* status. Rashi and Tosafot assume that the practice was to make an *Eruv* for Jerusalem.[34]

f) The area must be traversed daily by 600,000 people. In fact, whether this condition is necessary or not is a dispute between

---

29. *Eruvin* 59a. For this reason, Rockefeller Plaza, despite meeting the other requirements, is not a *Reshut harabim*, because it is privately owned.

30. *Shulchan Aruch Orach Chaim* 345:7.

31. Ibid.

32. This is the phrase the *Mishnah Brurah* quotes from the Ramban. Rav Moshe Feinstein, however, in *Iggerot Moshe, Orach Chaim* 140, writes that he doesn't know of any Talmudic source requiring the lack of *any* detour whatsoever. He therefore refuses to base a leniency on this point.

33. *Eruvin* 6b.

34. See Rashi to *Eruvin* 6b, Tosafot *Pesachim* 66a תוחב ד"ה. Rabbenu Ephraim (referred to by some early sources as a student of Rif) is quoted as disagreeing with Rashi and Tosafot. In his opinion, although the streets of Jerusalem did not constitute *Reshut harabim d'oraitha*, still there never was an *Eruv* made there. Rav M. Feinstein, in *Iggerot Moshe* Vol. I, p. 240, suggests that the reason for this might be that an *Eruv* should never be allowed in any central metropolis. People coming from far and near to visit the large city will carry there on Shabbat, relying on the *Eruv*; however, when they return to their small towns, they might continue to carry there on Shabbat too, not realizing that their community might not have an *Eruv*. Accordingly, Rav Feinstein opposed the erection of an *Eruv* in Manhattan, which is a central metropolis like Jerusalem of old. The fact that so many towns in Europe did have an *Eruv* does not indicate that the opinion of Rabbenu Ephraim has been rejected, for these towns are not considered centrally located metropolitan areas.

See, however, "Rabbenu Ephraim" by Rabbi Israel Shepansky, Mossad HaRav Kook 1976. pp. 352-356, where the early sources quoting Rabbenu Ephraim seem to indicate an entirely different understanding of his view.

Rashi and Tosafot on one side, and the Rambam on the other.[35] As we will soon see, later *Poskim* disputed the point as well.

Highways

It must be noted, however, that the above conditions are only required when we wish to declare that a *street* be labeled as a *Reshut harabim d'oraitha*. The *Magen Avraham*[36] rules that a highway *(derachim haovrim me'ir le'ir)* is a *Reshut harabim d'oraitha*. *Orchot Chayim*[37] quotes *poskim* who say that what the *Magen Avraham* means is that, in fact, the highway is the model *Reshut harabim*, the litmus test by which we determine whether any other area is public domain. Therefore, if a city street is *mefulash misha'ar lisha'ar* 24 hours a day and traversed daily by 600,000 people, we no longer consider it merely a street, but declare it, too, to be a "highway," and a *Reshut harabim*. It is the *street* which must fulfill these additional three conditions; but a highway itself, being the paradigm of a *Reshut harabim*, need not be accessible at all times to the public,[38] nor need it have traffic consisting of 600,000 people.

With the six conditions of the *Reshut harabim* in mind, we can now examine the different approaches as to why it is sometimes possible to construct an *Eruv* around a city. Each approach is based upon the assumption that some required conditions is not present, thus rendering the city in question a non-*Reshut harabim d'oraitha*, or maybe even a *Reshut hayachid*.

(A) Shishim Ribo

As mentioned previously, whether traffic of 600,000 *(shishim*

---

35. On *Eruvin* 59a.

36. סי' שמ"ה סק"ה

37. אורחות חיים (ספינקא) שם ע"ש תשובת בית יעקב

38. According to this understanding of the status of a highway, it would not be possible to render a highway a non-*Reshut harabim* by placing collapsible doors at the beginning of it. One might have thought that the highway now has דלתות הראוין לנעול and is no longer a *Reshut harabim*, but in fact, we see that a highway is a *Reshut harabim* even if it is not accessible at all times to the public.

ribo) people is a requirement for a *Reshut Harabim* is disputed among the *Rishonim*. For many years, it was accepted *psak* in Europe that the view of Rashi and Tosafot represented the majority opinions in requiring 600,000 people before labeling the area a *Reshut harabim d'oraitha*. Therefore, rabbinic authorities permitted the establishing of *Eruvin* in cities lacking *shishim ribo*, declaring that the cities were not *Reshuyot harabim d'oraitha*, and as such, could be enclosed by *Tzurot hapetach* according to the Maharam Rotenburg's approach.

In the early 1800's, however, Rabbi Ya'akov of Karlin,[39] the author of *Mishkenot Ya'akov*, challenged the very foundation of this leniency. It is only Rashi and Tosafot, he claims, who say that a *Reshut harabim* must be *traversed* by *rabim*, (multitudes) and that "*rabim*" is defined as the number of Jews in the desert at the time of the Tabernacle, from which period these laws are derived. The Rambam, though, denies such a requirement, saying merely that the area must be owned by the public. The *Mishkenot Ya'akov* contends that the majority of the *Rishonim* agree with the Rambam against Rashi and Tosafot, thus effectively depriving us of the basis for many of our *Eruvin*. The *Beit Ephraim*, in a letter to Rabbi Ya'akov of Karlin later published in *Mishkenot Ya'akov*,[40] defends the original approach against the attack of the Karliner Rov, contending that the majority of *Rishonim* do, in fact, agree with Rashi and Tosafot. Nevertheless, the strict opinion of the *Mishkenot Ya'akov* is cited by the *Mishnah Brurah*[41] and *Aruch Hashulchan*.[42]

(B) Aruch Hashulchan

A novel, if highly questionable, leniency is suggested by the *Aruch Hashulchan*, Rabbi Yechiel Michel Epstein of Navardok.[43]

---

39. *Mishkenot Ya'akov* 120 חלק או״ח
40. *Orach Chaim*, no. 106.
41. לס׳ שס״ד ס״ב בה״ל ד״ה ואחר
42. *Orach Chaim* 345:17
43. Ibid 345:19-24 See however דברי מלביאל Vol. III p. 267, by Rabbi Tannenbaum of Lomze, who feels that one may not rely on this "new" leniency as it is not found in the earlier classical sources.

In his opinion, only during the times of the Talmud was there actually a real status of *Reshut harabim d'oraitha* for streets of cities, because, for a street to be a *Reshut harabim* (with a *He hayediah* — a definite article) it must be *the* main thoroughfare of the city, with all other streets being minor. Nowadays, however, our cities have several such large streets, and, claims Rav Epstein, each one cancels out the importance of the others.

(C) Mefulash

R. Shlomo Dovid Kahana was once asked why the *Eruv* in Warsaw was still relied upon. In the days of the *Chidushei HaRim*, when the *Eruv* was originally established, Warsaw did not have a population of 600,000, but since then, the city had grown and, before the Second World War, had well over that size population. He responded[44] with yet another suggested leniency. The larger a city grows, he said, the less of a chance there is for any one street to go *straight through* the whole city, with no digression. Since one requirement for *Reshut harabim d'oraitha* is *mefulash misha'ar lisha'ar*, our cities are therefore not *Reshuyot harabim d'oraitha* and we may erect *Eruvim* according to the Maharam Rotenburg, as cited above.[45]

(D) Chazon Ish

A totally new idea is advanced by the *Chazon Ish*.[46] He claims

---

44. Quoted by R. Kasher in *Noam* referred to above.

45. Rabbi Moshe Feinstein (*Iggerot Moshe Orach Chaim*, Vol. 1, page 242) claims that this leniency is a very shaky one. Even if we assume that lack of *mefulash* means that an area is not a *Reshut Harabim d'oraitha*, nevertheless, Rav Moshe argues, such an area is a *Reshut harabim mi-d'rabbanan*.

46. *Hilchot Eruvin* סימן 43 especially אות 7. See also אורחות חיים Vol. I, p. 139, quoting earlier *poskim* who say the same. These *poskim* add that in such a situation, even according to the view of Rambam one would be allowed to carry. The *Mishnah Brurah* (# 362, note 59) recommends that Bnei Torah follow the stringent view of Rambam not to carry in an *Eruv* consisting of *Tzurot hapetach* spanning a gap of more than 10 *amot*. אורחות חיים points out that if there are actual walls enclosing the majority of the area (עומד מרובה על הפרץ) then, although there are gaps in the *mechitzot* of more than 10 *amot* for which there are constructed *tzurot hapetach*, the *Eruv* would be acceptable even according to the view of Rambam.

that not only are many of our cities not *Reshyuot harabim d'oraitha*, but, in fact, they can be proven to be *Reshuyot hayachid* on a biblical level. His calculation run as follows: since city blocks consist of rows of connected buildings, we automatically have two *mechitzot* bordering any street. (The fact that the *mechitzot* were originally intended only to enclose their respective houses is irrelevant, because the Gemara rules that a *mechitza* can create a *Reshut hayachid* even if they were not erected with that intention in mind). Then if anywhere along the course of the street we run into a dead end (and here a dead end need not be an absolute barrier — it must only impede forward traffic, but can allow one to turn left or right) we thus have our third *mechitza*. Since only three *mechitzot* are required biblically, we now have a street which is a *Reshut hayachid min haTorah*. (see diagram 1)

At first glance it would seem that the street crossings should present a problem, for we know that a breach of more than ten *amot* in a *mechitza* serves to disrupt the *mechitza*.[47] The crossings, being at least that large, should prevent the original two *mechizot* from being halachically connected to the third *mechitzot*. But in reality, the *Chazon Ish* shows how this is no problem. Assuming that the disqualifying effect of a breach of ten *amot* is only a rabbinic law,[48] the *Chazon Ish* points out that when only a rabbinic issue is involved, we do not say *Atu rabim umevatli mechitzta*.

Moreover, not only don't the crossings detract from the *mechitza*, but they even become part of it. We visualize the street as if imaginary lines were drawn extending from the two parallel *mechitzot* to the *mechitza* running in the opposite direction, and the space of the crossings is said to be enclosed as well. Once this is so, the crossings actually help us, for they become the third *mechitzot* of all the streets that intersect this particular street (see diagram 2). In this way, with one dead end street, an entire city can become a *Reshut hayachid d'oraitha*.

---

47. משנה עירובין

48. Whether indeed this disqualification is only rabbinic in nature is a point of controversy between the *Mishkenot Ya'akov* (109) and the *Beit Ephraim*. The *Chazon Ish* concurs with Rav Ephraim Zalman Margaliyot in labeling it only *d'rabbanan*. Rav Moshe Feinstein makes the same tacit assumption in *Iggerot Moshe Orach Chaim*, 139 ח״ב ס׳, without spelling it out.

Diagram 1

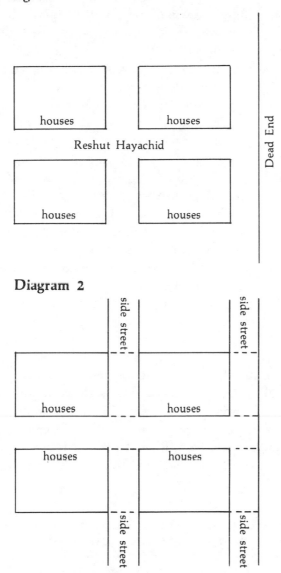

Diagram 2

— — —   represents the imaginary part of mechitza which serves
as third mechitza for side streets.

The *Chazon Ish* was very much involved in establishing several *Eruvin*. He himself would personally check the *Eruv* around Bnei Brak every Friday morning, even in the most inclement weather. Nevertheless, he himself did not carry in the *Eruv*, even to the extent of not wearing his watch, and recommended to "Bnei Torah" to do the same. Various reasons have been suggested by his followers for this behavior.[48A]

This ruling of the *Chazon Ish* is highly questionable. One point which can be disputed concerns the crossings which become, according to the *Chazon Ish*, *mechitzot* for the intersecting streets. It can be contended that while these crossings do not damage the *mechitzot* of the first street (because we assume that when there is more *mechitza* than breach, a gap larger than ten *amot* is only a rabbinic disqualification, and on rabbinic problems we do not apply *Atu Rabim*), nevertheless, they cannot serve as *mechitzot* for any side street, because with respect to that side street they are not just filling in a gap, but are being used as an entire *mechitza* (*Nifratz bemilu'o*). Such a use is not permitted.[50]

The *Chazon Ish* did not formulate his opinion on the purely theoretical level; he actually applied the approach in response to a practical problem referred to him by Rav Chaim Ozer Grodzensky of Vilna. In 1938, Rabbi Elie Munk of Paris turned to Rav Chaim Ozer for a ruling on whether it was possible to make an *Eruv* for the Jewish section of Paris. At first Rav Chaim Ozer, due to his failing health, did not want to get involved in the serious question. Only after repeated requests from Rav Munk did Rav Chaim Ozer pursue a halachic answer. He conferred with the Dayan in Vilna

48.a פאר הדור Vol. II, pp. 136, 285

49. This account is reconstructed from the letters we have which were sent by Rav Chaim Ozer to Rav Munk and the *Chazon Ish* concerning an *Eruv* in Paris. The letter sent to Rav Munk can be found in Rabbi M.M. Kasher's article in *Noam*, Vol. 6, pp. 34-65. In it Rav Chaim Ozer explains his initial reticence in deciding the question, his conferring with his colleagues, and the conclusions reached. The final *psak* does not mention the *Chazon Ish's* claim regarding city streets, but Rabbi Kasher suggests that it was this opinion of his which influenced the *Chazon Ish* in his counsel to Rav Chaim Ozer. In a second letter, also reproduced in *Noam* from *Kovetz Igrot (Chazon Ish)* v.2 p187, Rav Chaim Ozer writes to thank the *Chazon Ish* for his collaboration on the Paris question.

who was in charge of *Eruvin* and wrote a letter seeking the advice of the *Chazon Ish*, who by then was already living in Bnei Brak. The *Chazon Ish* replied by letter, apparently depending heavily upon his unique approach as outlined above. In the end Rav Chaim Ozer informed Rav Munk that, under certain conditions, carrying could be made permissible in Paris. Rav Munk, realizing that under the circumstances the conditions could not be met, sent a copy of Rav Chaim Ozer's letter to all the Rabbis of Paris, to inform them that carrying would be forbidden.[49]

Gaps in the Eruv

Assuming the reliability of one or a combination of the above approaches, the problem of gaps in the *mechitzot* still remains. Most assuredly, our *mechitzot* should not have breaches larger than ten *amot* long. In Rabbi Yosef Eliyahu Henkin's letter urging the Rabbis to go through with the Manhattan *Eruv*,[50] he stressed that all gaps be closed up with *Tzurot hapetach*. This, however, has never been taken care of.

But there is an opinion that even a breach of four *tefachim* is not allowed. The Ramo rules that our cities no longer have a status of *mavuy*.[51] The *Magen Avraham*,[52] however, understands this to mean that our cities are not entitled to the leniencies of a *mavuy*, but are subject to a *mavuy's* strictures nonetheless. One such stricture declares that a gap of only four *tefachim* is enough to disqualify a *mechitza* when there is some traffic passing through the gap. The Even HaOzer disagrees, saying that the Ramo's statement exclude our cities from the strictures of a *mavuy* as well.[53] The *Mishkenot Ya'akov*[54] takes the side of the *Magen Avraham* in this dispute.

---

50. See אור המזרח ניסן תשמ״א
50.a A facsimile of the letter appears in Rabbi M.M. Kasher's *Sefer Divrei Menahem*, part 2, page 2.
51. או״ח שס״ג סכ״ו
52. או״ח שס״ה סק״ד
53. Ibid.
54. חלק או״ח ס׳ קכ״ד

Karpef

Even if we have determined our area to be a *Reshut hayachid* or *Carmelit*, and have enclosed it with *Tzurot hapetach*, not allowing any gaps larger than four *tefachim*, an additional problem may arise. The Rabbis have declared that an enclosed area of more than 100 x 50 *amot* over which the owner wishes to prevent people from walking (such as a planted field) is designated a *Karpef* in which one may not carry.[55] Additionally, there is a rabbinic law that when a *Reshut hayachid* is contiguous to another area where one may not carry, then one may not carry even in the *Reshut hayachid* itself.[56] By combining these two rabbinic laws we emerge with a stringency concerning cities which have (as many European cities do) a public park in their center. This park will often have a large flower bed or similar area, where people are careful not to walk. Logically, such an area should constitute a *Karpef* in which carrying is forbidden. Moreover, since the city is connected to the park, it should then be forbidden to carry even in the city. The *Chacham Tzvi*[57] cites the lenient ruling of the *D'var Shmuel* that the flower bed is not a *Karpef* because it is for the beautification of the city and the enjoyment of the citizens, rather than being someone's private, off-limits farm. The *Mishnah Brurah*,[58] however, writes that this leniency, which is advanced by several *Acharonim*, has no basis in *Rishonim*. It would be best, therefore, to find a way in which we could build an *Eruv* without relying on the opinion of the *D'var Shmuel*. The *Chazon Ish*[59] suggests that one might build *mechitzot (Tzurot hapetach)* around the park to separate it from the city proper; thus it would be permitted to carry in the city, but not in the park. The *Mishnah Brurah*[60] was aware of this possibility and rejected it, writing that even if we accept the leniency of the *D'var Shmuel*, building such *mechitzot*

---

55. או״ח סימן שנ״ח

56. משנה עירובין דב׳, ומשנה עירובין דד׳, ועין גאון יעקב ריש עירובין ב׳ על המשנה הראשונה שבמס׳.

57. ס׳ נ״ט

58. שנ״ח ס״ט בבה״ל לס׳ ד״ה אבל

59. פ״ח: כ״ה

60. Referred to above in note 58.

would actually exacerbate the situation, making it forbidden to carry even according to the lenient view.[60A]

Nifratz LeMakom HaAssur Lo

In modern cities care must also be taken that the enclosed area not be touching an area where carrying is forbidden. If a highway or a thruway (which constitutes a *Reshut Harabim*) cuts through the city with entrances to or exits from the highway contiguous to the enclosed area, not only may one not carry on the highway, but even in the rest of the city carrying would no longer be allowed. *Tzurot hapetach* would have to be constructed at the points of contact between the roads leading from and to the highway and the city.

Two Ground Levels

There is, furthermore, another problem which must be avoided. The Gemara[61] records a dispute between Rav and Shmuel regarding *mechitzot she'einan nikarot* — *mechitzot* which aren't discernable. If, for example, two adjacent houses share one wall, but that wall does not extend ten *tefachim* over the houses to separate the two roofs, can we say that the *mechitza* which separates the two houses below extends up halachically[62] to the sky

---

60.a A second type of *karpef* which has practical ramifications today is discussed in *Shulchan Aruch* (*Orach Chaim* 358:11). This *karpef* is a river or lake covering an area larger than a *Beit satayim* and ten *tefachim* deep, which is located within the enclosed area. Such a body of water is a *karpef* and makes it forbidden to carry in the entire city contiguous to it, unless the water serves some purpose for the people of the city. Thus, if, for example, the local fire department uses the river or lake as a source of water for extinguishing fires, then it is no longer classified as a *karpef*. See also *Mishnah Brurah* 358:85. Regarding the minimum depth of the water in ponds or rivers which might pose a problem, there are several opinions. According to *Shulchan Aruch* (# 358:1) if the water is less than 11 *tefachim* deep, there is no problem. According to *Mishnah Brurah* (ביאור הלכה ד״ה והיא) one ought to consider it a problem if the water is ony 3 *tefachim* in depth. The *Chazon Ish* writes (ס׳ פ״ט אות ד) that even if the water is less than 3 *tefachim* deep there exists a problem. Rabbi Feinstein recommends that one follow the view of *Chazon Ish* on this point.

61. *Eruvin* 89a

62. This would be based on the Talmudic principle of *gud asik mechitzta* which

to separate the space on top of the roof as well? Or perhaps, since the roof is a new ground level, at which level the *mechitza* is not discernable, we cannot use the *mechitza* of one ground level — the street — for another level — the roof.

The *Chazon Ish*,[63] based on another Gemara,[64] points out that the dispute of Rav and Shmuel is limited to the case where the two families' roofs are adjacent to each other, with no separation between the two above the new ground level of the roofs. In *this case only*, Shmuel is lenient and relies on the *mechitzot* from the lower level. Since the only reason there is a problem is due to the fact that two different families are living in the two houses below, and thereby the houses with their roofs are designated as two different types of *Reshut hayachid, miderabbanon*; and on the ground level below, the houses are clearly separated with a wall serving as a perfect *mechitza*; therefore we do not declare either roof to be "*nifratz lemakom ha'assur lo.*" But, basically, even Shmuel would otherwise agree that *mechitzot* relating to one ground level would not be effective for any new ground level above.[64A]

Based on this assumption, the *Chazon Ish* agrees with other *Poskim* who disqualify the following *mechitza*: if an *Eruv* is made in a city, using a cliff as one of the four *mechitzot*, but that cliff has a bridge leading from it which allows people to continue travelling along the same ground level, then we declare the top of the cliff to be the new ground level at the point of intersection with the bridge. Consequently, the previously-used *mechitza* — the drop of the cliff itself — can no longer be used as a *mechitza* for the place where the bridge meets the cliff because, with reference

---

entitles us to consider a *mechitza* as rising to the sky. (*Sukkah* 4b) and elsewhere.)

63. *Orach Chaim* 108:1-2
64. *Eruvin* 90a
64.a Rabbi Moshe Feinstein (in *Iggerot Moshe Orach Chaim* no. 139) does not subscribe to this claim of the *Chazon Ish*. He maintains that although *mechitzot* for under the ground may not serve as *mechitzot* above the ground, nevertheless, *mechitzot* above the ground may indeed serve another ground level, also above the ground.

to that spot, the cliff is a *mechitza she'eina nikeret*. If the bridge is more than ten *amot* wide, we are left with a gap of more than ten *amot* in the *mechitza*, totally negating it. And even if the bridge is less than ten *amot* wide, the *Noda Bi'Yehuda*[65] disqualifies the *mechitza* nevertheless. The *Mishnah Brurah*[66] has accepted the view of the *Nodah Bi'Yehudah*.

Also, according to the *Chazon Ish, Tzurot hapetach*, or for that matter even actual *mechitzot*, constructed on one ground level, would have no effect for a different ground level directly above. Bridges or highways crossing above existing *mechitzot* would not be affected by these *mechitzot* since they only related to their own ground level.

It is highly questionable, also, whether one may construct a *mechitza* or a *Tzurat hapetach* in such a way that it extends from one ground level to another.[66A]

Conclusion

The *Aruch LaNer* in his preface to *Niddah* quotes the Zohar's interpretation of a verse in Zechariah.[67] There the Mashiach is described as an *Ani verochev al chamor* — a humble man riding upon a donkey. Instead of using the usual word for denoting humbleness — *Anav* — the verse chooses to use *Ani* to convey the same meaning. The Zohar[68] explains that the word *Ani* is an acrostic, standing for *Eruvin, Niddah* and *Yevamot;* it is through the conscientious study of these complex but essential laws, says the prophet, that the Jewish people can hasten the arrival of the *rochev al chamor*, Mashiach ben David.

It is based on this comment of the Zohar that these three *masechtot* are known in the yeshivot as *"masechtot Ani"*, and are considered more difficult than most others. The laws relating to *Eruvin* are especially complex and require more concentration than

---

65. אר"ח קמא (ס' מ"ב).
66. ס' שס"ג שעה"צ ס"ק צ"ה. A careful reading of Ramban in *Milchamot* (to *Eruvin* 22) would seem to indicate that he too agrees with *Noda Bi'Yehudah*.
66.a See בית יצחק שנת תשמ"ג בהערה למאמר בנדון מקום הדלקת נר חנוכה.
67. 9:9
68. *Raya Mehemna* to Ki Teitzei.

most other areas of halacha. This paper is intended only as an introduction to this vast topic. The details of different situations are never identical and must be studied carefully in light of many other halachic details not covered by the present paper.

Parameters and Limits of Communal Unity from the Perspective of Jewish Law

Rabbi J. David Bleich

Among the most pressing needs of the Jewish community in this country — and even more so in Israel — is the need for adequate communication between the various diverse sectors of which it is comprised. Absence of common cause directed toward common concerns, frequent misunderstandings and even acrimonious disputes between ideologically divergent factions of the community are directly attributable to simple lack of communication. The transcendent mandate of *ahavat Yisra'el* and our sacred obligation to reach out to every Jew with concern and love require that we actively seek areas of ongoing contact and cooperation. Unity within the community is clearly desired by all for reasons which are both ideological and pragmatic in nature.

Unity, not unlike mother love and apple pie, receives the approbation of one and all. Why, then, is the very quest for unity likely to be so divisive? The answer is to be found in the agenda of many — but not all — of the exponents of this utopian ideal.

Tafasta merubah lo tafasta — one's reach ought not to exceed

Rosh Yeshiva, Rabbi Isaac Elchanan Theological Seminary
Professor of Law, Benjamin N. Cardozo School of Law,
Yeshiva University

one's grasp. There are matters regarding which persons of diverse *Weltanschauungen* can neither agree nor cooperate — and indeed no one who espouses the concept of religious, moral or intellectual pluralism should anticipate either cooperation or agreement in such matters. One to whom the taking of fetal life is anathema cannot be expected to endow an abortion clinic. A pacifist can hardly be expected to participate in war games. A Marxist is an unlikely candidate for the position of Vice-President in Charge of Reducing Workers' Wages. The Jewish community is hardly monolithic, monoprax or monodox. No responsible call for unity has ever been predicated upon a platform calling for the setting aside of all differences. Rather, it has consisted of a call for (1) agreement to respect differences which do indeed exist; and (2) the forging of bonds of cooperation between various sectors within the Jewish community in order to promote goals and ideals to which we are all committed.

Were the agenda to consist of the second item exclusively, the goal would not be unattainable; certainly, there would exist no impediment rooted in principle or ideology. Problems arise with regard to the first item which is — not improperly — regarded by many as a necessary condition for the achievement of the second. Agreement to respect differences which do indeed exist may mean one of two things. Minimally, respect connotes awareness and concomitant abjuration of antagonistic words and deeds. On a different level, respect also entails acceptance. Acceptance is quite different from toleration. Linguistically, "toleration" is a term used to describe a mode of thought and behavior vis-a-vis that which is the subject of disdain. Individuals, each of whom professes to possess absolute truth, may indulge one another and one another's beliefs simply because there exists no other viable *modus vivendi*. The alternative is mutual abnegation and mutual destruction. Since the negative effects of the alternative are contrary to the self-interest of each of the parties there emerges reciprocal agreement to exercise restraint in interpersonal and intramural relationships.

Acceptance differs from toleration in that acceptance requires the legitimization of pluralism, i.e., acceptance requires not only sensitivity to the fact that others have differing viewpoints and ideologies but also tacit affirmation that espousal of those views and ideologies is endowed with equal validity. This form of acceptance and respect is hardly unknown to Judaism. The dictum *elu va-elu divrei Elokim hayyim* certainly implies transcendental legitimacy for conflicting views even though protagonists engaged in the *milhamta shel Torah* do not and dare not give quarter to conflicting positions. Ravad,[1] followed by Duran[2] and Albo,[3] was willing to accord precisely the same type of legitimacy even to certain contradictory propositions each purporting to express theological truth.

Nevertheless, it is the attempt on the part of some to require conferral of legitimacy upon their ideologies and practices as a condition of unity which has made attainment of this goal impossible. It is the fear that cooperation within certain frameworks will constitute *de facto* acceptance and legitimization which creates an insurmountable barrier to unity in the eyes of that sector of our community which is dedicated to uncompromising adherence to the traditional teachings and practices of Judaism.

Halacha is remarkably tolerant, nay, accepting, but only within certain rather clearly defined parameters. Those parameters involve matters of dogma primarily. To be sure, there are numerous controversies regarding various articles of faith which have never been resolved in a definitive manner. For the most part, such controversies pertain solely to matters of belief and have little, if any, impact upon how Jews comport themselves. It is presumably for this reason that adjudication between diverse doctrines concerning the nature of Providence or the unfolding of eschatological events was not deemed imperative. However, acceptance of Torah as the revealed word of G-d and acknowledgment of its immutable nature are matters which are both unbeclouded by controversy in traditional Jewish teaching and which are also of profound significance with regard to virtually every aspect of Jewish life. These principles are fundamental to an

---

1. *Hilkhot Teshuvah* 3:7.
2. *Magen Avot*, chaps. 8-9.
3. *Sefer ha-Ikkarim*, Book I, chap. 2.

axiological system which serves to define the intrinsic nature of Judaism. The distinction between the practices of Ashkenazim and Sephardim, of Hasidim and Mitnagdim, could be accommodated by normative Judaism and ultimately find acceptance rather than mere toleration. Sadducees, Samaritans and Karaites could, at most, anticipate toleration by rabbinic Judaism. The halachic differences between oriental and western Jews and even the theological differences between Hasidim and Mitnagdim could be accommodated within a single axiological system. The differences between Sadducees and Pharisees, between Karaites and Rabbanites, between Samaritans and Jews could not be accommodated precisely because of the renunciation of the Oral Law, in whole or in part, by these sectarian groups. Indeed, an ideological system based upon acceptance of the revealed and immutable nature of both the Written and the Oral Law could not accommodate such diversity without committing the fallacy of self-contradiction.

The fact that certain contemporary sectarians may reject these axioms or reinterepret them in a manner which makes it possible for them to claim equal or even exclusive authenticity for their beliefs is entirely irrelevant. The Sadducees proclaimed the Pharisees to be charlatans; the Karaites taught that Rabbanites had falsified the *mesorah;* the Samaritans asserted that Jews had emended the Pentateuch to serve their own purposes. In each case we are confronted with two conflicting axiological systems which cannot concede one another's validity. Rabbinic Judaism finds itself in an entirely analogous position at present.

Judaism has always distinguished between those who transgress and those who renounce. Transgression is to be deplored, but transgression does not place the transgressor beyond the pale of believers. Renunciation — even without actual transgression — is a matter of an entirely different magnitude. Even misrepresentation of Halacha is equated in Jewish teaching with falsification of the Torah and hence with denial of the divine nature of the content of revelation.

This position is eloquently expressed in R. Shlomoh Luria's analysis of a narrative recorded in *Baba Kamma* 38a. The Gemara

reports that the Romans sent two officials to the Sages in the Land
of Israel to study Torah. The officials expressed satisfaction with
what they learned with the exception of one aspect of tort liability
in which Jewish law seems to manifest prejudice against non-Jews
(viz., the Jewish owner of an ox which gores an ox belonging to a
non-Jew is not liable for damages, while the non-Jewish owner of
an ox which gores an ox belonging to a Jew must make
restitution). Despite their discomfiture with this legal provision, the
officials promised that they would not divulge this aspect of Jewish
law to the governmental authorities in Rome. R. Shlomoh Luria,
Yam shel Shlomoh, Baba Kamma 4:9, raises an obvious question.
Imparting this information to the Roman officials could easily have
had catastrophic consequences for the entire Jewish people. There
was, after all, no guarantee that the officials would be kindly
disposed and would not deliver a full report to the government in
Rome. Why, then, did the Sages not misrepresent the law by
telling the Roman emissaries either that, in the case in question,
both a Jew and a non-Jew would be culpable for damages, or that
neither would be culpable? *Yam shel Shlomoh* responds by
declaring that Torah may not be falsified even in the face of
danger; falsification of even a single detail is tantamount to
renunciation of the Torah in its entirety.

It would appear that *Yam shel Shlomoh's* position is reflected
in the well-known narrative related by the Gemara, *Gittin* 56a. Bar
Kamtza determined to betray the Jewish people to the Roman
Emperor:

> He went and said to the emperor. The Jews are
> rebelling against you. He said, How can I tell? He
> said to him: Send them an offering and see whether
> they will offer it [on the altar]. So he sent with him a
> fine calf. While on the way he made a blemish on its
> upper lip, or as some say on the white of its eye, in a
> place where we [Jews] count it as a blemish but they
> do not. The Rabbis were inclined to offer it in order
> not to offend the Government. Said R. Zechariah b.
> Abkulas to them: People will say that blemished

animals are offered on the altar. They then proposed
to kill [Bar Kamtza] so that he could not go and
inform against them, but R. Zechariah b. Abkulas
said to them: People will say one who makes a
blemish on consecrated animals is to be put to death.
R. Johanan thereupon remarked: Through the
forbearance [anvatnuto] of R. Zechariah b. Abkulas
our house has been destroyed, our Temple burnt and
we ourselves exiled from our land.

It is popularly assumed that the Gemara, in describing
anvatnuto of R. Zechariah ben Abkulas, is censuring him for
misplaced humility and lack of initiative. This understanding is
reflected in a note in the Soncino translation (page 225, note 2),
which renders this term as "humility." Yet Rashi renders the term
"anvatnuto" as "savlanuto," which must be translated as "his
forbearance" or "his patience." Forbearance is a matter quite
different from humility and does not seem to warrant censure. The
Gemara's categorization of R. Zechariah's action is thus a statement
of fact and is not a criticism.

The reaction of the Sages was quite predictable. The
prohibition against offering an animal with a blemish may certainly
be ignored in order to preserve life. Bar Kamtza, who instigated the
Roman Emperor, was certainly in the category of a rodef, an
aggressor who causes the death of innocent victims through his
actions. Causing the death of the messenger who had made a
blemish in the animal would certainly have been permitted as an
act of self-defense. But R. Zechariah ben Abkulas did not respond
in the obvious, intuitive manner of his colleagues. His concern was
not with any single infraction of Jewish law. He was concerned lest
"people will say that blemished animals may be offered on the
altar" and lest "people say that one who makes a blemish on
consecrated animals is to be put to death." The overriding concern
was that the act might not be perceived as an ad hoc emergency
measure designed to prevent loss of innocent lives, but that it
might be misinterpreted as normative Halacha. Falsification of
Halacha, opined R. Zechariah b. Abkulas, is not permissible even
in face of the threat of death, destruction of the Temple, and exile

of the Jewish people. Perversion of the *mesorah*, even with regard to a single halacha, is tantamout to denial of the Sinaitic revelation.

II

Religious issues which contribute to divisiveness within our community must be seen against this backdrop. This is not to say that these issues must remain divisive. They are divisive only because the solutions demand conferral of equal legitimacy upon conflicting ideologies. Toleration, if not acceptance, is certainly within the realm of possibility provided that the protagonists are willing to accept neutral pragmatic solutions and do not insist upon scoring points on behalf of denominational interests.

An analysis of some of these issues — and why it is that they are destined to remain divisive — is in order. Among the most divisive issues in the United States is the *issur* against membership in the Synagogue Council of America and the New York Board of Rabbis promulgated by a group of eleven leading *Roshei Yeshivah* in 1956.

The question of participation in such umbrella groups has often been portrayed as identical to that of *Austritt*, a matter that became the subject of controversy between Rabbi Samson Raphael Hirsch and Rabbi Seligman Baer Bamberger. Hirsch demanded that the members of his community resign from the Frankfurt *kehillah* which was dominated by Reform elements; Bamberger counseled against so divisive a step. However, the issue in the Synagogue Council and the New York Board of Rabbis dispute is not parallel to that involved in the Hirsch-Bamberger controversy. There are no grounds for assuming that even those who did not favor *Austritt* a century ago would approve participation in rabbinical and synagogal umbrella organizations. On the basis of the voluminous material written by the protagonists in the latter controversy it is clear that a paramount issue was the fear of possible negative influence which might be exercised by the members of the larger and more powerful group. Although Hirsch regarded secession to be mandated on ideological grounds, for many, the primary fear was that with the passage of time religious commitment and observance of the Orthodox might become diminished.

Accordingly, so eminent an authority as R. Chaim Ozer Grodzinski[4] was prompted to declare that Hirsch and Bamberger were in conflict, not over a matter of Halacha, but over an assessment of socio-religious realia and that, therefore, the question is one which admits of diverse answers in different locales and at different times. The European *kehillah* system was primarily ethnic in nature; religious groups within the *kehillah* were, in some cities, permitted to conduct their own affairs in an autonomous manner. Under such circumstances membership in the central *kehillah*, it was argued, did not imply endorsement of the activities of organizations and institutions subsidised by the *kehillah*. Even opponents of *Austritt* refused to sanction such participation when those conditions did not obtain. Indeed, it is often forgotten that Bamberger himself demanded *Austritt* in Carlsruhe, Vienna, Wiesbaden, and indeed in Frankfurt as well, at a time when the autonomy of Orthodox institutions was as yet not guaranteed.[5]

In contrast, the issue in the United States in not that of possible negative influence but of legitimization. Organizations such as the Synagogue Council of America and the New York Board of Rabbis are, by their very nature, religious organizations; their *raison d'etre* is to enable diverse religious groups to speak with a common voice. It is precisely a union of synagogal bodies *qua* synagogue bodies and/or clergymen *qua* rabbis which confers, or appears to confer, legitimacy and recognition of equal ideological validity.

And it is precisely for this reason that men of goodwill would not find this obstacle to be insurmountable. It would be entirely possible for the Synagogue Council of America to coopt a number of secular Jewish organizations, to engage in a *shinuy ha-shem* and to emerge as an organization doing exactly what it does at present but without any implication of mutual recognition of doctrinal legitimacy. The New York Board of Rabbis would find a similar expedient a bit more difficult but by no means impossible.

---

4. *Ahi'ezer: Kovetz Iggerot*, ed. Aron Sorasky (Bnei Brak, 5730), I, no. 150.
5. See R. Simchah Bamberger, *Teshuvot Zekher Simhah*, no. 130.

On the Israeli scene, *giyur ke-halachah*, the most emotion-laden of problems, is the easiest to resolve. The Law of Return of 26 Tammuz, 5710[6] confers automatic Israeli citizenship upon certain classes of people. Other persons are by no means excluded from Israeli citizenship. They must, however, undergo a naturalization process. The provisions of the Law of Return, as they apply to naturally-born Jews, pose no problem whatsoever. However, since the Law of Return confers citizenship in a like manner upon converts to Judaism a problem arises with regard to conversions performed under non-Orthodox auspices.

Halachic Judaism can never sanction conversion in the absence either of ideological sincerity or of unreserved acceptance of the "yoke of the commandments." Thus no candidate may be accepted for conversion in the absence of a firm commitment to *shmirat ha-mitzvot*. Sincerity of purpose in face of obvious ulterior motivation can be determined only by a competent *Bet Din* on a case-by-case basis.

Moreover, halacha recognizes the validity of a conversion only if performed in the presence of a qualified *Bet Din*. The qualifications for serving on a *Bet Din* are carefully spelled out by halacha. Conversion, even when accompanied by circumcision, immersion in a *mikveh*, as well as acceptance of the "yoke of the commandments," is null and void unless performed in the presence of a qualified *Bet Din*.

A number of proposals have been advanced in an attempt to satisfy the desires and aspirations of the Conservative and Reform movements without doing violence to the principles of the Orthodox. The crux of these proposals is that all conversions be recognized as valid, regardless of the auspices under which performed, provided that the halachic requirements of immersion and circumcision are properly carried out. Conservative and Reform groups would undertake scrupulously to adhere to these halachic requirements.

Alas, such proposals, well-meaning as they may be, are unacceptable because they ignore one crucial factor: conversion to

6. *Sefer ha-Hukkim*, no. 51, 21 Tammuz 5710, p. 159.

Judaism is valid only if performed in the presence of a qualified *Bet Din*. In both the United States and in Israel — as in most countries — a judge cannot sit on the bench without first being sworn to uphold the laws of the land. In the absence of such a commitment his judicial decisions are legally meaningless — regardless of whether or not they reflect the law correctly. Jewish law does not require an oath — other than the one sworn by each of us at Mount Sinai — but it does state clear requirements for holding judicial office. One need not necessarily be an ordained rabbi in order to serve on a *Bet Din* for purposes of accepting a convert, but one must be committed to the acceptance of Torah — both the Written and Oral Law — *in its entirety*. One who refuses to accept the divinity and binding authority of even the most minor detail of halacha is, *ipso facto*, disqualified. Long before the Law of Return became a controversial issue, it was the stated opinion of halachic authorities that ideological adherents of Reform and Conservatism fall into this category. One of the foremost rabbinic scholars of our generation, R. Moses Feinstein, has written in at least six different responsa which appear in his *Iggerot Mosheh* that all who identify themselves as non-Orthodox clergy must be considered to be in this category.[8]

For this reason, no serious halachist can be receptive to any proposal which would provide for inclusion of non-Orthodox clergymen as participants in the statutory three-member *Bet Din* required for conversion. However, proposals have been advanced in some quarters calling for the establishment of a *Bet Din* composed of at least three qualified Orthodox rabbis with additional participants drawn from non-Orthodox groups. Such proposals are designed to provide the appearance of participation without providing a substantive role for non-Orthodox members of such a body. This proposal, it has been argued, should be

---

7. See, for example, Jakob J. Petuchowski, "Plural Models within the *Halachah*," *Judaism*, vol. 19, no. 2 (Winter 1970), 77-89.

8. See *Iggerot Mosheh*, *Even ha-Ezer*, I, no. 135; *Even ha-Ezer*, II, no. 17; *Even ha-Ezer*, III, no. 3; *Yoreh De'ah*, I, no, 160; *Yoreh De'ah*, II, no. 125; *Yoreh De'ah*, III, no. 77. See also *Iggerot Mosheh*, *Even ha-Ezer*, I, nos. 76-77 and 82, sec. 11; and *Yoreh De'ah*, II, nos. 100 and 132.

acceptable to all. The concern of Orthodox Jews that validity of the conversion not be compromised by the absence of a qualified *Bet Din* is obviated by assuring that three participants are fully qualified. In effect, the Orthodox members — and the Orthodox members alone — would constitute the *Bet Din*. Other participants are entirely superfluous and hence, it is argued, from the vantage point of halacha they should be viewed as observers whose presence is non-participatory and hence entirely innocuous. Non-Orthodox sectors of the community would be able to ignore this salient consideration and to claim participation of their representatives as full-fledged members of the *Bet Din*.

In point of fact, there does exist a halachic analogue which provides a paradigmatic distinction between participatory and non-participatory members of a *Bet Din*. *Halitzah*, which provides for release from the obligations of levirate marriage, must be performed in the presence of a *Bet Din*. The *Bet Din* for *halitzah* is not composed of the usual three-man complement but consists of five persons. However, the additional two members of this body play no substantive role whatsoever. Since they are assigned no function other than that fulfilled by their mere presence, they are known in rabbinic parlance as *"die shtume dayyanim,"* i.e., "the mute judges." The proposed *Bet Din* for conversion would be entirely similar to the *Bet Din* recognized by halacha for purposes of *halitzah*. Non-Orthodox participants would in fact be *"shtume dayyanim."*

Establishment of a *Bet Din* of this nature is not acceptable to large sectors of the Orthodox community for reasons which, not surprisingly, find expression in the regulations governing the composition of the five-member *Bet Din* required for purposes of *halitzah*.

Although *halitzah*, in order to be efficacious, must be performed in the presence of a *Bet Din*, there is nothing intrinsic to that ritual which requires a five-member judicial body. The basic requirement for the presence of a *Bet Din* could be discharged by a three-man body; the enlarged bench is required solely for purposes of publicization of the ritual — either to assure that the woman's status be known to the public at large so that she will not subsequently marry a *kohen,* or in order that prospective suitors be aware that there is no longer an impediment to seeking her hand. The unusual presence of additional members, even though they are assigned no participatory function, serves to publicize the proceedings.

The non-participatory nature of the additional two members is reflected in the seating arrangements employed. According to some authorities, the two additional members are assigned seats opposite the three members who constitute the *Bet Din* proper; others maintain that it is the practice for the additional members not to be seated opposite the three-man panel but at the side of the bench or row of seats occupied by the three-member *Bet Din.*

Logically, since the additional two members are not participants in the *Bet Din,* there is no intrinsic reason why they must be qualified to serve as judges. For example, Jewish law provides that members of a *Bet Din* may not be related to each other or to those appearing before them. This restriction clearly applies to the three persons sitting together as the *Bet Din* for *halitzah.* But does it apply to the two non-participating members who are coopted solely for purposes of publicization? This issue is the subject of controversy among early authorities. Ritva, cited by *Nemukei Yosef, Yevamot* 101a, maintains that restrictions governing qualifications of members of a *Bet Din* do not apply to these additioinal two members. *Nemukei Yosef* further infers from the phraseology employed by Rambam, *Hilkhot Yivum ve-Halitzah* 4:6, that the latter disagrees and rules that all five should be required to satisfy the identical requirements; *Tur Shulchan Aruch, Even ha-Ezer* 169, and Ramo, *Even ha-Ezer* 169:3 espouse the position of Rambam.

The analysis of this controversy presented by *Bet Shmu'el, Even ha-Ezer* 169:4, is quite instructive. *Bet Shmu'el* notes that *Shulchan Aruch* and Ramo record divergent practices regarding seating arrangements for the additional two members: *Shulchan Aruch* 169, *Seder Halitzah,* sec. 12, records the earlier practice which provides for the two coopted members to be seated opposite the first three; Ramo announces the modified practice of adjacent sitting at the side.

Bet Shmu'el proceeds to explain that when the additional two members sit opposite the *Bet Din* it is apparent to all that the coopted individuals are in fact not members of the bench; hence authorities who propose opposite seating for the coopted participants would find no reason for them to meet the qualifications established for fullfledged participants. However, explains *Bet Shmu'el*, an onlooker finding a seating arrangement such as that described by Ramo might well be unable to discern the essential distinction between the two groups. Accordingly, were unqualified persons permitted to occupy the two additional seats on the five-man panel, the uninformed bystander might conclude that the same relaxation of requirements applies to all members of the *Bet Din*. In order to prevent such error, concludes *Bet Shmu'el*, even the two non-participating members of the *Bet Din* must meet the requirements for participatory members of the *Bet Din*. Accordingly, declares *Bet Shmu'el*, those authorities whose practice did not require separate seating required that all five participants be fully qualified. Thus Ramo, for example, adopts an entirely consistent position with regard to both matters.

It is thus evident that all who are perceived by the public as members of a *Bet Din* must be qualified for service on that body even though, in actuality, they are not members of the *Bet Din*. Surely, the same principle applies to a *Bet Din* which sits for purposes of accepting converts to Judaism. Halacha forbids even the appearance of participation in such a judicial body by any person not fully qualified for actual participation.

Participation of non-Orthodox clergymen in such bodies even as non-participatory *"shtume dayyanim"* is cause for even more serious concern since it serves to legitimize the credentials of such participants and of the ideologies they represent. The considerations giving rise to opposition to joint participation in umbrella bodies such as the Synogogue Council of America and the New York Board of Rabbis certainly apply with even greater cogency and force to establishment of a common *Bet Din* for purposes of acceptance of converts.

There is nothing in this position which should be a cause for animus directed against the Orthodox rabbinate. The Orthodox posture on this matter is based upon objective criteria of Jewish law and in no way reflects political, partisan or personal considerations. Those who differ ideologically may disagree, and even deplore, this position; but intellectual honesty should compel them to recognize that it is a sincerely held view which is the product of a firm commitment to halacha in all its guises.

Nevertheless, a solution does exist. The objection is based upon implicit State recognition of the validity of such conversions, not upon conferral of citizenship *per se*. Since no one has ever argued that non-Jews should not be granted citizenship by the State of Israel, there could hardly be an objection to bestowing citizenship upon a person who remains a gentile because of an invalid conversion procedure. The solution is as obvious as it is simple: restrict the Law of Return to naturally-born Jews and allow converts to apply for naturalization in the usual manner. Non-Jews affirming loyalty to the State are granted naturalization as a matter of course at the discretion of the Minister of the Interior in accordance with sec. 5 of the Nationality Law of 5712.[9] Surely, no one will object if State officials, without in any way passing on matters of halacha, use objective judgment in considering even technically invalid conversion as evidence of an applicant's sincere desire to identify with the aspirations and common destiny of the citizens of the State of Israel.[10] It must be remembered that the present law provides that economic and social benefits associated with citizenship are automatically conferred upon even non-Jewish spouses and children of Jews claiming citizenship under the Law of Return as amended on 2 Adar II 5730.[11] The relevant section states:

The rights of a Jew under this Law and the rights of

---

9. *Sefer ha-Hukkim*, no. 95, 13 Nisan 5712, p. 146.
10. There is even a biblical precedent for treating naturally-born Jews and proselytes differently in terms of their relationship to *Eretz Yisra'el:* A convert has no claim to *yerushat ha-aretz.* Similarly, it is not at all anomalous to accept the claim of a Jew to citizenship automatically but to subject the bona fides of a convert to at least cursory scrutiny via the naturalization process.
11. *Sefer ha-Hukkim*, no. 586, 11 Adar II 5730, p. 34.

> an *oleh* under the Nationality Law, (5712-1952), as
> well as the rights of an *oleh* under any other
> enactment, are also vested in a child and a grandchild
> of a Jew, the spouse of a Jew, the spouse of a child of
> a Jew and the spouse of a grandchild of a Jew, except
> for a person who has been a Jew and has voluntarily
> changed his religion.

No demurrer has been heard with regard to these provisions of the
law.

Unity requires neither legitimization nor acceptance, but it
does require tolerance. Tolerance, without which co-existence
becomes impossible, at times demands tht ideological issues be
skirted rather than solved. Removal of the "Who is a Jew?" issue
from the political agenda would serve as an ideological victory for
no one, but would constitute a definite victory for the cause of
unity.

Recognition of non-Orthodox clergymen and the question of
solemnization of marriages proscribed by halacha are problems
which do not readily lend themselves to a facile solution. The State
of Israel has, in effect, preserved the millet system which granted
autonomy to each religious community in matters of marriage and
divorce. The Samaritans and the Karaites have been granted
recognition as autonomous religious communities. In effect, such
autonomy implies recognition of the beliefs espoused by these
groups as sufficiently different from those of Judaism as to
constitute separate religious faith-communities. Orthodox Judaism
cannot recognize other trends as legitimate expressions of Judaism.
This, however, does not prevent the State of Israel from extending
recognition to such groups as dinstinct and autonomous faith-
communities. If the goal is to secure redress of grievances and civil
liberties such a procedure would produce the desired effect. If,
however, the goal is recognition of the legitimacy of those trends as
different but nevertheless authentic expressions of Judaism,
recognition as distinct faith-communities would be
counterproductive.

Most significantly, a solution of this nature is antithetical to
the fostering of unity. The danger of a new Karaite schism born of

rejection of matrimonial law, as was the original Karaite schism, is a very real one. Conferment of autonomy in matters of marriage and divorce upon non-Orthodox groups can only hasten the process. The threat to genealogical purity which existed in only an incipient form in the early days of the Reform movement prompted personages such as R. Moses Sofer[12] and, much later, R. Chaim Ozer Grodzinski[13] to propose a call for such a schism. Orthodox Judaism has made its stand very clear. It is regretfully willing to accept schism rather than enter into ideological compromise. The ball is in the other court. Others must ask themselves: Does there exist any ideologically compelling reason which requires them to destroy Jewish unity? Assuming a negative answer to this query, the sole remaining question to be asked is: Is a measure of denominational pride an unreasonable price to pay for preservation of some vestige of communal unity?

---

12. *Teshuvot Hatam Sofer*, VI, no. 89.
13. *Ahi'ezer: Kovetz Iggerot*, I, no. 150.

Ribis: A Halachic Anthology

Rabbi Joseph Stern

את כספך לא תתן לו בנשך ובמרבית לא תתן אכל

Do not charge interest *(Ribis)* while lending money or food.[1]

Do not cause your fellow Jew to charge interest (i.e. do not *pay* interest in return for a loan — a prohibition against the debtor paying interest).[2]

לא תשיך לאחיך נשך כסף נשך אכל נשך כל דבר אשר
ישך.

Do not act as an accomplice to the charging of interest (an injunction against even consigning or certifying any usurious financial transaction).[3]

הא למדת שהמלוה ברבית עובר על ששה לאוין.

A usurious creditor violates six biblical prohibitions.[4]

כל המלוה ברבית כאילו כופר באלקי ישראל.

Usury — charging interest — is equivalent to atheism.[5]

---

1. ויקרא כה, ל"ג
2. דברים כ"ג, כ
3. שמות כ"ב, כ"ד
4. רמב"ם, הלכות מלוה ולוה פ"ב הלכה ב
5. ירושלמי ב"מ פרק ה' הלכות ח

Rabbi, Cong. Ohav Shalom (New York); Assistant Professor of Business, Trenton State College

כל המלוה ברבית נכסיו מתמוטטין.

An entrepreneur who lends money with interest will
suffer financial reverses.[6]

חיו לא יחיה זה המלוה ברבית.

The usurer will not experience Resurrection.[7]

The above verses and rabbinic dicta express the *issur* of *Ribis*
— the giving or receiving of any sort of profit for the loan of
money or food.

Few committed Jews would deliberately lend (or borrow)
money in violation of the injunction against charging interest. And
yet some very commonplace business transactions pose serious
halahic problems. This article will suggest some contemporary
applications of the *Ribis* principle and discuss proposed remedies
for each situation. A second section will focus on the status of
banks, corporations, and other organizations that may be exempt
from the *Ribis* prohibition. A third and closing section will discuss
the evolution of the *Heter Iska* (a document structuring a loan as
an investment proposal) and its feasibility for modern business
exigencies. The purpose of this paper is to explore the parameters
of the *Ribis* laws, rather than to offer authoritative *psak*. Any
halachic verdict must be rendered by competent rabbinic
authorities.

PART I

Contemporary Business Applications

A. Terms of Trade

One of the most common business practices is to offer a
discount for early payment. Perhaps the most popular procedure is
to allow a 2% discount for payment within 10 days. If such prompt
payment is not possible, the full amount is due within a month
(2/10 net 30).

The basic halachic principle concerning terms of trade can be

---

6. ב״מ עא
7. שמות רבה לא, ו

derived from Tosafot's resolution of two dichotomous Talmudic statements:

Rav Nachman seems to prohibit any type of consideration for early payment or penalty for delayed payment.[8] In affect, it is paying a premium for use of his funds, a form of *Ribis*. A charge for the debtor's use of the creditor's fund in the course of trade is *Ribis*.

אמר רב נחמן כללא דרביתא כל אגר נטר אסור

As an example of a forbidden transaction, Rav Nachman suggests the following scenario:

Someone prepays a peddler of wax. As a result of this advance infusion of funds, the grateful merchant offers 5 cases of wax for the price of four. This transaction is prohibited unless the vendor is currently in possession of the merchandise (but is unwilling or unable to provide for immediate delivery).[9]

אמר רב נחמן האי מאן דיהיב זוזי לקיראה וקא אזלי ד״ד׳
וא״ל יהיבנא לך ה׳ה׳ איתנהו גביה שרי ליתנהו גביה אסור.

However, the following mishna seems to limit Rav Nachman's ruling: (ב״מ סה) אין מרבין על המכר.

One is not permitted to discount a commodity's selling price (because of early payment).

כיצד מכר לו שדהו ואמר לו אם מעכשיו אתה נותן לי הרי
היא שלך באלף זוז אם לגורן בשנים עשר מנה אסור.

For example, a field is sold for 12 *maneh* if payment is delayed until the harvest season. If, however, immediate payment is rendered, the seller *specifies* that 1000 *zuz* (a lesser amount) would be sufficient. Such a practice is considered to be usurious. The text seems to imply that discounting is only prohibited when the terms of trade are *explicitly* mentioned. To compound the problem, Rav Nachman himself, commenting on the mishna, says טרשא שרי.[10] It is permitted to charge more for delayed payment (or

---

8. ב״מ סג:
9. שם
10. שם ע״ה

to deduct for early payment), provided these conditions are only implied, not explicitly mentioned.

Tosafot resolves the apparent contradiction by distinguishing between commodities bearing a set (fixed) market price and those having no set value. Items bearing a set market value (in contemporary times, gold, platinum, anything traded on a commodity exchange) may not be discounted on the basis of early payment. On the other hand, anything that has no precise price (Tosafot's example — a cow, a cloak) may be implicitly discounted. Under no circumstances may the terms of trade be explicitly mentioned.[11]

Tosafot's formulation assumes the form of normative halacha (הלכה למעשה) in the Shulchan Aruch's ruling.

מכר לחבירו דבר ששוה עשרה בי"ב בשביל שממתין לו
אסור ... בד"א בדבר שיש לו שער ידוע או דבר ששומתו
ידוע כמו פלפל או שעוה אבל טלית וכיוצא בו שאין לו
שער ידוע ואין שומתו ידוע מותר למכרו ביוקר.

In essence, one may only discount items (or charge a premium for late payment) that have no set market price.

Even then, the terms of trade may not be specified.[12] Are all terms of trade acceptable? The Shulchan Aruch (citing the Ramban) only tolerates a small amount of consideration מעט מעלהו granted for early payment. If it is apparent to all that the debtor pays less מעלהו הרבה — that would be prohibited. Rabbi Yaakov of Lisa suggests that a discount or premium greater than 1/6 would be excessive.[13]

Rabbi Mordechai Yaakov Breish, in a special section of his responsa (Chelkas Yaakov) devoted to contemporary Ribis applications, considers the halachic status of 2/10 net 30. Seemingly, such explicit consideration (even if not verbalized, the terms are at least written on the invoice) would be Avak Ribis, אבק רבית (a rabbinic form of usury). If at all possible, a Heter Iska should be arranged or the vendor should avoid writing down the credit terms.[14] Rav Breish's "Mechuten," Rabbi Yaakov Yitzchak Weisz (author of the responsa *Minchas Yitzchok*), proposes restructuring the business transaction to overcome the *Ribis* problem. Basing himself on the opinion of the *Chavas Daas*, he suggests that the vendor first price the commodity on the assumption of immediate payment. If the customer then insists on delayed payment, cancel the initial deal and arrange for a new transaction, this time at a premium. Similarly, if the customer desires a discount for each payment, withdraw the first proposition (e.g. 150 at the conclusion of the month) and substitute a new offer (130 for immediate cash).[15]

Too often, the above suggestions are not feasible, nor is the customer (a non-observant Jew) willing to abide by a *Heter Iska*. Cognizant of the need for business credit, Rav Breish[15a] cites the opinion of the *Imrei Yosher*, who considers a premium for delayed payment to be no more than a hedge against inflation, not *Ribis*. He draws an analogy between borrowing money and renting utensils. The renter is permitted to pay a fee for depreciation — why not allow a debtor to pay for currency's depreciation? (In a marginal note, Rav Breish's sons[15b] dissent, noting that the debtor is not liable to reimburse his creditor for inflation — nor should he. Compensating the lender $120 for a loan of $100 (even assuming a 20% inflation rate) would be tantamount to רבית קצוצה, (a biblical prohibition of *Ribis*). Only if a particular currency has been removed from circulation (e.g. Confederate money) must the debtor pay his creditor according to current market values.[16] Rav Breish himself offers an ingenious solution to the problem. He draws an analogy between renting real estate and contemporary terms of trade. The mishna permits a discount for prepayment of rent.

---

14. שו״ת חלקת יעקב ח״ג סימן כ״ב.
15. שו״ת מנחת יצחק ח״א סימן כ.
15a. אמרי יושר ח״ג קצב.
15b. חלקת יעקב ח״ג קפ״ט.
16. שם סימן ר״ב.

מרבין על השכר כיצד השכיר לו את חצירו ואמר לו אם
מעכשיו אתה נותן לי קח הוא לך בעשר סלעים לשנה, ואם
של חודש בחודש סלע לחודש, מותר.

If the year's rent is paid in advance, 10 selaim is
sufficient. On the other hand, if you pay on a
monthly basis, the rent will be one sela per month.[17]
This is permissible.

Why is this permissible? Rent is only due at the end of every
month. Charging more for not paying in advance is not a premium
— Ribis — for use of the renter funds, but rather a free market
price. It is the landlord's prerogative to waive some of the rent
(מחילה) for early payment. Most business transactions — at least in
Talmudic times — were payable *immediately*. Any price differential
for later payment would be, in effect, charging the purchaser for
temporary use of the seller's fund — Ribis. According to the above
reasoning, it *may* follow that in today's business environment,
terms of trade would no longer pose halachic problems. Few if any
transactions are immediately payable. Credit is an accepted part of
the business milieu. 2/10 net 30 is not a fee for 20 days borrowing,
but rather a partial waiver of the purchase price, a rebate granted
for early payment. Ribis only exists if an *obligation* to pay is
delayed in exchange for some consideration to the creditor. Here no
financial obligation exists till the end of the month. Yet, despite all
possible justifications for the practice, Rav Breish advocates use of
the traditional *Heter Iska* wherever possible.

B. Mortgages

Real estate transactions can be structured in several formats.
The most common occurrence is for a bank to finance the purchase
of a house. The bank receives regular interest payments as well as
the gradual return of the principal. Generally, this type of
transaction poses no halachic problems, especially if a bank
controlled by non-Jewish interests is utilized. (The status of a
financial institution controlled by Jews will be discussed in a
subsequent section.) Occasionally, however, the financial

---

17. ב"מ סה:

intermediary is bypassed, and a mortgage agreement is contracted directly between the parties. Rav Moshe Feinstein[17a] considers such a transaction to be *Ribis K'zuza* (a biblical violation). He considers this to be analogous to the Talmud's case, קנה מעכשיו וזוזי ליהוי הלואה גבך "I am selling you a field. Take title now and pay me later."

Under those circumstances, the seller may not consume any of the field's produce nor may he derive any benefit from the purchaser.[18] Any consideration rendered to the seller would be in effect a reward for temporary use of his funds and, consequently, *Ribis*. Rav Breish agrees that any mortgage agreement contracted between Jews is prohibited without a *Heter Iska*, differing only slightly to assert that the *Ribis* involved would be *mid'rabbanan*,[19] of rabbinic origin.

He then considers the halachic ramification of a further sale of the property, a second mortgage. A sells a house to B, utilizing a *Heter Iska*. Now, B proceeds to sell the house along with its mortgage to non-committed Jew C. C refuses to accept (to comply with) a *Heter Iska*. Rav Breish considers the possibility that the original *Heter Iska* between A and B would apply to C as well. This hypothesis is only tenable if one maintains that A and B have a unique relationship, that A in effect has a שעבוד הגוף, personal lien, against B as well as the right to foreclose the house if payments are not met. If such a personal obligation exists and if one postulates that B maintains that relationship even after he has sold the house (e.g. if C can't meet his obligations B might be responsible to reimburse A), the original document of *Heter Iska* between A and B might devolve upon C as well. However, the *Chelkas Yaakov* proves conclusively that a separate *Heter Iska* is required between A and C, especially in light of *dina de'malchusa dina* (civil law), which asserts that B's obligation to A only exists while B is in possession of the home.

In a marginal note, Rav Breish's children question the

17a. שו"ת אגרות משה יו"ד ח"א סימן עט
18. ב"מ סה:
19. חלקת יעקב ח"ג סימן קצ"ה

permissibility of a far more frequent transaction. A's mortgage is
financed by a bank. He then sells the home complete with the
mortgage to B. Wouldn't this be analogous to the following case
cited in the Talmud?

ישראל שלוה מעות מעכו״ם ברבית וביקש להחזירם לו
ואמר לו חבירו ישראל תנה לי ואני אעלה לעכו״ם.

A, who had borrowed money from a Gentile, is now
ready to pay his debt. His colleague B proposes to
take over the debt and eventually pay the Gentile.
This transaction is prohibited.[20]

Despite the Gentile's presence in the deal, our Rabbis consider
such an arrangement to be אבק רבית. Similarly, the presence of the
non-Jewish bank should matter little. The mortgage is being
transferred from Jew to Jew and should be prohibited rabbinically,
if not biblically. Rav Breish strongly differs, noting that selling a
mortgaged house from Jew to Jew was a very common practice
even amongst the most devout.

דבר זה נהוג מקדמת דנא גם בערי פולניא וכל מקומות
מושבותם של יהודים חרדים.

This practice is not analogous to the above Gemara but rather
to a similar case cited in that context.

העמידו אצל עכו״ם ואמר העכו״ם הניחם ע״ג קרקע.

Jewish debtor A presents his colleague B to the Gentile
creditor, who instructs the debtor to place the money on the
ground. Only then does B take title to the money.[21] The *Chelkas
Yaakov* argues that so long as no money is transferred from Jew to
Jew (even if the Gentile doesn't instruct the debtor to place funds
on the ground), no *Ribis* prohibition exists.[22]

C. Penalty Fee

May a fee be levied for late payment? Unlike the ordinary
Ribis construct, the interest involved is only conditional. Only if

---

20. ב״מ עא
21. שם
22. חלקת יעקב ח״ג סימן קצ״ו

the funds are not returned by a certain date, is a surcharge imposed. Arguably, this payment could be considered a fine (קנס) rather than Ribis. This question, discussed at some length in the responsa *Chelkas Yaakov*, was in actuality already a matter of controversy among medieval commentators *(Rishonim).*[23] Both Rav Yosef Karo and Rabbi Moshe Isserles (codifiers of the Sephardic and Ashkenazic viewpoints in *Shulchan Aruch*, respectively) prohibit such an arrangement.[24] However, the *Sma*[24a] not only tolerated penalty fees but actually saw the practice as a preferred manner of structuring all loans so as to overcome Ribis. The *Sma's Heter Iska* was designed as a penalty fee in case prompt payment was not received.

Rav Breish suggests a compromise, proposing that if the creditor insists on payment of the penalty, the debtor should arrange for an agent's involvement.

The agent's primary function is to persuade the creditor not to sue in court. As compensation for his efforts, he is paid a sum equivalent to the penalty fee. If, despite the agent's best efforts the creditor still insists upon payment of the *Ribis*, the middleman is permitted to give this sum to the lender. In this instance, no *Ribis* is being transferred from the creditor to the debtor. Rather, the agent is giving his own funds to the creditor.[25]

D. Installment Plans

One of the most popular forms of consumer credit is the installment plan. Monthly interest fees are charged. Rav Breish notes that such a credit arrangement poses more serious problems than ordinary terms of trade. Here, the *Ribis* is specified on a monthly basis, not merely implied. Whenever possible, a *Heter Iska* should be used. In emergency situations, it *may* be possible to invoke the *Chavas Daas's* suggestion mentioned previously (i.e. to

23. עיין ברמב"ם פ"ו חלכות מלוה ולוה חלכח יג דדוקא בקצץ וע"ש בראב"ד ובהגהות מרדכי הובא בב"י סימן קע"ז
24. יו"ד סימן קע"ז סעיף ט"ז
24a. הובא בספר לחם הפנים קונטרוס אחרון אות ב
25. חלקת יעקב ח"ג סימן ר"ג
26. שו"ת הר צבי יו"ד סימן קל"א

include the interest charges in the item's initial price). Even if a lower price had been agreed upon, the vendor may cancel the deal upon being informed of the need for financing and then insist upon this new price).[27]

E. Purchasing Securities from a Jewish Bank

Most transactions involving *Ribis* can be restructured as an investment deal, היתר עיסקא. However, according to the *Chelkas Yaakov*, one could argue that purchase of securities from a Jewish bank may not even be suitable for a שטר עיסקא. Ordinarily, a fixed percentage of the stock's price is paid immediately to the bank, while the rest is financed at market interest rates. This procedure is similar to other *Ribis* contingencies with one important exception. Unlike all other transactions where the borrowed funds are at least in the debtor's temporary possession, here the borrower never obtains access to the money. It is difficult to set up an investment company without an investor.

On the other hand, many extenuating factors exist. Firstly, purchases of stock are דרך מקח וממכר, structured as a sale, not as an outright loan, and consequently are *Avak Ribis*. Furthermore, as previously discussed, commodities without a set market price are permitted to be sold at a small premium (up to 1/6 for delayed payment). Beyond that, the exact halachic status of a Jewish bank is not quite clear, as will be discussed. Rav Breish concludes that while these extenuating factors are not sufficient to permit stock purchases without a *Heter Iska*, they are potent enough to allow an investment structure to be established.[28]

F. Prepayment of Goods and Services

A very popular means of "beating inflation" (especially in countries with triple-digit inflation) is to prepay, a pay-now-buy-later scheme. This very innocous gambit may involve serious *Ribis* problems.

אין פוסקין על פירות כל זמן שלא יצא שער שלהם

One may not pay in advance for fruit (or virtually any other

---

27. חו"ד קע"ג ס"ק ב.

28. חלקת יעקב ח"ג סימן ר"ל.

commodity) in the hope of guaranteeing oneself a stable price.[29] The buyer is receiving a discount (today's price for tomorrow's commodities) in return for allowing the seller the use of his funds. If, however, the vendor already has this merchandise in stock or at least if the commodity is at the final stages of the manufacturing process, it is permissible to arrange prepayment. (According to some authorities, even under these circumstances, the goods may not be sold below cost).[30] In addition, if the commodity has a fixed price, one may pay in advance for future delivery but only at that price. It is debatable, however, if prices that commonly fluctuate (market prices in urban areas) can be considered as fixed for purposes of this halacha.[31]

As a practical example of the above principles, Rabbi Shlomo Englander, author of כללא דרביתא, discusses the common practice of paying in advance for Tefillin. The *sofer* (scribe) doesn't have the merchandise in possession and can't even guess the market price at the time of the completion. Without a *Heter Iska* it may not be feasible halachically to pay in advance.[32] Buying futures contracts at commodity exchanges may pose similar problems.

Similarly, it is not permitted to pay workers in advance and then obligate them to this (lower) pay scale later in the season (when wages have risen).[33] Rav Breish however suggests that this restriction applies only to a day laborer (שכיר יום) who is not contractually obligated to work. According to Jewish law, a laborer may withdraw at any time. Thus any funds advanced to him can not be construed as wages but merely as a loan and would be subject to *Ribis* laws. However, it is permitted to prepay a contractor (who according to halacha may not withdraw and is contractually obligated to complete his job) in exchange for submitting to a lower wage scale. In this case, any advance funds are interpreted as a prepayment of wages, not as a loan and are exempt from *Ribis* restriction. Rav Moshe Soloveitchik (of

---

29. עיין בטור ריש סימן קע"ה.

30. עיין בכללא דרביתא סימן ח הערה י"ט.

31. יו"ד סימן קע"ה סעיף א וברמ"א שם.

32. כללא דרביתא בהקדמה.

33. יו"ד סימן קע"ו סעיף ח.

Switzerland) in a counter responsum disagrees, arguing that no distinction exists.[34]

G. Rental Contract

It is permitted to rent utensils even though the renter is receiving consideration for the use of his property.[35] Why is renting (שכירות) different than lending money (הלואה)? Two explanations are suggested. Firstly, the renter (שוכר) shares responsibility with the vendor, whereas total responsibility for reimbursement of a loan devolves on the debtor. For example, if the funds were destroyed by fire the borrower would still be obligated to pay back his debt. On the other hand, the renter wouldn't be liable for any accident (אונס) occurring to the goods. Another approach views the rental fee as a form of reimbursement for the depreciation of the renter's equipment. If neither of these extenuating circumstances applies (i.e. rental of silver or gold utensils, renting coins to a trade show) and if the renter bears full responsibility for damages and no depreciation is likely, any charges levied for renting would be Ribis.[36]

H. Leasing with Purchase Option

Several questions appearing in contemporary שאלות ותשובות (Responsa) are clearly the results of an increasingly sophisticated business milieu. Rav Weisz was asked by a Rabbi in Gibraltar about a "hire-purchase" scheme (the British equivalent of leasing with an option to purchase). The contract provided for the lease of a car for a specified period of time. The lessee would be required to pay a down payment as well as a monthly fee. If the monthly payment was not received promptly, a penalty would be levied. In addition, the contract obligated the renter to insure the car, pay all taxes, and pay for any depreciation and all damages.

Rav Weisz recommended that the penalty fee be deleted from the contract (following the opinion of Rav Karo and the Ramo in opposition to the stance of the Sma, as previously discussed). In

---

34. חלקת יעקב ח״ג כ״ב-כ״ה
35. יו״ד קע״ו סעיף ב
36. עיין בשו״ת הר צבי יו״ד סימן קל״ו

addition, he urges that the contract be amended to provide for at least partial liability on the lessor's part. If not, any rental payments could be construed as *Ribis* (as in the previous section).

Concerning the core issue, the lessee paying more in monthly installments than he would on a lump sum basis (isn't that a form of *Ribis*, rewarding the lessor for temporary use of his funds?), *Minchas Yitzchok* offers an ingenious solution, an approach which not only permits paying more for monthly installments but actually requires it. Title (at least on a halachic basis) to the car remains with the lessor until the lessee has completed all payments. In a similar case, a field sold on installment basis, the Talmud prohibits the eventual purchaser from deriving any benefit until all payments have been completed.[37]

לכ' מיתית זוזי ליהוי גבך

If the buyer were allowed to benefit prior to full payment, he would be receiving special consideration for an advance of money to the seller, hence *Ribis*. Here too, the lessee has no legal title to the vehicle. The installment extra charges are not *Ribis* but rather compensation to the lessor for the lessee's use of his property prior to completing payment.[38]

I. Discounting Notes

The *Shulchan Aruch* explicitly permits discounting notes, provided that the seller (who in effect is borrowing money from the buyer) does not agree to reimburse the purchaser if the original debtor (who drafted the I.O.U.) does not pay.[39] If the seller accepts full responsibility for damages to the purchaser (e.g. non-payment by debtor) the transaction would be structured exactly as a loan and any discount for immediate cash would be *Ribis*. Rabbi Englander, however, maintains that notes may only be discounted if they are written according to proper halachic format and if they are sold according to Talmudic Law (i.e. a contract must be written for the sale of the note. In addition, the note must be transferred from seller to purchaser). In the introduction to his work כללא

37. ב"מ סה

38. שו"ת מנחת יצחק ח"ד סימן כ

39. יו"ד קע"ג סעיף ד

דרביתא, he opposed the discounting of checks inasmuch as they are not valid documents from a legal standpoint.[40]

J. Inflation Effects

The Jewish State has been subjected in recent years to ravaging, often triple-digit, inflation. As a result, Torah authorities have concerned themselves and written extensively about the feasibility of indexing (tying all debts to the inflation rate). Is it permissible to pay three shekels if I initially borrowed only one shekel and the current shekel is only 1/3 of its former value? Most authorities, among them the *Minchas Yitzchok*[41], prohibit such an arrangement. The *Minchas Yitzchok* bases his assertion on a responsum from the Chasam Sofer[43] and on the following assertion of *Chavas Daas*.

דוקא שהתנה לתת לו מטבע והמטבע הראשונה נפסלה לגמרי שאז אין שם מטבע עליו כלל... אבל אם רק פיחת המלך מכמות שהוא כגון שהיה הדינה זה בכ״ה דינרים והעמידו על עשרים ודאי דאנן משלד רק המטבע שהלוה לו דהא עדיין שם מטבע עליו רק שהוזל

Only if currency has been taken out of circulation must the debtor pay with the new currency. If the currency has been devalued and certainly if no official devaluation has taken place but merely its purchasing power has decreased as a result of inflation, even if a specific indexing clause was inserted into the contract the debtor may pay according to the old exchange rate.[44]

In an article in נועם, Rabbi Yitzchok Glickman concludes that without a *Heter Iska*, indexing a loan (i.e. tying payment to the cost of living index) would be inadvisable.[45]

---

40. כללא דרביתא בהקדמה (בסוף דבריו)
41. מנחת יצחק ח״ו סימן קס״א
42. יו״ד סימן ע״ד ס״ק ח ע״ש
43. שו״ת חתם סופר חו״מ סימן ע״ה
44. חו״ד קס״ה ס״ק א
45. נועם טז שנת תשל״ג קנ״ג-קק״ס

In times of economic instability black markets thrive, often to the point of rendering obsolete legitimate foreign exchange markets. Rav Breish rules that a debtor who borrowed 3.5 Israeli Lira (equal to one dollar at the official exchange rate) should not give his creditor one American dollar in return if the black market exchange rate is 4 Lira for one dollar. Any payment beyond the official exchange rate would be *Ribis*.[46] In an appendix to the responsum, he discusses the case of a borrower who pays a debt of 4 Lira with one dollar. In effect, he pays off his debt at the black market rate, whereas according to official exchange rate, one dollar would bring less than 4 Lira. He leans to the conclusion that it would be sufficient to pay the black market rate but does not decide the issue definitely.[47]

K. Insurance Schemes

The *Shulchan Aruch* rules clearly that a straightforward insurance contract (i.e. with no investment portfolio attached) is not *Ribis*.

הנוסע עם סחורות ששווין ק דינרים מעבר לים ונתן כ׳
דינרים למי שמבטיח את סחורתו מותר.

It is permissible to pay an agent 20 Dinars to accept liability for a cargo worth 100 Dinars, despite the appearance of impropriety (i.e. if the cargo is damaged, the insurer pays out 100 Dinars in exchange for the 20 Dinars he received as an advance) Nonetheless this transaction is structured as a sale of liability, not as a loan.[48]

L. Regional Price Differentials

A producer may give his agent merchandise worth 20 dollars and ask him to sell it on his behalf in another town for 24. However, two conditions must be met: (a) the producer must bear responsibility for all damages (unlike the typical loan where the debtor is liable) and (b) the agent must receive compensation for

---

46. חלקת יעקב ח״ד סימן ל

47. שם

48. יו״ד סימן קע״ג סעיף יט

his efforts. (If not, he is transporting the merchandise *gratis* in exchange for temporary use of funds, a form of *Ribis*).[49]

M. Non-Monetary Consideration

A creditor may not benefit from his debtor in any manner, even non-pecuniary favors. For example, he may not reside in the debtor's house even if he had done so previously. In general, anything ostentatious, even if the arrangement had existed prior to the loan, may not be performed by the borrower for the lender. A debtor may not purchase an *Aliyah* (opportunity to be called to the Torah) for his creditor. The creditor may not borrow the debtor's car. The debtor may not promise that any contracting work he needs will be done under the creditor's aegis. However, favors that would not be widely known may be performed, but only if the debtor had done so previously for the creditor. Thus, a debtor who previously taught Torah to his creditor may continue doing this.[50]

Even "verbal appreciation", expression of gratitude for the loan, is prohibited. The debtor may not even greet the creditor (*Shalom Aleichem*) unless he was accustomed to doing so before the loan. He may not even thank the creditor for lending him money.[51]

Rav Moshe Feinstein[52] as well as Rav Ovadia Yosef[53] agree that the author of a book may not thank those who loaned him funds for its publication. Rav Yosef permits public gratitude only if the creditor raises part of the debt. Rav Feinstein permits a blessing "May G-d Bless You" "יברכך מן השמים" but no direct thanks for the loan.

PART II

Exemptions from the *Ribis* Laws

The following sections consider some of the categories that *may* be exempt from the *Ribis* prohibition.

---

49. שם סעיף ט"ו

50. עיין שו"ע סימן ק"ס סעיף י וביש"ש ב"ק פ"ט סימן י"א ובשו"ע הגר"ז הלכות רבית סעיף י"ב

51. שו"ע סימן ק"ס סעיף י"א ובשו"ע הגר"ז סעיף ט

52. שו"ת אגרות משה יו"ד סימן פ

A. Deal consummated through a broker

The medieval commentator Mordechai,[54] quoting Rashi[55], permits Ribis if the loan was conducted through an intermediary (שליח). Although Ramo cites this opinion, most authorities disagree with Rashi's assertion, and *at the most*, consider the use of a broker when other mitigating factors exist (i.e. *Ribis* is being charged on behalf of a charitable institution). They opine that under no circumstances should a usurious deal be sanctioned merely by virtue of a broker's presence.[56]

B. A Partnership

Virtually all authorities agree that the *Ribis* provisions apply to a partnership as well as a single proprietor.[57]

The ט"ז[58] stipulates that any funds obtained on behalf of a partnership from a non-Jew (subject to interest payments) must be borrowed by all partners equally. (For example, if an IOU note is utilized, it must be signed by all.) He reasons that if only one partner were to negotiate directly with one Gentile, he would not be permitted to invest the borrowed funds in the business. In effect, the Gentile intended to lend money to only one Jew. For this Jew to now share the money with his partners, would be tantamount to a Jew's lending another Jew money while charging *Ribis*.

Corporations - Banks

With the emergence of a Jewish State and financial intermediaries operated by Jews, questions arose as to the permissibility of these institutions' imposing interest on loans and paying any interest to depositors: The larger implications of the question were if commercial banks in Eretz Israel (or Jewish-owned

---

53. שו"ת יביע אומר ח"ד

54. מרדכי פ"ה דב"מ סימן של"ח הובא בשו"ע ק"ס סעיף טז

55. בתשובות ורוב האחרונים (ובכללם העט"ז והט"ז והגר"א) חולקין ע"ז וגם הב"י דחה שיטה זו.

56. וכן היא מסקנת רוב האחרונים אבל הרב בד"מ וברמ"א והש"ך קיימו שיטת רש"י

57. ודלא כדעת הבאר עשק (הובא בשו"ת שבות יעקב ס"ס קס"ו ובחלקת יעקב ח"ג סימן קס"א) שהתיר רבית ע"י שותפות

58. ט"ז סימן ק"ע ס"ה יג ועיין בשו"ת מלמד להועיל יו"ד סימן נ"ט

banks in the Diaspora) may operate in a manner similar to their counterparts worldwide, or if a *Heter Iska* were necessary for every transaction.

Almost a century before the establishment of the State of Israel, Rav Shlomo Ganzfried[59] (author of the popular *Kitzur Shulchan Aruch*) and the author of שואל ומשיב, Rav Nathanson,[60] debated the merits of this issue, the former prohibiting not only *Ribis* levied by a Jewish bank but even depositing funds in any financial institution with Jewish stockholders, while the latter strongly disagreed (invoking such Talmudic principles as "*Rov*" and "*Breira*"), urging Rav Ganzfried to retract and in future editions of the *Kitzur* to delete his decision. However, both authorities seemingly agreed that a bank wholly owned by Jews would be subject to the *Ribis* laws.

However, some contemporaries of these scholars, most notably the Maharam Schick[61] and Rav Shlomo Greenfeld[62] (שו"ת מהרש"ג), considered a bank's unique status as a corporation; its owners are not personally liable for any debts incurred on their part. Thus any *Ribis* would not pass from creditor to debtor, but rather from a lifeless entity to real people. This unique state they perceived as a mitigating, but not totally exonerating, factor. They allow a corporation to collect אבק רבית (*Ribis* that is of rabbinic origin) or permits *Ribis* if the organization is also a charity or acting on behalf of an estate.

Proponents of the unique halachic status of a corporation cite an interesting argument of the Talmud.[63] The Gemara allows a farmer to advance a Kohen or Levi money and then collect the loan by withholding the tithe (תרומות ומעשרות) that they would ordinarily have been entitled to. According to Rav Greenfield's interpretation of the Gemara, the case involves granting an advance in exchange for a guaranteed price on commodities, a rabbinic prohibition of *Ribis*. Yet, it is permitted on the basis כיון דכי לית

59. עיין בקש"ע סימן ס"ה סעיף כ"ח

60. עיין בשו"ת שו"מ (מהד"ק ח"ג סימן ל"א)

61. שו"ת מהר"ם שיק יו"ד סימן קנ"ח

62. שו"ת מהרש"ג יו"ד סימן ה ̇

63. גיטין ל:

נמי ליה אית כי ליה יהיב לא ליה. Since if the farmer experienced such
a calamitous harvest that no produce was harvested he needn't give
that tithe; even if he can tithe, he is not subject to the *Ribis* laws.
He argues that a corporation is analogous to the above situation;
the *Ribis* prohibition only applies in case of a personal obligation to
pay, שעבוד הגוף, not where the corporation's liability is limited to
its business assets. Modern authorities, notably the *Minchas
Yitzchak*,[64] dispute the מהרש"ג analysis of the law and stress that
even according to him only an איסור דרבנן of *Ribis* may be
suspended for a corporation.

Modern responsa dealing with the corporate status in the eyes
of halacha (a topic with ramifications for other areas of Jewish life
as well, especially Sabbath observance and חמץ שעבר עליו הפסח),
frequently cite the insight of the renowned Talmudic exegetist Rav
Yosef Rosen (Rogatchover Rav).[65] He notes that a *Tzibbur*
(corporate entity) has historically been treated differently than a
syndicate of individuals, no matter how numerous. For example,
S'micha[66] (laying of hands on a sacrifice prior to slaughter) and
T'murah[67] (transference of the sacrificial status of one entity to
another) apply only to individuals and not to corporations.
However, the *Minchas Yitzchak*[68] disputes this assertion and
maintains that a bank may not collect or pay out interest without
benefit of a *Heter Iska*. He reasons that if individuals retain their
statutory rights in a corporate entity (e.g. one is permitted to sell or
to bequeath a reserved place in a Shul), surely a *Tzibbur* never
loses its own very personal identity. He notes that a Synagogue
congregation conducts the search for Chometz[69] and that it may
not pay interest.[70] Evidently corporations are considered as
individuals in the eyes of halacha. Rav Pesach Tzvi Frank suggests
that although state-owned bank may be exempt from *Ribis*[71]
problems, a privately-owned bank is certainly not.

---

64. שו"ת מנחת יצחק ח"ג סימן א
65. שו"ת צפנת פענח סימן קפ"ד
66. עיין מנחות צב.
67. תמורה יג:
68. שו"ת מנחת יצחק ח"ג סימן א
69. ירושלמי פ"ה דפסחים ה"א
70. יו"ד ק"ע סעיף כ"ב
71. שו"ת הר צבי יו"ד סימן קכ"ו

Other authorities (notably the *Darchei Teshuva*[72] and Rav Yosef Henkin[73]) justify borrowing money from a Jewish bank despite any interest charges. They argue that *Ribis* can be construed as a fee to help defray the bank's administrative expenses incurring from the loan. Despite the lively theoretical controversy concerning the status of banks and corporations in practice, few if any authorities permit these institutions to charge *Ribis*, without obtaining a *Heter Iska*.

D. Charitable Institutions; Estates

In the interests of benefiting philanthrophic institutions and of protecting the rights of heirs not legally competent (generally children), our Rabbis permitted estates and *Zedaka* (צדקה) organizations to lend money and charge interest if the infraction is *mid'rabbanan* (of rabbinic origin). Under no circumstances may these institutions engage in deals involving *Ribis d'oraitha* (prohibited by the Torah) even if the deal is arranged with a broker's assistance.[74]

E. State of Israel Bonds

One of the most popular and efficacious means of financing the State of Israel's burgeoning needs is the sale of bonds. Is a *Heter Iska* required for every transaction? Rav Pinchas Teitz, writing in *Hapardes*[75] some 30 years ago, rationalizes the practice of selling Israeli bonds without a *Heter Iska* on the basis that *Ribis* implies a known creditor and debtor. Here, however, one cannot identify the individuals backing the bonds. Nor at the time of the transaction does the lender know the debtor's identity. Furthermore, it could be argued that all bonds are sold through a broker, invoking Rashi's opinion that רבית על ידי שליח is not prohibited. He also raises the corporate status of the Jewish State, the fact that the *Ribis* involved in each bond is less than a *Perutah* (the halachic equivalent of a penny) per citizen of Israel, and interestingly enough, the argument that Arabs are also issuers of

---

72. דרכי תשובה ק״ס ס״ק ט״ו.
73. עדות לישראל דף קס״ט-קע״ב.
74. יו״ד סימן ק״ס סעיף י״ח.
75. פרדס תשי״א דף א-ד.

Israeli bonds, thus involving a non-Jewish partner in the transaction. However, a respondent in the periodical *Hamaor* (Jubilee Volume) strongly disputes Rav Teitz's assertion and requires a *Heter Iska* for bonds.[76]

PART III

The היתר עיסקא — Its Development and Structure

Rabbinical leadership, cognizant of the need for a steady flow of funds and a healthy investment climate so that Jewish businesses might thrive, always sought to structure business deals so as to obviate any *Ribis* concerns.

A. Penalty for Late Payment

The Mordechai proposed structuring every loan as a straight-forward transfer of funds, where the creditor can only demand that the principle be repaid. However, if the loan is not paid promptly, then a penalty (equivalent to the amount of the *Ribis*) may be levied. This scheme was not widely accepted because of the widespread opinion (shared by the *Shulchan Aruch*) that even a penalty is a biblical violation of *Ribis*[77].

B. *Heter Iska* — Half Loan, Half Investment

This approach called for establishing an investment company whereby the debtor serves as a trustee for half the funds while the other half is granted as a loan. The profits and losses are divided equally. However, it is mandatory to pay the debtor at least a token fee for his services as a trustee. If not, he is managing the creditor funds in return for a loan, a clear incidence of *Ribis*. Often, clauses are inserted in the contract (שטר עיסקא) concerning the debtor's management of the funds. The contract further stipulates that the debtor must swear in case of any dispute regarding the amount of profit earned and two witnesses must certify any losses. However, if the debtor forwards to the creditor a certain sum (equivalent to

---

76. המאור שנת תשכ״ז דף שנ״ד

77. יו״ד סימן קע״ז סעיף ט״ז

the amount of "interest"), the above requirements are waived.[78]
(Some authorities permit specifying a sum to be paid monthly,[79]
others only a fixed lump sum payment[80].) This format, with minor
variations, serves as the basis for most contracts of *Heter Iska* in
contemporary times. Rav Englander insists that if specific sums are
mentioned in an *Iska* document, only those sums may be collected
by the creditor. For example, the creditor depositing money in a
Jewish bank (assuming a bank requires a *Heter Iska*) may not
accept gifts offered by the bank unless they are specified in the
Heter Iska.[81]

C. A Revolving Fund

The *Chochmas Adam* favors another format of *Heter Iska*. He
advocates a contract structuring the transaction as a deposit -
whereby the "debtor" would be no more than a trustee and after
the desired "interest" would be earned, the funds would be
converted into an outright loan. As in the previous instance, the
trustee must receive compensation for his efforts. However, the
Vilna Gaon and Rabbi Yaakov of Lisa opposed this procedure.[82]

D. Trusteeship or a Rental of Fund

Rav Breish, while defending the traditional *Heter Iska*
structure for transactions between individuals, feels that it is not
feasible for lending operations of Jewish banks. Firstly, it is
impractical for every borrower to receive a fee for his trusteeship
of the bank's funds. Furthermore, the interest is paid in monthly or
quarterly installments, rather than in a lump sum, a controversial
procedure.

C. *Heter Iska* for a Mortgage

Rav Moshe Feinstein suggests an עיסקא form specially
designed for financing a mortgage. He advocates that the seller

---

78. עיין שם סעיף ב וסעיף ז
79. יו"ד קע"ז סעיף ט"ז ובנקודת הכסף שם
80. שם ט"ז ס"ה כ"א
81. כללא דרביתא בהקדמה
82. עיין יו"ד קע"ז סעיף א ובביאור הגר"א שם
83. שו"ת חלקת יעקב ח"ג סימן קפ"ח

retain partial sovereignty over the home and merely rent out that part. The "interest" then will be construed as rental payments, not as Ribis.[84]

D. Contemporary Concerns

As business conditions change, questions have arisen regarding the practicality of the traditional היתר עיסקא. The Chelkas Yaakov[85] defends this practice and answers effectively most concerns that have arisen.

1) Isn't the היתר עיסקא a הערמה — a devious scheme to counteract the Ribis law? Rav Breish responds that we find ample precedent for such a הערמה in the sale of Chametz and of a first-born animal (בכור) to a Gentile. On the contrary, even those who dispute some aspects of the sale of chametz (e.g. selling animal feed along with the animals)[86] will accept the היתר עיסקא.

2) Often the debtor or creditor are not observant Jews and don't intend to comply with the terms of the עיסקא. Despite the opinion of many authorities that both parties must observe the Ribis laws for an עיסקא to be effective, Rav Breish and the Minchas Yitzchak[86a] permit it if necessary even for non-observant Jews (Rabbi Breish[87] refers to the famous statement of Rambam[87a] that ultimately every Jew seeks to do right, it being only temporary passion that causes him to disregard halacha.)

3) Few, if any, deals are true investment deals, but rather outright loans. Often, the money is lent to people who are not even remotely familiar with financial matters (e.g. teachers, domestic help). Rav Breish proves that not all of these factors invalidate a היתר עיסקא.

4) May a היתר עיסקא be written once and apply for all forthcoming transactions (an approach favored by many Polish rabbinic authorities)? The Minchas Yitzchok opposes any such advance היתר עיסקא, requiring a separate contract for each deal.[88]

---

84. שו"ת אג"מ יו"ד ח"ג סימן ס"ב.
85. חלקת יעקב ח"ג סימן קפ"ח-קצ"ב.
86. דעת הבכור שור בחידושיו לפסחים.
86a. מנחת יצחק ח"ד סימן ט"ז.
87. רמב"ם פ"ד הלכות גירושין הלכה כ.
88. מנחת יצחק ח"א סימן כ.

Conclusion

Several salient themes should be gleaned from our discussion.

1) Virtually any type of financing scheme, if conducted between Jew and Jew, may involve *Ribis*. Careful consideration should be given to the *Ribis* ramification prior to structuring a transaction.

2) If at all possible, היתר עיסקא should be sought for any commercial transaction that may involve *Ribis*.

3) Where such an arrangement is not feasible, rabbinic counsel must be sought.

כספו לא נתן בנשך ... עושה אלה לא ימוט לעולם.

He who never collects interest will never suffer financial reverses.[89]

---

89. תהלים ט"ו, ה

THE INDIVIDUAL

Privacy: A Jewish Perspective

Rabbi Alfred S. Cohen

What is privacy, and why is it so important to us?

That is a question which is becoming increasingly and disturbingly relevant to the way the individual interacts with society; the manner in which society seeks to find solutions to this question is one dimension of its entire philosophy of the dignity of the individual, of the rights of society, and of the balance which ought to pertain between these spheres of interest.

◆§ Privacy: A Negative Approach

Invasion of privacy is feared in the Anglo-American tradition as an encroachment of government upon the rights of the individual, and a person's right to protect his privacy has more than once been the cause of overt defiance of Government, sometimes even of revolution. As a sacred perogative of the in-

Rabbi, Young Israel of Canarsie; Faculty Member, Yeshiva University High School for Boys—Brooklyn

dividual against the power of the Crown, it was hailed by Lord Chatam in Parliament in 1766:

> *The poorest man, may, in his cottage, bid defiance to all the forces of the Crown. It may be frail; its roof may shake; the wind may blow through it; the storm may enter; all his forces dare not cross the threshold of the ruined tenement.*[1]

The Twentieth Century has indeed been witness to the stark destruction of human nature and "civilization" which is the result of the ruthless elimination of privacy in modern police states. In Nazi Germany, in the Soviet Union and her satellites, in Communist China, the destruction of the individual's sense of his own privacy was one of the principal methods used to gain control over the minds and the will—and the bodies—of the populace. With ample justification, the invasion of privacy is resisted as the first step to a totalitarian state.

⋖§ Privacy: A Positive Approach

In America, the unwelcome realization that technology makes possible heretofore unbelievable incursions into the private domain and a concern with the all-encompassing nature of governmental intervention in social as well as commercial relationships, have led to many drives for formulating legislation which could protect the individual and curtail government (or some other agent) from invading the privacy of individuals. All this effort concentrates on a *negative* goal—preventing the violation of privacy. Although recognizing the value of protecting privacy, over the ages Jewish thought has concentrated rather on the *positive* values of privacy. Albeit we are

---

1. A Treatise on Constitutional Limitation, by Thomas M. Cooley, Boston: Little, Brown, & Co. p. 365, 1883.

concerned to prevent undue invasion of privacy we find that
our Sages wrote primarily on the many ways in which privacy
is a desideratum in itself, an essential ingredient in the formation of the complete human being.

Privacy in its simplest form can be understood as the
environment in which a person is able and free to develop his
unique talents without interference from external factors. The
Maharal of Prague had a beautiful insight into the great
wisdom of the Creator in His design of the human body. In expounding on a Talmudic passage in Ketubot (5b), the Maharal
comments—"why are a person's fingers shaped like rounded
nails or pegs? So that if he hears unworthy words, he may take
his fingers and place them upon his ears, so that he will not
have to listen . . . And were he not fashioned in this way, then
Man would have been considered created deficient. The explanation of this is . . . that there is a difference whether
someone beholds a scene which is unworthy of him, or whether
he overhears something not good . . . for if he sees an act of
murder or some other evil things, there is not in this seeing an
acceptance and acquisition. However, when someone hears
something, he has perforce accepted it—it enters into his mind
and has an effect on his thoughts."[2]

Under the American Constitution, a person's home and
his body cannot be violated. The Maharal sees an even more
basic protection of privacy—the privacy of the senses, privacy
of the human mind. Privacy is the primary need of an individual, a right which the Maker wants each person to exercise wisely. We are the ultimate arbiters of what thoughts, vi-
sions, words, and concepts will be allowed to enter our own inner sanctum, the privacy of our minds. G-d created Man with
the ability—nay, the responsibility—to guard carefully the
purity of his privacy. This moral lesson is even evident, ac-

---

2. ‏מהר"ל , נתיב הצניעות, פרק ב'‏.

cording to the above Talmudic passage, in the way the human
ear is formed. The entire ear is hard, but the little flap over the
aural opening is soft so that it can be readily pushed down to
cover the ear, preventing the intrusion of words that one does
not choose to hear.

In the *Mesilas Yesharim*, Rabbi Moshe Chaim Luzatto
considers the ways in which a person can develop moral
perfection. There are three things which will keep the person
away from perfection of character:

The first of these is the care and the concerns of the world.
The second is laughter and ridicule; and the third is society
(that is, the company a person keeps can prevent his achieving
high moral status).[3]

Even if one has worked on his own character to develop
good traits and to grow closer to the Al-mighty in holiness,
there are times when he will fail to do what he knows is right
because he will be afraid that his friends or associates will make
fun of him; at other times, a person's desire to be friendly with
people who are on a lesser moral level than he, may similarly
keep him back from doing what he knows is right.

Thus we must realize how the intrusion of other people's
deeds and values can invade the privacy of the individual; and
because of this invasion, the individual may fail to realize his
own potentials and become subject to the tyranny of public
opinion.

The world in which we live intrudes upon our senses,
forming and shaping our thoughts, whether we will it or not.
As the Maharal taught, a person must choose what he will permit to enter his privacy. The Rambam goes even further, and
writes that if a person finds himself in an environment which
he considers to be having an undesirable influence upon him,

---

3. "מסילת ישרים" פרק ה'.

and he is unable to guard himself sufficiently from its negative onslaughts—"let him then withdraw and go to live in caves . . . and deserts". (*Hilchot Deiot* 6:1).

Why is it that a person so desperately needs privacy? Surely it is to develop his own unique combinations of talents and abilities with which the Creator endowed him. Only by utilizing his innner abilities and talents can any individual attain fulfillment of his own self and approach an understanding of the personal relationship which exists between himself and G-d. This coming close to the G-dhead is what we term *Kedusha*—holiness, and it cannot be attained in a setting wherein the individual does not have the privacy of "inner space".

The pages of Jewish history are replete with holy individuals who understood the truth of that which is expressed in the *Mesilas Yesharim*. Moshe Rabbenu fled to the desert in order to be able to be by himself and communicate with G-d, and that is when he beheld the vision of the Burning Bush. In more recent times, the Baal Shem Tov, the Vilna Gaon, and the Chazon Ish are famous for the intervals during which they would totally withdraw from human society, even from the circle of family and disciples, in order to develop their own mind and character. Privacy was the essential prerequisite for the fulfilment of the great powers of intellect and spirit.

- - - - - - -

Hillel the Wise said, "If I am not for myself—who will be for me?" Yet Hillel ended his aphorism thus: "But if I am only for myself—then what am I?" (*Ethics of the Fathers* 1:14)

The individual needs the privacy of his own thoughts and ideas in order to fulfill his personal destiny—and as such he can contribute the greatest benefit to the community. We consistently advocate that the ultimate good is that which benefits not only one, but the community, and particularly the Jewish people as a whole. The most praiseworthy scholar is he who

learns in order to be able to teach others.[4] Man's perfection, attained in a vacuum, is not what G-d desires. Each person's individual moral growth, which will foster the excellence and
moral growth of his fellow human being, is the true direction of
Jewish teaching and endeavor. Consequently, there are occasions when the individual must set aside his private life in order
to fulfill the demands upon him as a member of society. This
principle is often illustrated in Talmudic literature:

Respect for the dead and comfort of the bereaved are
religious teachings which are commonly accepted even by
those who neglect most other mitzvos in the Torah. This
phenomenon is not based on any special status of the laws of
mourning in Torah law, but rather illustrates how highly
regarded and how deeply ingrained these concepts are in the
Jewish psyche. Nevertheless, the *Shulchan Aruch* directs that a
doctor (if he is needed) and a *melamed*, a Torah teacher of
young children, ought to observe the *Shiva* only for *three* days,
rather than the full seven, because the community needs their
services.[5]

This extraordinary halachic statement implies that the individual must allow the public to invade his private world—his
sorrow and his loss—for the welfare of the community which
outweighs his own need for and right to privacy.

Another startling example of the lengths to which privacy
may be invaded for the benefit of others is found in the following Talmudic account: (*Berachos* 62a)

> *Rabbi Akiva said, 'One time I followed Rabbi*
> *Yehoshua (his teacher) into the bathroom, and I*
> *learned from him three laws . . .' Ben Azai said to*
> *him: 'How could you have such nerve before your*

---

4. פרקי אבות.
5. יורה דעה שצ״ג.

> *own teacher!' To which Rabbi Akiva responded:*
> *'It, too, is Torah, and I must learn it . . .'*

In the same vein, the Talmud relates that Rav Kahana once hid under the bed of his teacher, Rav. Later, he even dared to question Rav about his (sexual) conduct with his wife, and when Rav expressed amazement that his disciple had violated this most personal aspect of his life, Rav Kahana too answered—"It is Torah, and I must learn it." (Ibid.) Nor do we find any censure of his behavior; apparently the privacy of the individual is of lesser value than the benefit of the community, which can learn how to improve their own behavior by copying the Torah leaders.

Elsewhere, the Gemara relates an incident of a rabbi whose sister had died, but he did not find out about it until much later. When the messenger brought him the report, he immediately took off his shoes. Then he turned to his student and said, "Let us go to the public baths." The Gemara tried to find explanation for his odd conduct, and the response is revealing: He did this because he wanted to teach his disciples three laws concerning mourning—that a mourner may not wear shoes, that a person who hears about a death long after it happened need only mourn one day, and that even a short part of the day is considered as a whole day (that was why he suggested going to the public baths, which a mourner would not be allowed to do; *Pesachim* 4a). Thus, even in his sorrow, the true Jewish leader realizes that his responsibility to instruct his disciples in the ways of Torah takes precedence over his private grief.

This last is a difficult concept for the modern Western mentality to accept. However, let us understand that it is not just that each individual has obligations to the group which override his private preferences. The other side of the coin is that each person is an integral and essential unit in the whole, and if he is deficient, then the whole is lacking.

On *Yom Tov*, there is a particular commandment

"vesamachta", to rejoice. "Availut", mourning, is forbidden during Yom Tov.[6] When the entire community rejoices, no individual is permitted to retain his private grief. He functions as part of the group, gaining with the entire nation the merit to be loved by G-d. The involvement in his personal grief would inhibit the individual from partaking in the elevation of the spirit which is possible only as a national experience. Thus each person draws sustenance and strength from his existential participation in the unique destiny of the Jewish people.

◄§ The Home

From the time of its formation as a nation, the Jewish people has lived with respect for the privacy of others. "How goodly are thy tents, O Jacob . . ." (Numbers 24:5) was the spontaneous hymn of admiration which burst from Balaam, who had actually come to curse the camp of the Israelites in the desert. What was so "goodly" about their dwelling places? Our Rabbis (*Bava Bathra* 60a) respond that Balaam was deeply impressed by the way the Jewish encampment was laid out, so that no one's door faced the doorway of anyone else. In this way, each person was assured that no one could look into his private world.

If the Jew's privacy at home is assured, how much more so is physical intrusion into his home forbidden! The Torah (Deuteronomy 24:11) prohibits a creditor from even entering the premises of the debtor to claim what is owed him or to take a pledge. Sifre (the Tannaic commentary to Numbers and Deuteronomy) notes that this prohibition applies also to a worker who comes to demand his pay. He must wait outside, and may not enter the employer's house to collect that which is rightfully owed him. This is particularly significant in that, by Torah law, the employer is expressly forbidden to delay the

---

6. ‏מועד קטן כא:‏.

prompt payment of a laborer's wages. What this means then is that, even when a person transgresses the Torah's command, his right to privacy remains protected; even to redress a wrong, the worker may not enter the employer's house.

The Talmud (*Bava Metzia* 113) teaches that the Court messenger who was instructed to carry out a judicial decision and seize a pledge for the creditor, could not enter the home of the debtor. The Rambam adds that if the creditor decides to seize it on his own initiative, he is punished by whipping if damage occurs to that pledge (although he is legally entitled to have it). We thus see how far human dignity is recognized and preserved by Jewish law.[7]

The concept of privacy was further expanded by the famous "*herem* Rabbenu Gershom" instituted in the eleventh century by the illustrious Rabbi Gershom of Mayence, the "Light of the Exile."[8] According to this universally acclaimed edict, it is forbidden for a person to intercept or to read someone else's letter. This ruling must certainly be recognized as a hallmark in the annals of legislation for protection of the privacy of the individual.

◆§ Hezek Re'Iyah—Impingement of Privacy

In Jewish law invasion of privacy was tantamount to

---

7. Rambam ד' הלכה ג פרק ולוה מלוה הלכות. If no damage occurred to the pledge, the man would not be lashed by the Court, in accordance with the rule לאו הניתק לעשה אין לוקין עליו.

8. יורה דעה של"ד — באר הגולה also ספר הלקט, Volume I, #173, based on the verse in Vayikra 19:16 לא תלך רכיל בעמך . There is some question as to why an edict of excommunication (herem) was required to forbid an act which is already forbidden by the Torah. It is suggested that people might not have taken seriously an admonition to refrain from reading private letters, not realizing that actually it was a Biblical prohibition (derived from the issur of לא תלך רכיל). Alternatively, it is possible that since confidentiality of the mails was absolutely essential for commercial enterprise, it was considered necessary to issue a herem for such an invasion of privacy.

trespass or theft, and similarly punishable. There are ample
precedents through centuries of Jewish legal writings to indicate that the individual is entitled to prevent the public from
intruding upon or sometimes even knowing about his private
doings, correspondence, and other aspects of his private domain. Included in this concept is "hezek re'iyah", "damage" incurred by visual prying. Thus, the famous Talmudic teaching
that a neighbor is obligated to share the expense of building a
privacy fence between two courtyards *(Bava Bathra* 60a). There
are many practical implications for this law, which is elaborated
upon in great detail in the *Shulchan Aruch.* For example:

> *Someone who wants to put a window in a
> wall facing upon the courtyard of his neighbor,
> whether it be a large or small window, whether
> high or low—the owner of the courtyard can pre-
> vent him from doing so by claiming that 'you will
> harm me by looking in. Even if it is a high win-
> dow, you can go up on a ladder and look in on my
> courtyard.'*[9]

In another case, where the neighbor had already installed a
window without objection from the courtyard owner, the Beis
Yoseph would allow it to remain, but the RaMo in his gloss
notes that many legal authorities dispute the right of the
neighbor to maintain even a long-standing window over the
objection of the courtyard owner. The invasion of privacy was
classified as a "hezek", an actual damage, against which a
property owner could sue in the Jewish court. In the Responsum literature, too, we find many questions posed to Rabbinic
authorities about "hezek re'iyah", which give evidence of its
wide practical application and vigorous enforcement.
Sometimes property owners attempted to prevent installation

9. אבקת רוכל תשובות ב"י קכ"א.

even of *non-transparent* glass windows, claiming that their privacy thus was less secure than when only brick walls faced their courtyards. We also find a complex analysis of the permissibility of installing a *movable* window pane to replace a *stationary* window pane. The courtyard owner objected that a movable window pane afforded the neighbor a clear view of the courtyard, whereas the fixed pane of glass often got dirty and gave more privacy![10]

In writing about the Fourth Amendment and the *Halacha*, Rabbi Norman Lamm analyzes the impact of the ruling that neighbors share equally in the expense of installing a privacy fence:

> Interestingly, the Halacha does not simply permit one of the erstwhile partners to build a fence for his own protection, and then require his neighbor to share the expense because he, too, is a beneficiary, but demands the construction of the wall so that each prevents himself from spying on his neighbor. Thus, Rabbi Nachman said in the name of Samuel that if a man's roof adjoins his neighbor's courtyard—i.e., the two properties are on an incline, so that the roof of one is approximately on level with the yard of the other—the owner of the roof must construct a parapet four cubits high. In those days, most activity took place in the courtyard, whereas the roof was seldom used. Hence, without obstruction between them, the owner of the roof could see all that occurs in his neighbor's courtyard and thus deprive him of his privacy. This viewing was regarded as substantial damage as if he had physically invaded his premises. Therefore, it is incumbent upon the

10. פתחי תשובה קנד ס"י ס'ק ט.

> *owner of the roof to construct the wall and bear all*
> *the expenses, and so avoid damaging his neighbor*
> *by denying him his privacy.*[11]

◄§ Privacy of a Public Figure

As in every legal or ethical system, no one value can be absolute. Inevitably, the clash of conflicting needs requires some modification in practical circumstances.

So, too, privacy, while important and protected by Jewish law, is nevertheless not viewed as the ultimate value before which all others must recede. Rabbinic teachings indicate that we must consider carefully what harm will devolve to a person from the invasion of his privacy—as against the possible benefit that will accrue to others as a result thereof.

In the following section I propose to explore the extent to which public figures are entitled to preserve the secrecy of their private lives.

The term "public figure", as used here, is not limited to famous individuals. It will be employed in a relative sense: in any social grouping, a person who by virute of rank, vocation, charisma, or other distinguishing feature is placed in a position where he or she takes precedence over others, or who is admired by others, may be considered a "public figure". Within this frame of reference, a teacher or principal, a Rabbi, an elected official, a judge, sometimes even parents, become people set apart from the crowd, people to whom others turn, whom they may emulate. In that sense, they bear a special responsibility.

It may sound trite, but in assuming "public office," a person undertakes a special trust. In such instances, even the most intimate facets of a person's lifestyle may at times rightfully belong in the public domain. (The "public" here can be

---

11. *Judaism* - Summer 1967 (Volume 16/Number 3).

defined to correspond to the scope of the "public figure's" sphere of influence). Parents are entitled to know not only that their child's teacher has qualified for a license; they also have every right to be assured about the moral probity of the person molding the delicate psyches of their offspring. Here it is very relevant to know not only a person's professional competence, but also his moral worthiness.

Jewish thinking takes this prerogative further, extending it to anything at all which would shed light upon the ethics or character of a person who holds a position of respect in the community, for that person will consciously or unconsciously be emulated by the public. The President may be a highly-accomplished diplomat and lawmaker, but if he is morally corrupt, he can cause untold damage to the national character, and the people have a right to be protected from his influence. Furthermore, if he already holds such a position of eminence, he is not entitled to be protected from revelations which might tarnish his image; on the contrary.

The Talmud instructs us to "expose the hypocrites", and Rashi explains that "those who are wicked but act as if they are righteous, it is proper to expose them . . . because people learn from their deeds, thinking that they are righteous people . . ." (Yuma 87b).

We know that the Torah considers the relationship between child and parent a hallowed one, akin to the respect which a person should feel for the Al-mighty.

Similarly, the student must have an overwhelming sense of awe for his Rebbe, his teacher. The Talmud taught that a true disciple will look upon his mentor "as one of the Angels who minister to G-d" (Chagiga 15b).

We might think that since admiration and respect are so desirable, the Torah would bid us foster these emotions in a child or student. However, in his vital book on the laws of

intra-personal relationships, *Shmirat Halashon*, the Chofetz
Chaim wrote:

> *Despite this, if one person sees in another*
> *person an ugly characteristic, such as conceit or*
> *pride or some other bad traits . . . it is proper that*
> *he report this thing to his child or student, to warn*
> *them not to associate with him in order that they*
> *not learn from his deed . . .*[12]

This is absolutely astounding in view of the great respect
the Torah demands for elders. Nor is the above an isolated or
anomalous instance. Elsewhere in *Shmirat HaLashon*, the
Chofetz Chaim notes the advisability of publicizing a person's
evil deeds (and this is not considered *lashon hora* (slander) "if
his intention is that people will, thereby, avoid these evil deeds,
when they hear how others despise evildoers . . .".[13]

The impact of his words are clear: It is not only permitted,
it is indeed a virtual *mitzva* to invade a person's privacy and expose the sordid truth so that the public will not be misled,
nor—and this is the operative purpose—be influenced to
emulate a person whose true character does not meet the standards of Torah. If we are bidden to shatter the very natural and
desirable admiration which a child feels for his parent or a student for his teacher, then it follows that the privacy of any
person who is in a position to be imitated must be violated in
order to protect the public.

Rabbenu Yonah wrote *Shaare T'shuva* (Gates of Repen-
tance) in the 12th century, and it is still a basic handbook of
Jewish morality and ethics. Choosing his words very carefully,
he wrote:

> *If you know well that a person is not truly G-d-*

---

12. הלכות איסורי לשון הרע כלל ד' אות ו'.
13. Ibid., כלל ו אות ד'.

fearing, and he continuously goes in a path which is not good, it is a mitzva to speak derogatorily about him and to reveal his sins, and to cause people to despise sinners, so that people will learn to have contempt for evil deeds (para. 218).

What it amounts to is that any person in the "public" eye has to be prepared to sacrifice his privacy, in part or in toto; the ordinary rules safeguarding a person's privacy just can not apply to him.

In the second century, during the period of Hadrianic persecutions in Israel, a Babylonian scholar undertook the functions of the Sanhedrin, which was unable to meet during the turbulent war years. Afterwards, however, when peace was restored, this scholar refused to relinquish those functions and defied the newly-reconstituted Sanhedrin.

Thereupon, the Sanhedrin sent two scholars to Babylon. When the two scholars entered the Yeshiva in Babylon where that scholar taught, he greeted them and asked them why they had come. "We have come to learn Torah from you," they responded. Upon hearing this, the Rabbi stood up and announced to all—"These two are the greatest scholars of the generation." However, as he began lecturing, they contradicted all his proofs: when he wished to permit something, they proved it should be forbidden; when he wanted to forbid, they showed it was really permissible. Annoyed, he wanted to brand them as imposters and fools, but they told him—"It is too late, you have already announced to everyone how wise and how great we are." What then was their purpose in coming, the Rabbi wanted to know, since it was obvious that they had no true desire to learn from him? Their actual purpose, they revealed, was to discredit him totally in the eyes of the people, who heretofore had so much respect for him. Why did they want to do this? Because he was unfit to exercise the prerogatives which he had assumed for himself, and only through discrediting him could they break the respect and allegiance which the people had undeservedly bestowed upon him.

In analyzing this incident, the Talmud asks a profound question: We understand why, when the Babylonian Rabbi permitted something, the two scholars forbade it—after all, no harm will come if people are a little more strict in interpreting the law. But when he forbade something which really was forbidden, and they permitted it—how could the two Rabbis allow something which is actually prohibited? To which the Talmud responded—all this is worth it, *just so that people do not follow a leader who does not merit his position.*[14]

It is told about Rabbi A. I. Karelitz, known as **Chazon Ish** (1878-1953), that he loved to reminisce about "gedolim" (outstanding Torah scholars and leaders), and incidents in which they played a role. Now, the Chazon Ish was well-known as a person who had spent decades closeted in his study, filling every minute of every day for years, engrossed solely in learning Torah. How then, could he waste his time in idle chitchat about other Rabbis? But he explained that we learn not only from the formal legal opinions published by brilliant Talmudists, but equally from their casual conversations and from their reactions to ordinary human occurrences. And if sometimes even a revered leader fell short of the ideal in his actions, the **Chazon Ish** did not hesitate to relate that as well—so that the masses would not blindly follow. (Interestingly, however, one time a visitor launched into a story about a certain public official, and the Chazon Ish held up his hand to stop him. "No, no," he admonished, "that person is by no

---

14. .ברכות סג׳

means a *Gadol,* and to talk about him is certainly not allowed;
it is only gossip."[15]

*   *   *

The above references serve to show why a public figure
cannot be treated in the same way as a private individual, and
why it is sometimes important to invade his privacy, in order to
prevent his having a detrimental influence upon the character
of people. In America in the past few years particularly, we
have all become familiar with the deleterious effects upon
public morality of the pecadilloes of public officials. Cynicism
has become so prevalent that many feel we cannot even blame
anyone for engaging in the virtual epidemic of falsity,
chicanery, cheating and theft which plagues our society. After
all, if Presidents and Senators can do it, why shouldn't
everyone? Of course, this is not a justifiable excuse for
wrongdoing, but the very expression of such a sentiment
echoes the erosion of public morality which such actions have
caused. Recent history reflects how well our Sages understood
the human condition.

✺ Necessary Information—Or Gossip?

A word of caution: Due to the unrestrained excesses of the
news media nowadays, it is necessary at this point to qualify
what was explained above. The permissible invasions of
privacy which we noted extend *only* to those data which are essential for protection of the public. But while it is necessary for

---

15. This is a personal experience of the Chazon-Ish's grandnephew, as related
to this writer.

The Chazon Ish in one of his letters (חלק ב קלג) notes that once his
Shabbat was disturbed since he feared he had spoken evil against a
scholar, but assures the reader that it had to be said for one is obliged to
know the ways of scholars. However, he admonishes his audience not to
add on even an extra word lest he be speaking evil talk against a Torah
scholar.

me to know that the bank president has been jailed three times for embezzlement, it is not my right to know that he has been married three times. In other words, the permission to invade another's privacy, once granted, is not all-inclusive. Since it arises from my right to know what I need to know in order to protect myself, it logically and rightfully ceases at the point where the intrusion into the other's personal life does nothing other than satisfy my curiosity or prurience.

A beautiful example of this is found in a Talmudic passage expounding the Torah. In Bamidbar, we read about the five daughters of Zelaphchad, who wanted to inherit land in Israel, since they had no brothers and their father had died in the desert "for his sin". That is all that the Torah says about Zelaphchad, (Bamidbar 27:1-11); but in the Talmud (Shabbos 96b), Rabbi Akiva identifies Zelaphchad as the man who chopped wood on the Sabbath and was put to death for the desecration (Bamidbar 15:32-36).

"Rabbi Judah ben Bethaira said to him: 'Akiva, one way or the other, you will have to answer for what you said. If you are right (and Zelaphchad was the Sabbath-desecrator), the Torah concealed (that fact) and you divulged it . . . and if he was not (the Sabbath-desecrator), then you have maligned a righteous person." Thus we see how seriously our Rabbis took the infraction, as an unwarranted revelation of a person's private life. The yardstick to measure permissibility of exposure can only be the perceived benefit to the group, whether that entity is as small as the family unit or as large as the nation. And if there is no benefit, there can be no excuse for intrusion.

In the Talmud (Sanhedrin 31a) the rule is set that the debates and deliberations of judges in the Sanhedrin could not be divulged. No member of the Sanhedrin court was even permitted to say, "I voted to acquit, but my colleagues voted to find the person guilty, and what could I do, they were in the majority and would not accept my view." The confidentiality of the deliberative process in judicial proceedings is absolutely essential if the members of the court are to act without constraint, without fear of reprisal from the guilty parties. One time, one of the jurors revealed how he had acted in a case— *twenty-two years* after it happened. Rav Ami immediately expelled that scholar from the Sanhedrin, for a judge who reveals such secrets cannot serve as judge. One who has no regard for the privacy of the judges has no right to be one of them.

There has been a great deal of publicity in the past few years about the news media's prying into every remote corner of a person's life in order to satisfy the curiosity of the masses (and to sell papers). Some of the violations are justifiable, but others clearly are not. A few years ago, Jacqueline Kennedy Onassis was constrained to sue in court for the invasion of her privacy by one photographer, who dogged her steps and hounded her continually. Mrs. Onassis unquestionably is a famous figure, but it is hard to imagine how the invasion of her privacy in any way operated to the benefit of the world. On the contrary, that was probably just the kind of action that Justices Warren and Brandeis had in mind when they castigated the "yellow press" as publishers of gossip, which serves only "to occupy the indolent" and "belittles" the object of the gossip.

On the other hand, the news media did the American public a great service a few years ago when they revealed the unsteady psychiatric history of the Vice-Presidential nominee, Thomas Eagleton. Although it was clearly an invasion of his privacy, it was a fact which was vital for the electorate to know. That does not necessarily imply that the resultant brouhaha which forced Eagleton to withdraw the nomination was justified. The impact of the revelation is separate from the essential necessity for the revelation. Once the revelation was made, it was up to each voter to decide if the fact of such a history was relevant to the office being sought.

As far as public figures are concerned, easily the most notorious incident in recent history is the accident at Chappaquidik, in which Edward Kennedy nearly drowned and a young campaign worker lost her life.

Let us discuss this incident only to illustrate our point. Should Edward Kennedy have to suffer the limelight's being turned on his role in this tragedy? Is he entitled to have the Court records sealed, as other defendants have? Why should the American people be entitled to know whether or not he was having an affair with his secretary?

As far as the Jewish viewpoint applies, we have to say the following: people are entitled to know the true facts regarding the accident for a number of reasons. How does this man—who might well be President and hold in his hands the lives of millions—react in a crisis? What will he do when his split-second decision can spell life or death for someone else? Does he "lose his cool" or does he function well in stress? Clearly, this invasion of his privacy is a crucial bit of information for the intelligent selection of a national leader.

As to the question of his possible liaison with the dead young woman—many will say that that has absolutely no bearing on his competence to carry out the weighty responsibilities of a President. In a limited sense, they are right. But we know that a public figure such as the President surely represents to the country far more than a mere office-holder with many responsibilities. He is admired, imitated, and respected, particularly by the young. And if he is deficient in his moral probity (and for most people, even in modern America, adultery still fits into that category), then he is not worthy of filling a position which has such a central influence in molding the moral character of the generation. Jimmy Carter was ridiculed when he announced that he would seek to fill high administration posts with people who had a solid family life. But on the other hand, we are all aware that there has been a serious breakdown of morality in America and at least part of that is due to the example set by leaders of society. So maybe a person can be a good Commerce Secretary even if he is unfaithful to his wife—but directly or indirectly, it is bound to have a negative effect on the moral outlook of the public.

◦§ The Truth Even When It Hurts

The tendency to gossip is an almost universal failing, despite the fact that it is strictly forbidden as *"lashon hora"*. In speaking *lashon hora* we are perpetrating a terrible invasion of another person's privacy, by publicizing that which he would want to keep hidden. Yet even here, there are some surprising twists in the halacha, which can perhaps be illustrated by a personal experience:

The young man sitting across the desk from me was visibly perturbed. After exchanging perfunctory pleasantries, he blurted out his problem. "Rabbi," he said, "you keep telling us that Torah offers the guidelines for any and all situations that may arise, that it is eternally relevant and modern. Well, I'm faced with a very serious dilemma, and I would really appreciate it if you can advise me . . .

"We live in a two-family house, and the girl upstairs is dating a friend of mine. My problem is, Rabbi, that long ago he confided to me that he suffers from diabetes, since childhood. I know that the girl doesn't know. What should I do? If they ask me about my friend, should I tell them this? If they don't ask, should I offer the information anyway? What about my friend—I don't want to hurt his chance at happiness, but I feel guilty about hiding this from the girl. What should I do?"

It was not just the young man seeking advice who was unsure of what justice really demanded. There are many others among us, as well, who do not know the correct response. So I decided to explore the question with him and present the resolution in a way that would help him understand the principles behind the decision.

Most of us at one time or another are endowed with the power to reinforce or destroy a prospective undertaking, purely by what we say. It was this type of situation—whether a *shiduch*, or a contemplated business partnership, or a job application—that Rabbi Meir Hacohen, the sainted Chofetz Chaim z''l, addresses in one part of his classic treatise, *Shemiras HaLashon*.

In a recent address, Justice Lewis F. Powell described the current thrust of Supreme Court decisions as "a more traditional and in my view a sounder balance . . . evolving between the rights of accused persons and the right of a civilized society." When the Chofetz Chaim spoke from Radin, not Washington, a hundred years ago, it was precisely this type of delicate balance that he sought, realizing that while a diabetic young man seeking to marry has the right to keep his personal affairs private, the young woman is also entitled to know fully the circumstances of the situation she is entering. It took a *gaon* of the Chofetz Chaim's caliber to show how to walk the tightrope between the commandment not to speak evil of one's fellow man—*"Lo seileich rochil be'amecho"*—and the mitzva not to stand idly by as another person is being harmed—*"Lo sa'amod al dam re'acho"* (both in Vayikra: 19,16).

I quoted the Chofetz Chaim's decision: that one must tell a suitor or businessman about serious deficiencies in the prospective partner.[16] In rendering this *halachic* decision the author of *Shemiras HaLashon* was well aware of the con-

---

16. The Chofetz Chaim does not elaborate upon a most vital point—at what point should one volunteer information about deficiencies in a prospective partner? There is certainly going to be a very great difference in the reaction of a girl who learns that a young man is seriously ill *before* she ever meets him—and that of a girl about to announce her engagement to the fellow. One obviously must consult a competent authority on such a matter.

troversy his words could generate. As if anticipating the challenges and arguments, he prefaced his *psak* with a detailed explanation of the reasoning and sources upon which he relied in **permitting the invasion of privacy.** *

His decision is predicated upon two Talmudic sources: In *Sanhedrin* 73, the *Gemora* describes the Biblical prohibition "*Lo sa'amod . . .*" as referring to a situation when "one sees his friend drowning in the river or threatened by bandits and does not help him." Thus we see that one is obligated to try to save his friend not only from death but also from financial or other losses. A further proof is deduced from a requirement stated in the *Gemora*[17] that one *must* (—not just *may*) —publicize illegal land acquisition to protect the lawful owners.[18]

My young visitor was quite surprised. He had been worrying that he was tempted to resort to a most blatant type of *lashon hara* (tale-bearing)—and I was telling him he was not only *permitted*, but that he was actually *obligated*—to tell what he knew. "Yes," I assured him, "your duty to save your fellow man from harm takes precedence, provided certain conditions are met."

---

*It is interesting to note that the Chofetz Chaim admits his hesitation, realizing some people would seize upon certain paragraphs as a "heter" for lashon hora, or that they might unjustifiably elaborate upon or draw conclusions from what he wrote. Nevertheless, he decided to set down the halacha so that those honestly seeking the truth might find it. He relied on an incident in Bava Bathra 89b: Rabbi Yochanan ben Zaccai was perplexed, for he had become aware of devious business practices being used by some Jewish merchants. If he denounced such activities publicly, perhaps some heretofore honest persons would learn how one could cheat; but if he remained silent, people would lose respect for the Rabbis, as being unaware of the realities of life. The Gemara concludes on the verse כי ישרים דרכי ה' צדיקים ילכו בם ורשעים יכשלו בם "The ways of G-d are straight; the righteous will walk in them, the sinners will stumble on them."
17. Bava Bathra 39b.
18. Ibid.

The young man had been motivated by a conflict of two admirable instincts. In presenting the decision emphasizing one of them, it was essential that the other not be lost. So even while outlining his duty to "tell it like it is," I took special pains to stress the necessity of being on guard against careless gossip—a much more prevalent vice than not saying enough. Even in this case where "telling" is warranted, there are strict guidelines to be considered, as outlined by the Chofetz Chaim:

a) *Do not exaggerate or dramatize the situation that you are reporting.* Diabetes or heart disease are serious health problems—but just how seriously are the persons affected, and how greatly may their disabilities affect their children? Did the prospective bride have a brother who died of Tay-Sachs disease? That does not mean that she is necessarily tainted or even a carrier. Keep things in perspective. One is obligated to state the situation simply, so that the person involved can then determine on his or her own the implications of the problem.

b) *Weigh your words carefully.* Don't blurt out the first thoughts that come to mind. First ponder whether that which *you perceive* as a fault is *actually* a flaw, or only your personal judgment. —If Chaim is a quiet fellow, that doesn't mean he is "depressed" or "odd." —If Berel is a trusting soul, that doesn't make him a simpleton. The information rendered must be *relevant and important to the decision being made.*

Surprisingly, the Chofetz Chaim did not stipulate that one must have first-hand knowledge of the problem before reporting it. On the contrary, even hearsay has to be passed on! The *Gemora*[19] criticizes Gedalia ben Achikom (the Jewish governor whose assassination precipitated a total exile of Jews from Eretz Yisroel), for ignoring the warnings of a man called Yochanan that there were plots against him. Since they were "only rumors," he did not give them much thought—and was

---

19. Nidah 61a.

indeed murdered by those plotters. Even if one only overhears rumors that damage is being contemplated against another, he is bound by *halacha* to pass on these suspicions.[20]

c) In telling about these deficiencies or flaws, one's motive must be *purely* to prevent some loss or damage to the recipient of the news, and not even incidentally to pass on a juicy piece of gossip or to satisfy a grudge against the offender. For example: *Rosenberg want to hire Hilda as a maid. Levy knows that Hilda is a thief; moreover, she once insulted him. Levy must inform Rosenberg, to alert him against being robbed; but if he also wants to even the score with the insolent maid, he would be guilty of "tale-bearing."* (The solution to this problem is not to withhold the information, but rather to purify one's heart.)

However, if we are convinced that the detrimental knowledge will not sway the person to break the partnership or the *shiduch*, we are forbidden to tell him at all. Since we cannot ward off the damage, why heedlessly besmirch someone's reputation?

d) Even if all the above conditions have been met, one should still seek an alternative to being the bearer of evil things. The Talmud[21] tells us that when Joshua prayed to the Al-mighty to reveal to him who had taken from the *cheirem* (sanctified booty) of Jericho, G-d answered—"Do you think I am an informer? Draw lots and find out for yourself!" We need no clearer indication that the role of "tale-bearer" is an undesirable one. If there is information your friend *must* have, try to help him get it through some means other than directly informing him.[22]

---

20. Ibid., commentary of the *Rosh*.
21. *Sanhedrin* 11a.
22. There is also no obligation to volunteer information that a person could easily ascertain for himself, if he would bother to investigate.

e) Perhaps the most elusive and difficult condition to meet is the last one the Chofetz Chaim stipulates: One has to gauge the effect one's words will have upon the person spoken *about*. Sometimes the harm that will come to the subject through such revelation will outweigh the prevention of harm to the other party. Recent studies have shown that people known to suffer from sickle-cell anemia or epilepsy or who have had (successful) cancer operations are often stigmatized, fired from their jobs, and treated as pariahs. The person with flaws or deficiencies has rights, too, and they must likewise be protected.

> *If Reuven is considering entering a business partnership with Shimon, should I inform him that Shimon was expelled from school for forgery? Only if my words nullify the advantages that might have accrued to Shimon—becoming Reuven's partner—but affect him no further. But if, by telling Reuven about Shimon's past I not only prevent his promotion to partnership, but cause him to be fired altogether, then I am doing him more harm than I would have spared Reuven, and I must remain silent.*[23]

It is obviously impossible to lay down universal guidelines for the legitimate invasion of privacy. The underlying message must be awareness and restraint.

◂§ Privacy in Marriage

The difficulties inherent in selecting a marriage partner fade into insignificance before the far more complex challenge of building a solid marriage.

---

23. The Chofetz Chaim explicitly writes that in this case one must disregard the possibility that the offender has repented. The prospective partner has a right to know about events in his past that may shed light on his character.

There is no relationship in human experience which is so based on mutual trust and love as the marital union. Closeness between husband and wife is essential to the full flowering of the harmony and trust which form the foundation of a good relationship. Nevertheless, every marriage counselor (and millions of ordinary individuals, also) will attest to the fact that *too much* closeness, too much identification with the spouse can spell the death of a healthy relationship. A person can feel stifled in a smothering closeness. It is wise and healthy for each person in a marriage to retain some measure of his or herself that is private.[24] I am not advocating that each necessarily have a private or secret bank account, or go on separate vacations, although there are those who recommend such actions. But each person in a marriage must retain his or her individual identity; privacy is a human need which must be realized, even in a marriage.

It is not only psychology which advises that it is unwise to "tell all." The Prophet Micah warns, "From her who lies in your bosom, guard the gates of your mouth," which Mezudas David explains, "Do not tell your wife something which ought to be hidden."[25]

To what extent does Jewish law circumscribe conversation between a married couple, and are there any religious boundaries to revelations between them? After all, "A man's wife is like his own body"—why should there be any restrictions at all?

As we have noted previously, a man or woman is fully entitled to inquire and seek to find out information he or she

---

24. The laws of tziniut which apply even to the intimacies of marriage also indicate the desirability of each person's retaining some part of himself private. This is true not only in the physical sense.

25. Michah 7:5. See Gemara in Taanit 11b and Chagiga 16b. However, אין מקרא יוצא מידי פשוטו.

needs to know about a prospective spouse. A person has the
right to enter into a relationship knowing all the facts.
However, once married, a little discretion is more than wise;
certain aspects of a person's thoughts or past are better buried.
The *Shulchan Aruch* (Code of Jewish Law), for example, writes
that a widow who remarries should not continue to observe the
"yahrzeit" (anniversary of death) of her first husband.[26] While
her second husband surely is aware of it, it is not desirable to
bring the fact to his conscious attention. A woman's privacy is
so important that the Talmud says one of the four types of people whom G-d abhors is a person who enters *his own home*
without warning. If he is not expected, let him knock first, lest
he disturb his wife's privacy.[27]

Conversations between married partners should be cir-
cumspect as well. In seeking to determine the *halachic*
guidelines for permissible revelations between them, we have
to consider three categories:

(1) "I have never found anything better for a person than
silence," comments Rabbi Shimon ben Gemaliel (Avot, perek
1:7) and this piece of advice applies equally to marriage. It is
not necessary for a husband or wife to reveal to each other
every thought, every oversight, every unworthy incident,
whether in the past or in the present. A person is entitled to
preserve some privacy of thought—and indiscretion.

(2) One might feel that it is unnecessary even to mention
that a revelation to others of personal aspects of a marital
relationship is strictly forbidden for either partner. Unfortunately, it does have to be said. Human nature being what it is,

---

26. ‎כל בו פרק ב ס׳ ד אות ל״ד, שו״ת ציץ אליעזר ח״ה ס׳ ל״ד‎.
27. Pesachim 112a. See the Rashbam, who applies the verse concerning
 the Cohen Gadol, whose garments had little bells sewn to the hem, ‎ונשמע‎
 ‎קולו בבואו אל הקודש‎. Especially interesting is the comment of the Avot of
 R. Nossan, the seventh chapter, third Mishna.

numerous tidbits may well slip out over a casual cup of coffee with a neighbor or a co-worker. But your spouse certainly has as much right to privacy as a stranger—and since it is strictly forbidden to talk about another person (lashon hora), certainly your spouse should feel secure that you will not reveal things about him or her! Even when the relationship is breaking up, each partner must guard against the natural tendency to explain to relatives and friends just what a beast, what a monster the other was, and why he/she is the aggrieved party in the divorce action.

(3) The most sensitive area governed by the halacha is that which dictates what a husband or wife may properly repeat to the spouse, concerning what was told to them in confidence. A lawyer, a doctor, a Rabbi, a principal, or others, may be privy to intimate information. What can such a person rightfully share with his/her spouse? Most people would think that if one can trust the discretion of his or her partner, it would be permissible to tell. But it happens that this is a common fallacy, for *the exact opposite is true.* The Gemara (*Yuma* 4b) teaches that when a person tells you something, do *not* think that you can repeat it to others unless you are warned—"Don't tell, it's confidential." On the contrary, *anything* at all which someone tells you must be treated with strict confidentiality, unless or until he gives you permission to repeat it.

Sometimes a family counselor or Rabbi or teacher will have information about a person or family which he has to know as a consequence of his involvement with them. Often this information is of the most intimate nature, and quite often it concerns family situations which nobody would want anyone to know. It is essential to guard oneself from revealing or even alluding to anything of this sort—not to colleagues, not even to one's husband or wife. It would be a breach of halacha.

◄§ Professional Confidences

The laws which have been discussed till now are basically guidelines for the individual in his customary social milieu, in dealings with family or friends. However, a new vista in halacha is opened when we consider these religious restrictions in their application to certain professions, wherein there is a great potential for conflict between professional ethics or requirements and the dictates of halacha.

The twentieth century has introduced us to the concepts of psychoanalysis, the healing of a troubled mind through revelation and unburdening of secret experiences deep within the psyche. Where must a doctor, or psychologist, or lawyer draw the line—may he reveal what was told to him in his capacity as a professional counselor? To do so would be to violate the principle of strict confidentiality which is the cornerstone of the trust upon which these relationships are founded. On the other hand, the professional counselor is bidden, like any other Jew, "lo ta-amod al dam re-acha"—he may not fail to act to save his fellow Jew from harm. Thus if a psychologist knows that one of his schizophrenic patients is dating another Jew, doesn't he have an obligation to warn the prospective spouse, in the same way that every Jew is obligated to warn another Jew of a potential hazard?

It is a complex problem, and the halachic indications are difficult to specify. The questions can be divided into two areas of inquiry: First, let us examine the problem from the point of view of the professional counselor's right to protect his own professional standing and secure his livelihood. It is quite obvious that if a lawyer reveals his clients' peccadilloes to others, he will shortly have no clients. Moreover, an individual whose professional ethics demand strict confidentiality, such as a doctor or psychoanalyst, may lose his job or even his license to practice if he does not hold his tongue. Would Jewish law then require him to reveal detrimental information about his patients, even if in doing so he endangered his own livelihood?

The rule of thumb followed by poskim is that a Jew is not required to spend more than 1/5 of his income in the fulfiliment of a mitzva. For example, if a man has $100, and an ethrog costs $50, he would not have to purchase one (Ramo אורח חיים תרנ"ו). However, there is disagreement between the authorities as to whether this rule applies only to positive commandments (mitzvot asai) or also to negative ones (mitzvot lota'aseh). The Ramo (Ibid.) cites the Rashbo and Raavad in his contention that it is forbidden to violate a negative commandment, no matter how much it costs him. For example, even if a person would lose half his customers were he to close his store on Shabbos, he is nevertheless forbidden to keep it open. But the Chasam Sofer, among others, does not wholly accept this dictum. In his commentary on Shulchan Aruch, and also in his Responsa (חשן משפט קע"ו) the Chasam Sofer distinguishes between violating a mitzva through *doing* some action or violating it by *failure to act;* for him, this is the criterion rather than whether there is a positive or negative mitzva involved. For example, he states that it is absolutely forbidden to eat produce of Israel which was grown in the Sabbatical year (Shmita), since this is an act which violates the positive mitzva; no matter what the financial loss incurred in order to buy produce which is not grown in the Sabbatical year, a person may not do anything to violate the mitzva. Following the same line of reasoning, the Vilna Gaon (Yoreh Deah קנ"ז אות ה'), relying upon a text in Sanhedrin 83a, maintains that one need not incur an expense of more than 1/5 of his income in order to avoid transgressing a negative commandment, provided that the person did no action, but merely failed to act to prevent the violation. This view is shared by the Pischay Tshuva, Sefer HaChinuch, and Pri M'gadim.[28] [29]

---

28. פתחי תשובה יורה דעה קנ"ז ס"ק ד, חינוך מצוה תקפ"ח, פרי מגדים אורח חיים תרנ"ו.

Our research shows that the majority of Halachic authorities accept the position that a person whose livelihood depends upon maintaining the confidentiality of revelations made to him, need not jeopardize his position by telling those secrets. Although keeping silent might violate the negative mitzva of not standing by and allowing another Jew to be harmed, yet as long as he is not violating the mitzva by *doing* any action and, were he to act he would endanger his own livelihood, then he is permitted to remain silent.

- - - - - - -

The second Halachic issue to be explored regarding the revelation of professionally-acquired secrets is somewhat less direct. Even if there would be no monetary loss involved for the counselor nor danger to his ability to practice his profession, yet there remains the question whether professional counseling could continue as a viable activity if the public could not rely upon the absolute inviolability of a confidence. Would a person ask a lawyer's help in defending himself against a charge if he feared that thereby the secrets of his business or behavior might be revealed to society? Would parents turn to a child psychologist for guidance if thereby the child's deficiencies became known to others? Obviously, fear of exposure would preclude many persons from seeking help which they desperately need.

Therefore, we have to consider not only the personal professional status of a Jewish lawyer or doctor or psychologist, but also the welfare of the Jewish community as a

---

29. Even the Ramo is not totally opposed to this principle. Although as previously cited, Ramo wrote that one must not violate a negative mitzva no matter what the case, yet in another context (יורה דעה קנ"ז), Ramo wrote that one need not go to extraordinary expense to bury a corpse found by the side of a road. This is a negative mitzva, not to leave the body unburied. See גיליון מהרש"א ibid.

whole. Is it beneficial for the community to have available to it
people with the skill and knowledge to help those in pain, or in
confusion, or in confrontation with the law? I think yes, very
much so. Can we then allow this benefit to the community to
take precedence over the rights and prerogatives of the individuals within that community? Or do our obligations to the
individual—in our case, to warn a person of a hazard he may
be facing—have a prior validity?

Although this specific question is not directly answered
by poskim, the preponderance of Rabbinic opinion in this area,
as we will explain below, leads clearly to the conclusion that the
public need overrides the personal welfare of the individual.*

The Gemara sets a rule: "Ain podim et ha-shevuim yotair
me'al demayhem." We do not pay an excessive ransom for a
hostage, even if it is within the power of the community to
meet such an expense. Why? Because if the community allows
itself to be thus victimized once, there will be no end to the kid-
nappings for exorbitant ransom. Therefore, to save the community from such a threat, we simply do not ransom the individual who is being held for exorbitant ransom. He may die,
but in the long run the community will benefit. The Israeli
Government's absolute refusal to ever ransom hostages is a
modern example of the relative efficacy of such a policy.

In the Talmud and elsewhere we find a variety of amend-
ments made to Jewish law, "mipnei tikkun olam", to improve
society. An instance of this is the report in the Gemara
(Sanhedrin 81b) that the Beth Din used to *execute* persons who

---

* The glaring exception to this rule: If a city is beseiged by the enemy, and
they declare: "Give us one **person**, and we will kill him and let all of you go
free. And if not, we will kill **all of you**," the Halacha is that all of them must
die; that they may not turn over an innocent person to be killed, even if that
will save the entire community. See Maimonides פרק ה' יסודי התורה, quoting
ירושלמי תרומות, פרק ה'.

transgressed by moving muktzeh on Shabbat. Now, muktzeh is a relatively minor restriction enacted by the Rabbis, certainly not deserving of death for its neglect. However, since that generation was lax in Shmiras Shabbos, the Courts applied the death penalty even for minor infractions, so as to re-establish strict Shmiras Shabbos. Another example of the principle that the law may be bent for the ultimate welfare of the community is in the "takkana" (Sanhedrin 2b) that any three men, even if they are not truly competent and conversant with all the halachos, may act as a Beth Din in certain cases of borrowing and lending money. This enactment was passed so as to make it simple to borrow and lend money. The Rabbis feared that if there were a lot of "red tape" involved, people would hesitate to lend money to the needy, and since this was seen as a desirable and necessary service for the poor, the Rabbis made it very easy to form a Beth Din, so there would be no excuse not to lend.

The outstanding Responsum on this topic was penned by the Chasam Sofer,[30] in a case where the Rabbis of a town wanted to declare a "herem" on a certain sinner (excommunication), but they were afraid that this action might drive him away from Judaism altogether. In his Responsum, the Chasam Sofer distinguishes between privately rebuking a person for his misdeeds, if one fears that the reprimand might drive him away from the religion—this is forbidden—and excommunicating a person who has publicly flouted the religion. In the latter case, the Rabbis are clearly required to declare him in herem, in order to "remove a 'michshol lo-rabim' ", a public menace. Even if banning a sinner publicly may drive him from the religion, the Rabbis cannot allow public and flagrant violation of the Torah to go unpunished, for if they do, others will

---

30. See רמ"א יורה דעה של"ד.

think that there is nothing wrong with such sinful behavior, and they too will sin. Therefore, regardless of the outcome to the individual, the public must be protected.

From these examples we can derive the principle that the good of the entire group, the amalgam of many individuals, is of a higher value than the welfare of any particular individual. It may unfortunately be true that if a lawyer does not reveal to his friend that the person with whom he plans a business partnership has an unsavory criminal record, that person might indeed enter into a disastrous relationship—yet to do otherwise and betray the confidence of a client may do even greater harm to the community as a whole.

What has been written herein ought to be considered only as a general guideline for the professional counselor faced with a conflict between his religious morality and his professional ethics. Let each person take great care in choosing the proper course of action in each particular situation.

◆§ Privacy in Communications

One of the most famous laws regarding the protection of privacy is the *herem Rabbenu Gershom* which forbids the reading of another person's letters. Upon pain of excommunication the *herem* forbids the opening or reading of a letter belonging to someone else. Even Sephardic Jews, who were not within the area of Rabbenu Gershom's direct influence, adopted this ban almost universally.

The ban derives from the Torah's prohibition: "Be not a tale-bearer among your people." Reading personal correspondence is another form of invasion of the privacy of an individual, and must be proscribed. The *herem* continues in force today and has at least equal validity in our time as it did in the more simple lifestyle of the Middle Ages; by extension it undoubtedly applies to electronic forms of spying and eavesdropping as well.

Wire tapping and other invasions of privacy by electronic methods used to be devices employed only by government agencies or master spies in exotic novels. However, as the electronics industry emerges from its infancy, their use is increasingly commonplace, from the businessman spying on the competition to the rejected spouse seeking evidence in a divorce suit. As electronic communications replace or join the written word in importance, they pose a serious potential threat to the confidentiality of communications. The *herem* banning the reading of someone's mail would equally forbid clandestine eavesdropping.

We have little difficulty in accepting the *herem* of Rabbenu Gershom as a necessary barrier protecting the privacy of individuals. But how far does that ban reach? Is the confidentiality of communication a value of high priority or of relatively minor importance? Let us explore that question with regard to familiar recent events.

◄§ National Security

Former President Richard Nixon was responsible for more than just two years of upheaval on the American scene. The entire Watergate scandal with its concomitant cover-ups and mud-slinging, revealed a true Pandora's box of chicanery and generally sordid activities which certain officers of the Government tried to shield under the blanket of "national security". The President also refused to hand over his private tapes, and justified certain actions, on the grounds of "national security".

The issues he raised have not yet been resolved and continue to be a source of controversy and confrontation in our society. Although "national security" during Watergate was quickly recognized as a code-word for cover-up, we do nevertheless have to address the underlying question, which is a valid one: May the Government of a country claim that the requirements of national security shield it from being forced to reveal its "private" activities? In addition there is an allied problem, arising from the revelations of Watergate excesses, of whether or where there are limits to the Government's right to invade the privacy of an individual for "national security" purposes.

The President argued, and was echoed by the F.B.I. and C.I.A., that those sworn to protect the nation from danger could undertake any means they found necessary to accomplish that goal. According to this argument, if the C.I.A. or F.B.I. have good cause to think someone is a spy or is somehow dangerous to America, or is (even possibly inadvertently) helping someone who is dangerous, then they can resort to any form of invasion of privacy in order to gather evidence or information. Eavesdropping, spying, wiretapping, theft of files—all can be rationalized.

Theoretically, at least, Jewish legal thinking would probably support this position, even though it seems extreme. (I say only theoretically, because I realize that recent experience has taught us that we must police our policemen.)

We have mentioned that Rabbenu Gershom enacted numerous *takkanos* and *haramim*, not only the one concerning letters. An equally famous *herem* is his edict forbidding a man from being married to more than one woman at a time.[31] One of the circumstances where the *herem* is not in force is if the *herem* would have the effect of preventing the performance of a mitzva. For example, if a man dies without children, his brother must marry the widow, the mitzva of *yibum* (the levirate marriage). If we follow the *herem* however, a married brother will not be able to perform the mitzva of *yibum;* therefore, our Rabbis indicate that we would suspend the *herem*, for Rabbenu Gershom *never intended it to apply in such a case.*

---

31. אבן העזר א:י.

Another edict of Rabbenu Gershom is that a man may not
divorce his wife against her will. However, here, too, there are
exemptions. If his wife is considered a *overes al das*, if she does
not adhere to the laws of the Torah, he may divorce her even
without her consent.[32]

Now, if Rabbenu Gershom did not intend for the restrictions to apply in the above instances, if he himself in legislating
them specified that they were not absolute, then it is in-
conceivable that he would not have set aside these edicts when
it came to *pikuach nefesh*—a dangerous situation involving life
and death.[33]

What is "national security" if not the life-and-death of a
national state? If we are being spied upon by foreign governments, if some of our nationals are betraying our military
secrecy, should we not use any means at our disposal to find
out and prevent its continuance? Is the spy's privacy more
sacred than the country's security? It would seem illogical for it
to be so.

Actually, there is precedent for this approach within the
framework of Jewish jurisprudence. The Jewish courts were
very strictly governed by a code of evidence which gave an alleged criminal every benefit of every doubt. There had to be
two witnesses against him, and their testimony had to be virtually identical in every detail[34] (if one observed the event from

---

32. Ibid.
   אבל ביבמה לא החרים והוא הדין בכל מקום שיש דיחוק מצוה כגון ששהה עם אשתו שנים ולא
   ילדה. אמנם יש חולקים וס"ל דחרם ר"ג נוהג אפילו במקום מצוה.
33. This line of reasoning was also followed by Rabbi Chaim David Halevy,
   Chief Sephardic Rabbi of Tel Aviv, in a question involving a teacher's
   claim that he should be allowed to intercept mail of a certain student in
   order to secure information necessary to prevent him from following sinful ways. However, no clear-cut decision was reached. Sh'maatin, an
   Israeli periodical, Tammuz 5736, as reported by Rabbi J.D. Bleich in
   Tradition, Spring 1977.
34. מכות ו:

the roof, while the other was facing the criminal, and they did not see each other, their testimony is inadmissible). Even if two witnesses saw a murder take place, but did not warn the murderer that it was forbidden—and specify what punishment the Courts would mete out—then he could not be executed!

In the entire panorama of Jewish law, there is only one exception to these rules—when the accused is a *maisis*—one who incites a fellow Jew to commit idolatry.

"The one who incites to idolatry needs no warning (to be found guilty)", writes the Rambam (Hilchos Avodas Kochavim 5:3). Furthermore, although we never resort to entrapment in seeking a conviction, it is permissible when someone is suspected of inciting to idolatry (Ibid.). In all capital cases, the judges are exhorted to exercise mercy, to try and find some saving grace. But it is forbidden to seek to justify a "maisis" or seek clemency on his behalf.

Why is the law so harsh for a "maisis?" One possible answer is that the actions of a "maisis", who tries to wean others from the service of G-d and to join him in idolatry, *jeopardize the very existence of the Jewish people*. G-d, so to speak, will tolerate a great deal of evil from Israel—but when we reject our covenant with the Al-mighty and abandon His worship, then we have abandoned our *raison d'etre*, our very cause for being a nation. The "maisis," in modern terminology, threatens the *national security*. What our *halacha* teaches us in such a case is that we abrogate our rules protecting suspects, we close our hearts to pity, indeed we must be ruthless in defense of national security.

Thus it follows that a State must be given wide latitude in defense of its national security, which is vital to its very existence. Whereas wire-tapping and eavesdropping cannot be condoned under ordinary circumstances, for the protection of the State we must apply a different measure.

◄§ The Individual and Society

We have noted previously that there cannot be a law which governs all situations equally. The revelation of a person's private life may become desirable as the benefit to the public increases, and as a function of the harm which might ensue upon retention of that privacy.

In the past few years, as American privacy law has grown through numerous judicial decisions and legislation by the states, certain developments have occurred which are not always in consonance with Jewish teaching. Here again, we will inspect the new trends in order to come to a better understanding of our own religious teachings on the subject.

In 1971, a very interesting verdict was rendered in a suit involving invasion of privacy. A disabled veteran named Dietmann had been pretending to be able to cure all sorts of ills, employing powers which were totally imaginary. Hearing about this, a magazine reporter posed as a potential patient seeking a cure for cancer, and managed to record the ensuing "medical" advice which Dietmann prescribed for him. Secret recordings were made and pictures clandestinely taken; shortly thereafter, the magazine published an expose of the quack, and he was arrested for practicing medicine without a license.

The noteworthy feature is this case, which is now part of the law of the land, is that notwithstanding the fact that Dietmann was found guilty of quackery, he subsequently filed suit against the magazine, *and won*, for invasion of his privacy! Albeit he was doing something illegal and potentially detrimental to the public welfare, the Court ruled that his right to privacy remained inviolate.[35] *

---

35. "The Press, Privacy, and the Constitution", New York Times Magazine, August 21, 1977.

* Recent Supreme Court cases have upheld the right of a woman to have an abortion as she sees fit, because the Constitution guarantees her the privacy of her own body. Jewish law is unequivocally opposed to such reasoning. No person's privacy entitles him or her to use his body contrary to the dictates of the One Who made that body.

Jewish teaching could not approve of such protection of privacy. While it is true that an individual has an *a priori* right to privacy, society has its prerogatives as well. Foremost is the right of the social group to be protected, which it cannot be if vital information is withheld from it. If a doctor is not qualified—why should he be privileged to hide that fact from those to whom he offers services? It flies in the face of logic (and, of course, *halacha*), to say that the law protects his privacy.

If a lawyer is unscrupulous or a dentist inept or a mechanic incompetent, it is not only permissible, it is a virtual *mitzva* to save people from becoming their victims. Once a person places himself in a position where people entrust to his care their children or their health or wealth, that part of his character or past which is relevant (but *only* that part) to the proper performance of his task cannot be shielded from public scrutiny.

Conflict between two opposing rights is inevitable when we have on the one hand a person's desire to keep his personal life private as opposed to the equally legitimate wish of the consumer (or patient or employer) to be well informed.

This antagonism of interests leads us to discussion of a broad area of human relations which is becoming increasingly the subject of debate: what are the proper limits to the information which a prospective employer—including the government—may require from the candidate for a job?[36]

---

36. The wonders of technology have made possible situations right out of "1984", and we are hard-pressed to know how to deal with them. New York State has recently completed a project (other localities will surely follow) to put all employment and earnings data on a master computer. The data stored in this computer bank is seen, by many opponents, as a further unwarranted intrusion into people's private affairs. Since the data

Focussing on this problem, *The New York Times* reported:

> Fill in name, address, Social Security number. List past employers and dates of employment. Give three references. Indicate salary expected, hours available. Note all health problems. Sign here if all information given in this application is true to the best of applicant's knowledge.
>
> Finally, take lie detector test.
>
> This request is becoming the bottom line in job hunting. . .[37]

When he published *Shmiras Halashon* a century ago, the Chofetz Chaim had already anticipated our modern problems:

"It is an important principle to know that if a person wants to let someone into his affairs—for example, to hire him in his business, or to go into partnership with him . . . it is permissible for him to go around and ask and inquire from others . . . so as to prevent possible loss to himself (by hiring an un-

---

bank is used by a variety of government agencies to check on a wide range of information, the data stored for each individual is often far more extensive and detailed than is necessary for any specific inquiry. This conjures up nightmares of government clerks (or perhaps some unscrupulous outsider) privy to the private details of a person's life. It also leaves great problems—who will decide which details will be divulged—and to whom.

Jewish law teaches that the good of the individual must at times be abrogated for the good of the group. However, here it is hard if not impossible to weigh such ephemeral concepts. Is it sufficiently important for the state to catch welfare cheats to endanger the privacy of millions of people, who might now be prey to blackmail or unfair revelation of derogatory information? I do not think we can easily posit a rule which will fit all situations, and I view the technological marvels with great unease.

37. The New York Times, August 19, 1977.

qualified or dishonest employee). And it is permissible to reveal even very derogatory information, since his intention is not to harm (the prospective employee) but he is telling the truth in order to save his fellow man from potential harm . . ."[38]

The crucial question in the invasion of an applicant's privacy, as Jewish law sees it, has to be the relevance of that information to the proper performance of the employee's job. Most companies should not be entitled to require polygraph (lie-detector) tests as a routine prerequisite for employment, but certainly there are numerous instances when such inquiry would be wholly justified. To ask a person if he or she is a homosexual is a blantant violation of that person's rights, if the position applied for is a bank teller or a sales clerk. There is no evidence whatsoever that homosexuals are any more or less dishonest than heterosexuals. However, the exact same question is very properly vital information when a school board wants to hire a teacher or bus driver. If the individual is strongly attracted to little children, that should be known before he is hired.

---

38. שמירת הלשון הלכות רכילות כלל ט also שמירת הלשון הלכות הלשון כלל ד' אות א'.

The source of this is Rashi's commentary to Shavuous 39. Further, in Yevamot 87b, we find an incident involving a woman whose husband died. Since they had a child, the widow required no yibum or chalitza, and thereafter remarried. Subsequently, the child of the first marriage died, and since the first husband now had no offspring, the Rabbis had to decide whether the woman now required chalitza. The Courts decided that she did not, based on the logic of the verse, "For her (the Torah's) paths are pleasant ones . . ." It could never be the wish of the Torah to force an action which would engender ill-will between a man and his wife. Since the second husband would possibly feel revulsion for his wife if she underwent chalitza, it was not required. The Chofetz Chaim therefore concludes that we cannot seriously believe that the Torah, whose ways are pleasant, would place restrictions upon a businessman which could result in his joining with a partner who could cause him tremendous financial damage.

We cannot posit a rule regarding lie-detector tests which will apply equally to all involved; it will depend on the nature of the job sought as well as the nature of the questions asked in each situation.[39]

- - - - - - -

Judaism places a great emphasis upon the dignity of the individual, and there are numerous statutes which make it a sin to remind a person that at one time he used to be a sinner; it is even forbidden to remind or mention that a proselyte was once not a Jew. We will accomplish no good and only shame a person by reminding him or others of his unfortunate past.

Would we then approve of laws such as have recently been passed, which would permit the expunging of criminal records after a period of time has passed without another arrest? In Rhode Island a statute has been passed to allow destruction of misdemeanor records after completion of sentence, and in other states records of marijuana convictions may be destroyed.

This may sound very noble, giving the repentant sinner a "clean slate," but it is a terrible disservice to people who may want to enter into relationships of trust with a former thief or addict, unaware of the full dimensions of the situation in which they intend to be involved. Jewish law, while sensitive to the rights of the individual, does not give them precedence over the rights of other individuals to be protected and forewarned, and to enter into situations knowing all the facts beforehand.

---

39. The many restrictions and conditions surrounding character investigation are considered elsewhere in this article. We should note that all restrictions governing checking the background of a prospective spouse apply also to one investigating a prospective partner, with the added reservation that one should be careful not to ask an evaluation from a person who might harbor professional jealousy.

Also, as noted earlier, the application of principles to a wide cross-section of the population, without thought to the myriad inconsistencies of life, cannot but result in laws which are unfair, resulting inevitably in travesties of justice.

> *In Britain, the situation is ... forbidding: There, it is a crime to publish the fact of a prior conviction if an individual has not served more than 30 months in prison and has not been arrested again within seven years. Thus, if an English equivalent of Spiro Agnew (if that can be imagined), should run for Parliament eight years after his felony conviction, no mention could be made of the conviction in the British press.*[40]

Our Rabbis teach that if one exercises mercy at a time when he should be firm, he will end up being cruel to those whom he ought to be treating with mercy. This is happening in America today, with the courts and legislators floundering, unable to arrive at an equitable philosophy of privacy law. Halacha has no such problem. Our laws are specific, and carefully detailed. Nevertheless, that is not enough to assure justice—that is up to each individual, to the extent that he is dedicated to learning the Law and following its dictates.

◄§ The Privacy of a Mitzva

One cannot complete a study on the topic of privacy without touching upon one aspect of that subject about which people are generally oblivious. We refer to the relationship between man and G-d.

So accustomed are we to hearing lavish praise heaped upon public benefactors at testimonial dinners, so inured have we become to the fulsome and extravagantly-phrased lauding

---

40. The New York Times, ibid.

of honored persons, that possibly we have lost sight of the reality that this is antithetical to Judaism's teaching.

Through all history, there are many persons who have pondered deeply and sought to find an answer to the eternal question: "What does the L-rd require of man? What does G-d want us to do?" And through the ages, we have been given many answers. But the Prophet Micah condensed all the laws, all the teachings of the Torah and the Rabbis into one pithy response:

"Know then, what it is that G-d requires from thee— naught but to do justice and follow righteousness—*and walk modestly with G-d".*

The words of the Prophet are striking: "hatznea leches" Of all the descriptive words which Micah could have chosen to illustrate the manner in which one should "walk with G-d," tzinius (modesty) seems the least likely. We could appreciate "walk honestly" or "go with alacrity", "walk in purity", "walk with kindness . . . love . . . humility. . ." But "hatznea leches"? What did the Prophet have in mind?

If we ponder the experiences of our people, as we observe the behavior of the great individuals whose activites and beliefs shaped our national character, we will find exemplified that quality of "hatznea leches." Our forefathers worshipped G-d privately, without fanfare and not for the public admiration which would accrue to them as "holy men." The relationship between a person and his Maker is the most intimate, the most private of all. The individual neshama strives for the heights of spiritual achievement in the privacy of anonymity, lacking any audience but One. Purity of deed, single-minded sanctification occurs when a person seeks to impress only the Creator, when he is not performing for the public, seeks no admiration and expects no credit. Sincere devotion to G-d is a private encounter of the most personal nature.

Avraham Avinu

Let us re-examine the Biblical accounts of our forefathers, and we will recognize this to be true. The pinnacle of the Patriach Avraham's dedication to G-d was expressed in the series of events which we call the *Akeda*, wherein G-d tested Avraham by asking him to sacrifice his son Yitzhak. After all the trials and hardships which Avraham Avinu had to overcome, this was the most difficult to undertake.

We can well be amazed at the fortitude and love with which Avraham accepted that trial. Yet we must be astounded at the way he went about it—he did not even tell his wife Sarah where he was going. It was strictly between himself and G-d, and no one else need know. Imagine the heartbreak in a father's heart; think of the stupendous heights of dedication to G-d which Avraham achieved at that moment—and yet he wanted no one to know. At least gather the disciples around, or the leaders of the neighboring tribes—let the world recognize how great is the belief which moved Avraham to sacrifice his entire life's endeavor for the sake of his G-d. But no, Avraham prepared for the Akeda without telling anyone. Even the servants who accompanied him on the way were left at the foot of the mountain. Avraham and his son go, alone, up the mountain. There will be no audience. This is not being done for glory, not even as a lesson in Divine devotion *(kiddush hashem)*. It is a private encounter, closed to the view of any being. The relationship between G-d and man is a private bond. "What is it that G-d wants from man? . . . *hatznea leches* . . ." go quietly, without fanfare. Do your mitzva in a hidden manner.

Yaakov Avinu

After Yaakov had an encounter with the Angel of Esau, he was given the name Israel instead of Yaakov. The Angel explained the choice of name: "Israel, because you fought *im Elokim*" and the Targum Onkelos renders this—because you fought *before G-d*—you engaged in your religious activities only before G-d, you were not interested in the adulation of the masses, but only in satisfying the will of the Al-mighty. Therefore, he merited the elevation from Yaakov to Israel.

Moshe Rabbenu

Moshe Rabbenu was the one individual in all history, chosen from the millions who have peopled this earth, to be the link between G-d and His people in the giving of the Torah at Mount Sinai. Of Moshe, the Torah writes that Hashem found him uniquely suited to be the ultimate "servant of G-d." Even in the early stages of his career, we find Moshe Rabbenu as a "loner," a shepherd in the desert, one who searched for communion with G-d by himself. It was in the desert that G-d appeared to Moshe in the Burning Bush, and it was indicative of the circumstances in which man can hope to reach out to his Creater—alone, without an audience, with no motive other than service to G-d.

So total was Moshe's dedication of his entire being to Hashem, that after *Mattan Torah*, Hashem instructed him to separate from his wife, so that he would always be ready for a visitation from the Al-mighty. *But nobody knew that Moshe had separated from his wife.* So private was the relationship, so modest was Moshe, so unconcerned with admiration for his unique election by G-d to a role unparalleled in world history, that not one person other than his own wife was aware of the fact that G-d had elevated him beyond the status of any other prophet. Only when Tzippora his wife let slip a sigh, did Moshe's own sister and brother become cognizant of his exalted position. Here we see again that the relationship between the individual and Hashem rightfully is totally private, not a subject for the knowledge of others.

* * * * * *

It is not only prayer and devotion which ought to be performed privately. Many mitzvos should ideally be performed without thought to public approbation or notice of the act. Of course, the best-known of this category is *tzedaka*, whose highest pinnacle is "mattan besaiser," giving in secret—a private act in which neither the donor nor the recipient knows the identity of the other—nor does anyone else even recognize that tzedaka is being given. For us, who are so accustomed to munificent donations being publicly announced and applauded, it is a startling feature of the *mitzva*, that it is preferably done privately. (There are certainly compelling reasons why we have found it necessary to abandon *mattan besaiser* in favor of public acclaim for giving charity, but this is not the place to dwell upon those reasons. Nevertheless, the weaknesses of human nature do not alter the desired mode of performing mitzvos.) If no one is aware of a great financial sacrifice, if neither admiration nor gratitude will accrue from an act of kindness, then the mitzva is being done *lishma*, purely for its own sake, as a private act of devotion to G-d, and as *chesed* to another human being. In this, it is akin to care of the dead prior to burial, which our Rabbis call *chesed shel emes*, true generosity of the heart. When a person expends time and effort in the necessities of preparing a corpse for burial, he expects no thanks from the dead and he knows no recompense will come to him. It is an act done purely for the *mitzva*. When charity is distributed privately, it approaches the elevated level of *chesed shel emes*.

- - - - - - -

"How goodly are thy tents, O Jacob, thy dwelling places, O Israel." We return to the blessing of Balaam, a paean of admiration torn from his unwilling mouth. As we indicated, the beauty of the Jewish home which so impressed Balaam was the privacy of the tents, pitched in such a way that no doorway faced another doorway. The family and the home have ever been the bulwark of the Jewish nation, the secret defense against the vicissitudes of environment, hate, and distractions of the world.

We would do well to give thought to those things which we permit to encroach upon the private sanctuary of our homes. Whether they be material posessions or books, TV, friends, let us recognize that they influence us, that they constitute an instrusion of the outside world upon the privacy of the home. We have every right to be selective, therefore, in determining what people, ideas, words or even physical objects we allow entrance. As the Maharal teaches, Man was created with overwhelming wisdom by the Creator. He was given the physical means to maintain the privacy of his mind and body. Let him exercise those prerogatives wisely.

Chukat Ha'Akum: Jews in a Gentile Society

By Rabbi Zvi Y. Teichman

Many years ago, America was introduced to the Jewish consciousness as the faraway "goldene medinah", a mecca of freedom and opportunity which beckoned to all who aspired for a better life. To a remarkable degree, that dreamt-of promise has been kept—Jews in America have achieved great success, enjoying complete freedom to integrate into the society and economy.

This freedom is in sharp contrast to the millenia of persecution and deprivation in the Diaspora. Given the enforced separation of the Jew from general society, living in ghettoes and restricted in the professions he might enter, there was little need to be concerned with the Biblical injunction *"Bechukosehem lo tailaichu"*, "You shall not follow the Gentile customs". However, modern life brings its own dilemmas, and the thinking Jew in America now needs to devote serious thought to this injunction.

In the following pages, we shall examine the classic interpretations of this verse and seek to measure our customary practices by its standard. Are Thanksgiving and Mother's Day observances which a Jew may join, or are they proscribed by *"Bechukosaihem"*. . .? Does the verse preclude our acceptance of

---

Chaver Kollel, Yeshiva Bais Yosef

each new whim of fickle fashion? Should it affect the manner in which we act or dress, cut our hair, or call our children?

Even a cursory study indicates that many areas of behavior which we take for granted are indeed within the purview of this *issur*.

It is adherence to mitzvot which insures the uniqueness of the Jewish people, and some were given to us specifically for the purpose of preserving this uniqueness. It is no coincidence that in regard to the covenant of *Milah*, circumcision, the *Sefer haChinuch* writes:[1] "Of the fundamentals of this command is the desire of G-d to affix to the nation, which is separated by being called in his name, a particular sign in their bodies to separate them from other nations in the form of their bodies, just as they are differentiated from them in the form of their souls." With the very first mitzva given to the Jew, the Torah wished to insure our preservation as a unique people.

Rambam writes:[2] "The Jew should be distinguished from them and distinct in his dress and his actions just as he is distinguished from them in his knowledge and his understanding."

In commanding us "*Bechukosaihem lo tailaichu*" (Vayikra 28:3) the Torah did not specify which habits or customs of the Gentile are intended. What then is the nature of this law?

The root of the word "*Bechukosaihem*" is "*Chok*" which usually would be understood to apply to statutory enactments. In this instance, however, it is not referring to those laws that are duly legislated but rather to customs and practices which are validated by convention.[3] However, this surely is not a sufficient clarification of the term "*Bechukosaihem lo tailaichu*", for indeed we do share many modes and manners with other nations. We must therefore discern what are those customs that are regarded as

---

1. חינוך מצוה ב'

2. רמב"ם פי"א הלכות עכו"ם ה"א

3. The Targum translates "chok" as "nimusin", which is Aramaic for "customs".

"their laws", also referred to by the Talmud as *"Darkei Ha-
Amori"*, ways of the Amorite.

It would be beneficial to offer a brief summary of two texts in
the Talmud that deal with this prohibition. The differences of
opinions concerning these texts form the various criteria upon
which the prohibition is based.

The Gemara in *Avoda Zora* (11a) relates that it was customary
for Gentiles to burn the beds and artifacts of their kings after their
demise. Initially, the Gemara was under the impression that this
was an idolatrous act, but the question is then asked —

> How can this be? For we learned in a Braitha
> that the burning of articles at (Jewish) kings' funerals
> is permitted, and there is nothing of the ways of the
> Amorite about it? If it is an act of idolatry, how could
> such a burning be condoned? Is it not written "And
> you shall not walk according to their laws?"

The Gemara then proceeds to answer, "The burning is not an
idolatrous act, but is merely a mark of high esteem for the
deceased."

In *Sanhedrin* (52b), the Mishnah states:

> The death penalty of beheading by sword was
> performed thus: the condemned man was decapitated
> by the sword, as is done by the civil authorities.
> Rabbi Yehuda said, "This is a hideous disfigurement;
> rather, his head was laid on a block and severed with
> an axe." They replied: "No death is more disfiguring
> than this." Whereupon the Gemara continues - "We
> learned in a Braitha; Rabbi Yehuda said to the
> Chachomim" (Sages): 'I, too, know that this is a
> death of repulsive disfigurement, but what can I do,
> seeing the Torah has said - *"You shall not walk
> according to their laws"*! (Therefore the method used
> by the Civil Authorities cannot be followed.)' To this
> the *Chachomim* responded: 'Since the Torah already

decreed the method of the sword, we did not derive
this practice from them, and if you will not agree to
this, then how about that which was taught: "The
burning of articles at a king's funeral is permitted,
and there is nothing of the ways of the Amorite
about it?" But since this burning is referred to in the
Torah, as the prophet Yirmiyah said to King Zedkiah
(Yirmiyah 34:5): "You shall die in peace, and as with
the burnings of your fathers, the former kings that
were before you, so shall they make a burning for
you." It is not from them (Gentiles) that we derive
this practice, and hence, it becomes permissible'."

Tosafot[4] notice an inconsistency between the two texts. The
Gemara in *Avoda Zara* seems to indicate that this (the burning) is
not considered a custom to be prohibited by the laws of *Chukat
Ha'Akum*, since it was an honorable rite customarily administered
to those kings, rather than a practice directed at their idols. On the
other hand, the text in *Sanhedrin* seems to indicate that it is by
virtue of the fact that it is prescribed in the Torah, albeit possibly
an act accepted by idolators, that it becomes permissible.

To clarify these conflicting passages, *Tosafot* conclude that
these are two types of customs that are prohibited by the Torah:
Firstly, those customs that are related to idolatrous religion, *Chok
L'Avoda Zora*, and secondly, those customs that, although not
related to idolatry, are performed for foolish or vain reasons.
Tosafot go further and state that those customs which fall in the
category of *Chok L'Avoda Zora*, even if they are sanctioned by the
Torah, nevertheless, if subsequently they are adapted by the
Gentile nations as idolatrous rituals, they become prohibited. To
prove this point, *Tosafot* refer to the usage of a *Matzeva*, a single
stone upon which sacrifices were brought. The book of *Bereshith* is
replete with the usage of the *Matzeva* by our forefathers; yet, the

---

4. ע"ז שם בד"ה ואי חוקה ובסנהדרין שם בד"ה אלא.

Torah in *Devarim*⁵ prohibits its use, since it was eventually
adopted by the Gentile world.⁶

However, those customs which are not related to their religion,
but rather are practices which are based on their own attitudes, if
they are warranted by the Torah, do not become prohibited. It is
for these reasons that the Gemara in *Avoda Zora* must first
establish the nature of a custom to be unrelated to idol worship.
Similarly, in *Sanhedrin*, the Sages first must state that execution by
means of a sword is preferred for its more humane administration,
rather than for idolatrous reasons. After this is established, the
Gemara in *Sanhedrin* can then state that since the rite is sanctioned
in the Torah, even if it is practiced by other nations, it remains
permitted.

The *Ran* and the *Maharik* take exception to *Tosafot's*
understanding of the Gemara in *Avoda Zora*. The *Ran*⁷ sees the
prohibition of following *Chukat Ha'Akum* as including *only* those
customs which are idolatrous in nature - i.e., customs that are
obviously related to idol worship as well as those practices which
have no apparent reasons, for they too are suspect of having an
idolatrous relationship. Therefore, the acceptance of the burning
ritual among the Jewish people is contingent on the fact that its
origin is honor, and not idol worship. It is allowed even without
being specified as permissible in the Torah. Apparently, the *Ran*
concurs with the views expressed in *Avoda Zora*⁸, rather then with
the text in *Sanhedrin*.

The *Maharik*⁹, in a responsum, offers a unique insight. He
says that any practice which we adopt, which makes us appear to
be following the ways of the Gentile, serves as an acknowledgment
of them, and is for this reason prohibited. The *Maharik* postulates

5. דברים טז:כב
6. See רמב"ן ויקרא יח:ג who discusses *Matzeva* as opposed to an altar and sacrifices
which are also customarily found amongst the nations.
7. על הרי"ף בע"ז שם וע"ע בחי' הר"ן לסנהדרין
8. כך העלה בתשו' מהרם שיק - חיו"ד סי' קסה בתירוץ א'
9. שו"ת מהרי"ק שורש פח'

two categories by which we define those customs that are
prohibited: Firstly, those practices which have no inherent
justification, as is understood from the usage of the word "*chok*",
which denotes those laws which are given without a logical
explanation. These practices are prohibited, not because they are
suspect of being related to the religion of the Gentile as the *Ran*
explains, but rather because by practicing these customs we appear
to be imitating the Gentiles who initiated them. Why else would we
do something that makes no sense, if not for the sake of
conforming?

The second category of prohibited acts includes those practices
which depart from the modest or humble ways in which a Jew
should conduct himself. This idea is derived from *Sifre's*[10]
commentary on the verse: — השמר לך פן תנקש אחריהם
דברים (יב:ל). "Take heed lest you be ensnared by them", where
it is written: "One should not say - just as they go with red
garments, so will I; just as they go with *kilusin*, so will I; just as
they go with *avtiga*, so will I." The *Maharik* explains that all these
are garments arrogant and haughty in nature, and therefore not
characteristic of the Jewish attitude in dress, which is one of
humility and modesty. (The *Maharik* is discussing customs related
to manners of dress. The same idea, however, can be applied to
any practice which departs from our moral codes of behavior.)

Inasmuch as the definition of "humble" or "modest" is a
subjective classification, the *Maharik* clarifies that there must first
be a decision by the community as a whole to depart from a
specific mode of dress or practice, for reasons based on our
principles. It is only after the community has decided to
differentiate itself from a specific mode, that one who decides to
dress as the Gentiles do is deemed to be "acknowledging" them.
Furthermore, if the departure from Gentile customs was not based
on religious mandates, but evolved for other reasons, although it is
not our way to implement these customs, they are not prohibited.

ספרי - פרשת ראה - פיסקא, כט .10

As the *Maharik* writes - "and the Jew is not *obligated* to be different from the Gentile at all."

A further rationale for Jews' diverging from the Gentile mode is that we are required to separate ourselves from immodest colors or fashions.[11]

Conversely, the *Maharik* states that because the essence of the prohibition is not to imitate and thereby acknowledge the ways of the Gentile, if there is a custom that does have an apparent reason for it, it is not prohibited. By adopting these customs, we are not acknowledging the Gentile, but rather accepting the *concept*. He goes further to state that even in regard to a custom that would commonly fit the requirement of being of Gentile nature, if the Jew's intention is not solely to imitate the Gentile, but rather for lucrative or other reasons, it, too, would be permitted. He applies this rule to the following question:

An inquiry was made in regard to a local custom: a physician used to wear a specific type of cape, in order to denote his profession. The inquirer questioned whether a Jewish doctor was permitted to use this garment, although its usage originated with the Gentiles. The *Maharik* answered that, firstly, there was no decision on the part of the community at large not to dress in such a fashion, and secondly, even if there were reasons not to dress that way, since the Jewish doctor's intention in doing so is not to imitate, but rather to be associated with his profession, it is permitted.

It would then seem that the *Maharik* understands the text in *Avoda Zora* that "burning of the king's possessions is an act of honor and therefore not prohibited" to mean that since it is a custom that is done for rational purposes, in adopting it we have acknowledged not the Gentile but rather the underlying concept. It would then appear that the *Maharik*, too, is accepting the Gemara in *Avoda Zora* in preference to the text in *Sanhedrin* which requires the custom to be warranted by the Torah.

---

11. רי"ף סנהדרין עד:א, רש"י שם, בפירוש ערקתא דמסאנא, וע"ע ברמב"ם הלכות יסודי
התורה פ"ה ה"ב ובכסף משנה שם, ובתשובת המהרי"ק.

Taking the *Maharik's* principle even further, *Maharam Schick* rules that even the appearance of accepting Gentile customs is proscribed.[12] It should be implicit that the Jew is following a custom for his own reasons and not as an acknowledgement of Gentile standards; otherwise, the practice would be prohibited *de facto*.

The *Bach*[13] also seems to concur with the *Maharik*, in his interpretation of a text in *Baba Kama* (83a). There it is related that in a certain era, there was a hairstyle that was common and inasmuch as it was characteristic of the Gentile, it should have been prohibited by the laws of *Chukat Ha'Akum*. Nevertheless, it was permitted for one Avtulmus Bar-Reuven to cut his hair in that style because he was influential in the ruling circles. The *Rambam*[14] implies that had he *not* cut his hair in such a manner, the Gentiles would have shunned him for not appearing as one of them. The *Beit Yosef* explains that saving Jewry overrides the prohibition of *Chukat Ha'Akum*, so that what would be prohibited under normal circumstances may be permissible to those who need to associate with Gentiles for the security of the Jewish community. On the other hand the *Bach* explains that a practice is permissible not only in extreme cases, but even under normal circumstances, provided that it is motivated by intentions to have an influence on the authorities rather than a desire to acknowledge them.

The Vilna Gaon[15], in his commentary on the Shulchan Aruch, is not satisfied with the synopsis presented by the *Maharik*, because of its inconsistency with the Gemara in *Sanhedrin*; and similarly, he rejects the explanation offered by the *Ran*. He then states his own understanding of the term *Chukat Ha'Akum:* The Gaon ‎states that the two texts concerning *"Bechukosaihem"*, although technically different, share a common denominator, i.e., customs which could possibly evolve in Jewish circles without the

---

12. שו״ת מהר״ם שי״ק חיו״ד סי׳ קסה.

13. ב״ח יו״ד סי׳ קעח בד״ה מי שקרוב.

14. רמב״ם פ״יא הלכות עכו״ם ה״ג בנוגע לקרוב למלכות.

15. בביאור הגר״א יו״ד סי׳ קעח ס״ק ז׳.

initiation of Gentile influence. The Gaon says that this *alone* is the
prerequisite for a custom to be sanctioned, regardless of other
factors. This is drawn from the phrase cited in the Gemara - "We
did not derive it from them (the Gentiles)." His point is well seen
in the reasons offered in the texts. Burning of a king's possessions
is a symbol of honor, an idea possibly conceived on our own, and
as such, permitted. The second reason, the Torah's explicit sanction
of the custom, is further proof that its practice by us has its origin
in the Torah, our own source of concepts, rather than in the
Gentile code of behavior. As the Gaon sees it, the case brought to
the attention of the *Maharik* about the physician's cape would be
prohibited, since we would never have devised that particular mode
of dress of our own accord.

We should note that in discussing the Gentiles, the vast
preponderance of the *Poskim* assume that the term connotes all
non-Jews.[16] Halacha apparently does not consider Islam as idolatry,
and therefore Muslim customs are not subject to the prohibitions
of *Chok L'Avoda Zora*.[17] However, regardless of whether or not
Christianity is classified as idol-worship (due to belief in the
Trinity), acceptance of Christian customs would certainly come
within the scope of the *issur* "*Chok L'Avoda Zora*".[18]

In summation: Albeit there is a plethora of controversy as to
the intent of "*Bechukosaihem. . .*", normative Judaism is guided by
the *Psak* of the Shulchan Aruch and the gloss of the *Ramo*.[19] The
latter rules in acccordance with the principles expressed by the *Ran*
and *Maharik*:

---

16. א. ק"ס ם"עכו הלכות א"פי מיימוניות הגהות ע"וע — (ח"פ) סימן יראים
The *Yeraim* argues that since the Torah specifically mentions the seven nations
and Egypt, the injunction was only applicable to their ways. The commentary
המלך עבודת on the Rambam reasons that since the Torah includes (three verses
later) "And I have separated you from the other nations" we can clearly see
that the prohibition was intended to all nations.
17. ג"קל ענין צג, ענין ץ"תשב ת"שו
18. ז"ט חיים אורח ,"להועיל מלמד" — הופמן ד.צ. הרב
19. א ק"ס עה דעה יורה קעח ערוך שלחן

... אבל דבר שנהגו לתועלת כגון שדרכן שכל מי שהוא רופא מומחה יש לו
מלבוש מיוחד שניכר בו שהוא רופא אומן, מותר ללובשו וכן שעושין משום
כבוד או טעם אחר, מותר.
ברכי יוסף יורה דעה קע״ח

Those things which were adopted for a benefit,
such as the custom that any one who is an expert
doctor wears a distinctive garment which indicates
that he is a professional doctor, it is permitted to
wear it. And also those things that are done for
respect or some other reasons, are permitted.

* * *

We will now turn to specific areas of behavior where these
principles might be applied.

Dress

An obvious area of concern for the principle of "do not follow
the ways of the Gentile" is the manner in which we dress.

Even as far back as the era of the sojourn in Egypt, Jews were
already distinguished from other nations. The well-known Midrash
is often quoted: "In the merit that they did not change their
names, clothing and language they were redeemed." The *Meshech
Chochma*[20] points out that Jacob foresaw the danger of assimilation
during the long exile, and to assure the preservation of *Klal
Yisroel*, devised this plan of being distinct in name, clothing and
language, which was passed down throughout the generations.

The prophet Zephaniah admonishes the Jewish nation: "And
it will be on the day that G-d will slaughter, and I will take notice
of the officers and the princes, and of all those who wear alien
dress." (Zephaniah 1:8) Rambam, writing in *Sefer Hamitzvot* on
the prohibition of *Chukat Ha'Akum*, directs us to this verse.

---

20. משך חכמה בחוקתי כו:מד

Similarly, Yirmiyah refers derogatorily to the Jews' acceptance of the Gentile dress. "And you...what do you accomplish when you wear red garments, when you adorn yourselves with gold ornaments, when you cover you eyelids with blue shadows..." (Yirmiyah 4:30).

Despite these negative indications, *Maharik* points out that even in Talmudic times, there does not seem to have been any distinction in dress between Jew and Gentile.[21] Apparently, this was *not* required by Jewish law, as long as no breach of modesty or humility was involved. An incidental question is whether immodest dress, although it is naturally forbidden by halacha in its own right, might possibly also be in violation of the issur *"Bechukosaihem lo tailaichu"*.[22]

Of particular interest in the context of our discussion is the question of distinctive "Jewish" clothing, such as a frockcoat or special style hat. Rabbi Moshe Feinstein in a responsum[23] deals with this issue, basing his conclusions on the principles set forth by the *Maharik*. He first establishes that in America there is no prohibition to dress in the secular fashion, since the mode of clothing is not any more designed for the Gentile than for the Jew; styles are set for everyone without distinction. Even following the strict interpretation of the Vilna Gaon, it would be permissible, since the clothing styles are not a derivative of Gentile mores, and could equally be regarded as Jewish style rather than Gentile styles.

---

21. מעילה יז:א - The incident under discussion was as follows: A decree was issued that Jews must abstain from *Milah, Niddah* and *Shabbos*. Rabbi Reuven ben Istroboli cut his hair in the style of the Gentiles in order to gain entree in government circles so that he might plead the case for the Jews. Since the Gemara does not relate that he changed his garments to those of the Gentiles it would seem that their garments were identical. (See also יוסף יורה דעה קע"ח ברכי). The Gaonim wrote: "We are scattered in the four corners of the earth. And every corner is different in their clothing, their deeds, and their adornments. Therefore whatever people of that place do, is also permitted to the Jews who dwell among them." אוצר הגאונים לנזיר, 200.

22. שו"ת דברי חיים חיו"ד ח"א סי' ל ויעויין שם שהבין ברעת המביט בקרית ספר שאף באין כוונתו להתדמות עובר על לאו. שו"ת אגרות משה, חיו"ד ח"א סי' פא.

23. שם

24. שבת קנו

Furthermore, although it may be historically true that Jews in
Europe did adopt special styles based on their moral principles
(black, simple) and on their wish to be different from the rest of
society, however, once a Jew has left that European community
and moved to a new community where the Jews dress differently,
he is free the follow the customary Jewish style in his new abode.

Kippa

Another area of distinction in our clothing is the custom of
wearing a yarmulka (kippa.) The underlying principal in covering
the head is to show our constant cognizance of the Divine Presence
above us, as the Gemara tell us,[24] that the mother of Rabbi
Nachman bar Yitzchok instructed him always to cover his head in
order to have the fear of G-d upon him. (The word yarmulka is a
contraction of two words 'yorei malka' - fear of the king (G-d).)

In Shulchan Aruch[25] there is much discussion as to whether
this is a *midas chasidus* (pious characteristic) which would not be
obligatory, or whether it is mandatory, and, if mandatory, under
which circumstances. The *Taz*[26] seems to settle at least part of this
dispute with his interjection that this custom pertains to the laws
of *Chukat Ha'Akum*. He explains that although in earlier times
there was room for debate, this question took on a different nature
later, when it became customary among the Gentiles to purposely
remove one's head covering when sitting.

The Chasam Sofer claims that covering the head is an
indication of humility.[27] If this is so, then its initiation is motivated
by a desire to be distinct in a manner based on the principle of
humility. And citing a responsum from *Mahari Bruna*,[28] the
Maharsham[29] learns that wearing a kippa should be considered as a

---

25. אר"ח סי' ב סעי' ו, אר"ח סי' צ"א סעי' ג, אר"ח סי' עד סעי' ב, אר"ח סי' ח סעי' ב

26. ט"ז אר"ח סי' ח ס"ק ג בסוף

27. עיין בשו"ת חתם סופר חח"מ בהשמטות סי' קצא ובספר צמח דוד חלק שני אלף הרביעי
— ליקוטים בשו"ת חתם סופר בסוף חאבה"ע סי' ב, וע"ע שדי חמד מערכת ה,,חית" כלל
קל"א

In reference to the evolution for the custom of going with an uncovered head.

28. תשובת מהר"י ברונא סי' לה

29. בדעת תורה אר"ח סי' ב

Dat Yehuda (Jewish religious practice). One who does not follow a *Dat Yehuda* is as if he were "following the way of the Gentiles". Perhaps this case of *Dat Yehuda* would also fulfill the requirement of the *Maharik*, inasmuch as it is a conscious departure by the Jewish community from societal norms, even if not related to areas of modesty or humility.

For whatever reason covering the head became the accepted Jewish mode (in the Ashkenazic community) — if an uncovered head qualifies as "following the ways of the Gentiles", we need to address a problem which arises therefrom. There are many offices and institutions that either require or intimate their desire that a Jew not wear his yarmulka while at work. This problem existed previously too, when it was obligatory to remove one's yarmulka in courts and government offices in deference to their institutions. Is it permissible to accept a job or attend a place where it is necessary to remove the yarmulka?

Rabbi D. Z. Hoffman cites various sources on this topic.[30] His inquiry is in regard to swearing in court without a head covering which, in addition to the aspect of *Chukat Ha'Akum*, involves the prohibition of pronouncing G-d's name with an uncovered head. In regard to the aspect of *Chukat Ha'Akum*, he implies that since our motive is not to imitate them but rather to follow their laws in deference to them, as it is common knowledge that we are just adhering to their rules, it would be allowed. The *Mishnah Brura*[31] in an annotation and the *Aruch Hashulchan*[32] state clearly that when going to court or in the audience of a government official, one may defer to the law of the land. This idea also follows the guidelines of the *Maharik*, that if one's motive is not to imitate but rather for monetary or other acceptable gain, it does not serve as an acknowledgement of the Gentile way. Thus we can extend the approach with respect to jobs as well; if a person feels he would lose the job if he persists in wearing a head-covering, then he is

30. מלמד להועיל יורה דעה סי׳ נו
31. או"ח סי׳ ב
32. שם

adopting their ways not for the sake of acknowledging them but for his own financial benefit, and this is permitted.

In a letter written to this author, Rabbi M. Feinstein, *shlita*, expresses his opinion that it is obvious that nowadays men all over America and Europe go around with uncovered heads, whether at home or in the office or even in the street, and that they do this as it suits their comfort and not for any ideological reason or religious motive. Consequently, a Jew who uncovers his head during his hours on the job, regardless of the motives of the employer in requiring it, is not transgressing the prohibition of *"Bechukosaihem lo tailaichu"* even according to the *Taz*.

Hairstyles

The Midrash in *Shir HaShirim*[33] states that Jews are distinguished by the way they cut their hair.

The Gemara and *Sifra* refer to two hairstyles that were characteristic of the Gentile - the *Kumi* and the *Bluris*. In the first style, the hair was cut short in front, leaving the other half of the head towards the back uncut. The second style could have taken either of two forms: the hair was cut around the head in a circular shape, and the central area of the head was uncut,[34] or maybe only the very sides were cut.[35] Both categories of styles were adopted by the Gentile with respect to their idols.[36] The *Bach* also includes in this prohibition growing hair long and loose to appear attractive in a vain and haughty manner. The *Chida*[37] categorizes the long and loose hairstyles of the soldiers in his time as being of such a nature, and admonishes the contemporary Jewish youth not to copy it, saying that this style is prohibited not because it is a form of worship to idols, but rather because growing long hair for the sake of vanity is associated with the Gentile manner.

---

33. איכה רבה פרשה ב:יז

34. כן נראה מהב״ח יו״ד סי׳ קעח ומ״ש בד״ה ולא יגדל

35. כן נראה מהב״י יו״ד סי׳ קעח ומ״ש בד״ה ולא יגדל

36. שם

37. ברכי יוסף יו״ד סי׳ קעח

In regard to cutting the beard, the Rambam[38] says that the reason for the Biblical prohibition of shaving with a razor is because it was a custom of the idolatrous priests.

The *Minchat Chinuch*[39], however, points out that whether or not shaving the beard is considered imitation of the Gentile depends on the nature of the Gentile practice in each generation. Although at the initiation of this custom by the priests, it might have been prohibited according to the laws of *Chukat Ha'Akum;* but if in the meantime the custom changed and Gentiles now do wear beards, shaving one's beard cannot be considered an adoption of their way. He draws a parallel between the custom of shaving and of dressing: as we are permitted to dress in a style that at one time was popular among Gentiles but is now outdated, so too with hairstyles. He goes further to state that if in fact it is a habit of Gentiles to purposely shave their beards, even if a Jew shaved without a razor (or in any manner which does not qualify for the prohibition of "*Lo Tashchit*") it could still be prohibited under the law of *Chukat Ha'Akum*, since one looks like the Gentile regardless of how the beard was shaved.

In an interesting historical aside in his lengthy responsum about shaving the beard, the Chasam Sofer traces the custom of being clean-shaven to an era when there was a eunuch king who could not grow a beard. In a desire to make his deficiency less noticeable, the king decreed that his subjects should all remove their beards. Continuing, he states that shaving is a common practice and no longer serves as a distinction between Jew and Gentile; therefore, one who shaves will not be considered as following a style which is distinctly Gentile, and it is not prohibited.

In America, the practice of shaving would be analagous to wearing the prevalent styles of dress, and would be no more indicative of the Gentile than of the Jew.

---

38. פי״ב מהלכות עכו״ם ה״א
39. מנחת חינוך מצוה רנ״א ס״ק א

Thanksgiving Day Celebration

Some halachic questions arise regularly in each generation: finding solutions for familiar problems is relatively easy — one studies the writings of our predecessors. However, when a new situation develops, it is difficult to know what is right, since often the current situation is not analogous to one of the past.

Such a quandry exists with the halachic status of observing national holidays such as Thanksgiving or Mother's Day, and there are scarcely any responsa on this topic. At first glance, we might think that there would be no problem about Thansgiving, which was instituted as a token of thankfulness for the success of the early colonies. Since it is a custom that was undertaken for a reason, then following the guidelines of the *Maharik*, it should be permissible to participate in this observance.

However, Rabbi Moshe Feinstein himself is not altogether certain that this is so. He questions whether indeed we can say that since a few colonists decided to celebrate their success, this is a valid enough reason for there to be a holiday for years thereafter. If it is not a valid reason, then the custom would be considered *Chukat Ha'Akum.*

Perhaps one would argue that the Thanksgiving feast is similar to that recorded in *Kiddushim 76a,* where the Jews participated in a meal tendered by King Yannai in celebration of a massive victory. The Thanksgiving Day feast is also a celebration for living in a free country. However, Rabbi Feinstein counters that the Jews in the time of Yannai held a feast only that one time, when they had the victory. However, to enact a yearly celebration on the basis of the actions of a few colonists may be a questionably valid source for this custom, as far as halacha is concerned. In his set of (as yet) unpublished responsa, Rabbi Feinstein expresses his hesitation on the subject, and recommends that one should not observe Thanksgiving and eat turkey each year. However, he notes that eating turkey then, without making a party, is certainly permissible; he also states that he does not consider Thanksgiving in any way a religious holiday, since it is not mentioned in their religious books. Yet he does feel that it is appropriate to be strict in this matter, and surely not to look upon it as a mitzva.

Names

We have previously cited the Midrash that in the merit that Jews did not change their names, they were redeemed.

The Midrash continues:[41] "Reuven and Shimon they went down and Reuven and Shimon they came up; they did not call Yehuda-Leoni, and not Reuven-Rubino..." (Rabbi D. Luria explains that these are the Roman translations of the meanings of the Hebrew names.)

There is a dispute between the *Maharshdam*[42] and the *Maharam Schick*[43] as to whether the adoption of Gentile names is prohibited by the laws of *Chukat Ha'Akum*. The *Maharam Schick* states forcefully that this is clearly prohibited, since those who call themselves by Gentile names do so specifically to imitate the Gentiles. (This practice seemingly does not fit the prerequisite of the *Maharik*, inasmuch as it is not a custom without reason, nor a breach of humility or modesty.) He relates an interesting experience which sheds some light on the significance of a Jewish name. He was once involved in a community transaction which brought him to the office of a governmental official. There, the official told him that he was a bit puzzled by an apparent enigma and asked for clarification. He did not understand why the Jews called themselves by Gentile names. All the other nations deem it an honor to use the names associated with their nationality, and would never contemplate changing them. Yet the Jews, one of the most ancient nations, shame themselves when they consider it an embarrassment to retain their ethnic names.

The *Maharshdam*, who preceded the *Maharam Schick*, states clearly that it is not prohibited. He cites a Gemara in *Gittin* (11b)

---

40. שו"ת חת"ס חאו"ח סי' קנט בסוף
41. ויקרא רבה פרשה לב
42. שו"ת מהרשד"ם חיו"ד סי' קצט
43. שו"ת מהר"ם שיק חיו"ד סי' קסט

which records that most of the "*gittin*" (divorce papers) from
outside of Israel were signed by witnesses who had Gentile names
(even so outstanding a Gentile name as Lucas). Since those who
customarily adopted Gentile names nevertheless remained
unquestionably valid witnesses, it is clear that this practice was not
prohibited.

Manner of Speech

The *Smag*[44] is the only authority who includes the aspect of
dibur - manner of speech - in his discussion of the laws of *Chukat
Ha'Akum.*

What is meant by *dibur* is unclear.

We do find that the Midrash previously cited ascribes the
Redemption in part to the merit that they did not change their
language.

The Mishnah in *Shabbat* (13b) tells us that there were
"eighteen decrees" that the pupils of *Beit Shamai* and *Beit Hillel*
decided to implement. They were prohibitions which would serve
as extra precautions in preserving the laws of purity, and some in
preventing the Jews' assimilation with the Gentiles. Among those
in regard to assimilation were such prohibitions as not to partake
of the Gentile's wine or bread. In the *Yerushalmi*,[45] the prohibition
against adopting the language of the Gentile is also listed among
the eighteen, as this, too, would serve as a precaution against
becoming too close to the Gentile.

The Chasam Sofer,[46] in fact, writes, that in light of the decree
made against adopting the language of the Gentiles, many revisions
were deliberately made by Jews in the German dialect, which
became known as the Yiddish language. However, the historical
fact that Gentile language was banned is a clear indication that it is

---

44. סמ"ג ל"ת נ'

45. פ"ק שבת

46. שו"ת חת"ס חאה"ע ח"ב סי' יא

not originally included in the Biblical prohibition of *Chukat Ha'Akum*. It is thus difficult to know exactly what is meant by "Gentile speech." Rabbeinu Hillel, in his commentary to *Sifra*, suggests that it may refer to incorporating avant-garde parlance into our speech, meaning the "with-it" words and phrases which deviate from the standard vernacular — i.e. to avoid 'lingo' or 'jargon'.[47]

Rituals

In practice, *Chok L'Avoda Zora* has diverse applications and is always a factor to be reckoned with in any undertaking. As we noted previously, *Tosafot* even go so far as to recommend cessation of a Jewish practice if it is later adopted by Gentiles as an expression of their religious worship, and halachic decisors do attempt to meet this additional criterion.

A famous controversy arising from the issue of *Chok L'Avoda Zora* centered upon the introduction of the organ into the synagogue, which was one of the many innovations the Reform movement tried to implement in the nineteenth century. Defending the use of an organ during prayer services, the Reformists cited the precedent of musical instruments which were played in the Beth Hamikdash, and even attempted to identify the organ with the *Ugav* or *Magrepha* which were played by the Levites there. Alternately, the Reformists defended musical accompaniment to the prayers as not being *Chok L'Avoda Zora* since it was neither a mindless practice nor a breach of modesty. However, in attacking the innovation (on many grounds), the Orthodox camp also proved that it definitely *was Chok L'Avoda Zora* since it was a form of worship employed in the church, which *ipso facto* made it impermissible in the synagogue.[48]

As for the issue of using music, whether in conjunction with

---

47. רבינו הלל בפירושו על ספרא, אחרי מות פרשתא ט הל' ט, וכך שמעתי מהגרי"ד עפשטיין והגר"ד קאהן בביאור כוונתו.

48. מלמד להועיל אורח חיים סימן ט"ז

tfilla or for other occasions, there are those who warn that we must refrain from using songs that might be considered in the Gentile mode or identified with their worship;[49] however, others disagree as to the impermissibility of adopting music of the Gentiles, if it was not used for their religion. In writing on this question, the *Chida* cites an authority who wrote that he himself "set most of his poems to the music of the Arabs, and although some of the sages were displeased with this practice, the law is not with them and there is absolutely nothing wrong with doing so.[50]

Some people may be surprised to discover that a fiery polemic was also aroused by a custom which is practiced in a large percentage of shuls - adorning the shul on Shavuoth with flowers, branches, and greens, in commemoration of the miraculous sprouting of foliage on Mt. Sinai at the time of the giving the Torah on Shavuoth. No less a personage than the Vilna Gaon ordered that this custom be abandoned,[51] for he identified the practice with the Christian custom of decorating their churches and homes with greens at holiday time. Albeit decorating the shuls was an ancient *minhag*, he objected to it with the contention that in the interim it had become *Chok L'Avoda Zora*. Although there were those who took exception with the conclusion of the Gaon,[52] in a responsum sent to this writer, Rabbi M. Feinstein notes that the *Aruch Ha-Shulchan* also agreed that previous generations had decided to accept the dictum of the Gaon and abolished the practice.

Within the laws of *Chukat Ha'Akum* we find a sub-category, *Darkei Ha'Amori*, which includes giving credence to superstitions or good-luck and healing charms (even *kemayot* or *segulot*) which have not been proven effective.[53]

The limitations placed upon us by the principle of *Chukat*

49. מעשה רוקח על הרמב"ם בפ"ח מהלכות תפלה ה"יא בהבנת תשובת הב"ח סי' קכז.

50. חיד"א בברכי יוסף או"ח סי' תקס

51. חכמת אדם כלל פט ס"ק א

52. דעת תורה להמהרש"ם או"ח סי' תצה, יוסף דעת בחידושים על יו"ד לסימן שמח

53. תוספתא שבת פ"ז ופ"ח Also see Encyclopedia Talmudit, Darkei Ha'Amori.

Ha'Akum are sometimes difficult to delineate with specificity. The Rambam in *Sefer Hamitzvot*[54] writes, "We are warned from following the ways of the Gentile and from accustoming ourselves to their customs even in regard to their clothes and their assemblies in their places." Elaborating on this halacha in *Mishneh Torah*, Rambam notes "...and one should not construct edifices similar in structure to their temples, for the purpose of assembly."[55] It would appear from here that the prohibition is in regard to imitating them, even in the style in which we construct our buildings. In writing on this halacha, the *Taz* adds that not only building as they build, but even calling Jews to assembly as they do is prohibited.[56] According to some, that is why shuls were never constructed with a bell tower to summon Jews to prayer.[57]

Based on the Rambam's understanding of *Chukat Ha'Akum*, Jews have always taken care that the forms of our synagogues do not resemble the style of churches, and also that we do not place the *Bimah* in the front of the synagogue as they do.[58]

*   *   *

In studying the particulars of the injunction of *Chukat Ha'Akum*, it is difficult to escape the conclusion that the Torah wants the Jewish people to maintain an exclusive and distinct identity among the family of nations. Rather than viewing this as a restriction upon our freedom, we might approach it as a philosophical desideratum, an ideal to inspire our beliefs and imbue our lives with worthy goals.

The prophet Yirmiyah compared the Jewish nation to an olive.[59] Clarifying the analogy, the Midrash notes that all liquids blend with one another except for oil of the olive, which remains

---

54. ספר המצוות להרמב"ם ל"ת ל'

55. פי"א מהלכות עכו"ם סוף הל"א

56. ט"ז יו"ד סי' קע"ח ס"ק ג - Based on the opinion of the ראב"ד.

57. שבילי דוד אות ב', הובא בדרכי תשובה סי' קעח

58. See ספר רוח חיים אות ב' regarding cantors wearing black robes בדרכי תשובה שם הובא

59. ירמיהו יא:טז

by itself. So, too, are the Jewish people, who stand apart and do not blend with other peoples.[60]

At the conclusion of his discussion on the topic *Chukat Ha'Akum*, the *Sefer ha-Chinuch* notes that it is in our best interest to remain distinct.

> One who separates himself from all foreign behavior and mannerisms and applies all his thought and his heart to G-d, to understand his wondrous ways, is rewarded in that his soul will abide with all that is good, and his seed will inherit the earth.

It would be appropriate to close with the words Rabbi Yaacov Emden chose in addressing his community regarding following the Gentile ways:[61]

> "And what else can I add to my words, in quest for their good, to save their lives from destruction.
>
> Who will give that they will heed me, and I will find solace that my efforts were not in vain.
>
> That it is befitting to Israel to be outstanding in their customs and in all their concerns.
>
> So that the Legion of the King should be known throughout the nations.
>
> His seed, his glory, his honor
>
> So that when he will come, the true Shepherd (*Moshiach Tzidkanu*) he will recognize his flock.
>
> Who will supply us with the day of the arrival of the master for whom we yearn.
>
> And how, then, will the people be recognized?"

---

60. שמות רבה לו:א

61. בסידורו עמודי שמים הל' תשעה באב שער הדלק חלון השביעי (חלון המצרי)

Cigarette Smoking and Jewish Law

Dr. Fred Rosner

Tobacco was first implicated as a cause of cancer in 1761[1]. There is no longer any doubt that cigarette smoking is a hazard to health. Overwhelming medical evidence has proved that cigarette smoking is associated with a shortened life expectancy. In January 1964, an Advisory Committee appointed by the Surgeon General of the United States Public Health Service issued its report[2] on the relationship between smoking and health. The conclusions of that report were summed up in the sentence: "Cigarette smoking is a health hazard of sufficient importance in the United States to warrant appropriate remedial action."

1. Redmond, D.E. Jr. "Tobacco and Cancer: The First Clinical Report, 1761." New Engl. J. Med. *282:* 18-23, 1970.
2. *Smoking & Health*, Report of the Advisory Committee to the Surgeon General of the Public Health Service, 387 pp. U.S. Gov't. Printing Office, Washington, D.C. 1964.

This article is an expansion by the author of a theme which he first developed in "Modern Medicine and Jewish Law,", published in 1972.

Director, Department of Medicine, Queens Hospital Center Affiliation of the Long Island Jewish-Hillside Medical Center; and Professor of Medicine, Health Sciences Center, State University of New York at Stony Brook.

Nearly four years later, after reviewing more than 2,000 research studies published since the 1964 report, the U.S. Public Health Service published its follow-up report[3]. The report concludes that: "epidemiological evidence derived from a number of prospective and retrospective studies, coupled with experimental and pathological evidence, confirms the conclusion that cigarette smoking is the main cause of lung cancer in men." Other findings include the fact that cigarette smoking is the most important cause of chronic obstructive lung disease (emphysema) in the United States. It is also a significant risk factor contributing to the development of coronary heart disease, cancer of the larynx and probably cancer of the bladder. Pregnant women who smoke have smaller babies and greater fetal complications than those who don't smoke.

In the United Kingdom, the Royal College of Physicians of London followed its first report on smoking and health[4] with another report[5] restating the medical hazards of smoking. The reports claim that cigarette smoking has become as important a cause of death as the great epidemic diseases such as typhoid, cholera and tuberculosis.

By act of Congress, the following warning appears on every pack of cigarettes manufactured for sale in the United States on or after November 1, 1970:

"The Surgeon General Has Determined That Cigarette Smoking is Dangerous to Your Health."

Television advertising for cigarettes was abolished by government decree as of January 1. 1971. Complete or partial bans on cigarette advertising are in effect in England, Holland, Norway,

---

3. *The Health Consequences of Smoking.* A Public Health Service Review: 1967. 199 pp. U.S. Gov't Printing Office, Washington, D.C. 1968.
4. *Smoking & Health.* Royal College of Physicians. Pitman Medical Publishing Co., London. 1962.
5. *Smoking & Health Now:* A Report of the Royal College of Physicians. Pitman Medical Publishing Co., London. 1971.

Sweden, Italy, Poland, Russia, Switzerland and probably other countries[6].

Yet in Brazil, the Secretary of Federal Revenue recently suggested to cigarette companies that they should organize an even more massive sales campaign than previously to increase the income to the Brazilian government from taxation on industrialized products[7].

The U.S. Public Health Service's 14th report on the health consequences of smoking appeared in 1981[8] and concluded that there is no such thing as a safe cigarette. The report states that "the smokers of lower tar and nicotine cigarettes who compensate by smoking more or by inhaling more deeply might thereby increase their risk of developing obstructive airway disease." In addition, lower tar cigarettes do not decrease the risks among pregnant women of spontaneous abortion, premature birth, or low-weight babies. Filtered cigarettes are no safer. A new concern relates to the use of new additives for tobacco processing for flavoring, some of which may give rise to carcinogenic substances when burned thus offsetting the potential benefit from lower tar and/or nicotine content of cigarettes.

There are new alarms for women who smoke. Deaths from lung cancer among women have increased dramatically in the past twenty years and may soon overtake breast cancer as the leading cause of cancer death in women. Also worrisome is the sharp increase in smoking among teenage girls who are entering their childbearing years. Babies of smokers weigh less than those of non-smokers and show slower rates of physical and mental growth. Prematurity, miscarriage and fetal death are also more common in smokers.

An earlier report in 1979 had already emphasized an array of other warnings to   smokers:

---

6. Best, E.W.R. *A Canadian Study of Smoking & Health.* Dept. of National Health and Welfare. Ottawa. 1966.
7. Barros, F.C. A Government that Encourages Smoking. *Lancet 2:* 366, 1981.
8. *The Health Consequences of Smoking: The Changing Cigarette.* Report of the Surgeon General, Public Health Service (Dept. of Health and Human Services) 1981, U.S. Gov't Printing Office. 252 pp.

a) A smoker has a seventy percent greater risk of death in any given year than a non-smoker. For two-pack-a-day smokers, the risk is one hundred percent greater.
b) Smoking poses a major heart-attack risk in both men and women. The danger of heart attck for women who both smoke and take birth-control pills containing estrogen is ten times higher than for other women.
c) Smoking can be especially hazardous to workers in certain occupations, including the asbestos, rubber, textile, uranium and chemical industries. Substances in smoke may act synergistically with chemicals to greatly increase a smoker's chances of contracting lung cancer.
d) To further emphasize the value of quitting cigarette-smoking, the report noted that after fifteen years, the mortality ratio for former smokers is nearly as low as for people who never smoked[9].

Yet people continue to smoke. To some people, cigarette smoking is the greatest single public health problem this nation has ever faced. The present essay is an attempt to show that in light of the overwhelming medical evidence proving the causal relationship of cigarette smoking to cancer of the lung, heart disease and chronic bronchitis, Jewish law absolutely prohibits this practice, notwithstanding several Rabbinic opinions to the contrary (vide infra).

The Torah tells us not to intentionally place ourselves in danger when it states take heed to thyself, and take care of thy life (Deut. 4:9) and take good care of your lives (Deut. 4:15). The avoidance of danger is exemplified throughout the Bible, Talmud and Codes of Jewish Law in the positive commandment of making a parapet for one's roof (Deut. 22:8) so that no man fall therefrom. R. Moses Maimonides (Rambam), in his classic Mishneh Torah, enumerates a variety of prohibitions, all based upon the consideration of being harmful to life. They are quoted verbatim (Hilchoth Rotze'ach, chapter 11:4ff) since they eloquently illustrate the point under discussion:

9. Clark, M. & Hager, M. Slow-Motion Suicide. Newsweek. Jan. 22, 1979. p. 83-84.

"It makes no difference whether it be one's roof or anything else that is dangerous and might possibly be a stumbling block to someone and cause his death — for example, if one has a well or a pit, with or without water, in his yard — the owner is obliged to build an enclosing wall ten handbreadths high, or else to put a cover over it lest someone fall into it and be killed. Similarly, regarding any obstacle which is dangerous to life, there is a positive commandment to remove it and to beware of it, and to be particularly careful in this matter, for Scripture says, *Take heed unto thyself and take care of thy life* (Deut. 4:9). If one does not remove dangerous obstacles and allows them to remain, he disregards a positive commandment and transgresses the prohibition: *Thou bring not blood* (Deut. 22:8).

"Many things are forbidden by the Sages because they are dangerous to life. If one disregards any of these and says, 'If I want to put myself in danger, what concern is it to others?' or 'I am not particular about such things,' disciplinary flogging is inflicted upon him.

"The following are the acts prohibited: One may not put his mouth to a flowing pipe of water and drink from it, or drink at night from rivers or ponds, lest he swallow a leech while unable to see. Nor may one drink water that has been left uncovered, lest he drink from it after a snake or other poisonous reptile has drunk from it, and die ...

"One should not put small change or *denar* into his mouth lest they carry the dried saliva of one who suffers from an infectious skin disease or leprosy, or lest they carry perspiration, since all human perspiration is poisonous except that coming from the face.

"Similarly, one should not put the palm of his hand under his arm, for his hand might possibly have touched a leper or some harmful substance, since the hands are constantly in motion. Nor should one put a dish of food under his seat even during a meal, lest something harmful fall into it without his noticing it.

"Similarly, one should not stick a knife into a citron or a radish lest someone fall on the point and be killed. Similarly, one should not walk near a leaning wall or over a shaking bridge or enter a ruin or pass through any other such dangerous place."

This quotation from Maimonides certainly emphasizes the point that placing one's health or life into possible danger is absolutely prohibited. Hence, the smoking of cigarettes, which constitutes a definite danger and hazard to life, should *a fortiori* be prohibited. The subterfuge of "it is no concern of others if I endanger myself" is specifically disallowed by Maimonides.

Similar prohibitions against endangering one's life are found in most later Codes of Jewish Law including R. Yosef Karo's *Shulchan Aruch*. The latter devotes an entire chapter (*Choshen Mishpat* #427) to "the positive commandment of removing any object or obstacle which constitues a danger to life." Elsewhere, (*Yoreh Deah* #116), R. Karo reiterates the prohibitions against drinking water left uncovered, putting money in one's mouth, putting one's hand or a loaf of bread under the armpit, leaving a knife in a fruit. He further states (*Orach Chayim* #170:16) that two people should not drink from the same cup, and (*ibidem* 173:2) that one should wait between eating fish and meat because of danger.

Rabbi Moses Isserles, known as Ramo, in his glossary on R. Karo's *Shulchan Aruch* (*Yoreh Deah* 116:5) concludes:

"... one should avoid all things that might lead to danger because a danger to life is stricter than a prohibition. One should be more concerned about a possible danger to life than a possible prohibition. Therefore, the Sages prohibited one to walk in a place of danger such as near a leaning wall (for fear of collapse), or alone at night (for fear of robbers). They also prohibited drinking water from rivers at night ... because these things may lead to danger ... and he who is concerned with his health (lit.: watches his soul) avoids them. And it is prohibited to rely on a miracle or to put one's life in danger by any of the aforementioned or the like ..."

Ramo thus prohibits reliance on miracles when one's health is at stake. The fact that so many Jewish people smoke is no justification for this dangerous and life-threatening practice. If many Jews commit a transgression, others should certainly not follow; rather they should try to teach the sinners to repent from their evil ways. The "pleasures" of adultery are not condoned by even the most liberal-minded Jew. Why then should the pleasures of smoking which also involve biblical prohibitions *(vide supra)*, be relegated to an inferior status, to be treated more leniently?

Not only is the intentional endangerment of one's health or life, such as by smoking, prohibited in Jewish law, but also wounding oneself without fatal intent is also disallowed. The Talmud (Baba Kamma 91b) quotes Rabbi Elazar Hakapar Berabbi who maintains that a man may not injure himself. He learns this point from the Scriptural phrase *And make an atonement for him, for that he sinned regarding the soul* (Numbers 6:11) which refers to a Nazarite who is called a sinner because he deprived himself of wine. Certainly, says Rabbi Elazar Hakapar, a person who deprives himself of his health by injuring himself is considered a sinner. One can extend this reasoning to include smoking.

Maimonides, in his *Mishneh Torah (Hilchoth Melachim* 6:10) states that he who smashes household goods, or destroys articles of food, with destructive intent, transgresses the commandment *Thou shall not destroy* (Deut. 20:19). Our Sages (Shabbath 140b) deduce from this phrase a prohibition against the wanton destruction of anything useful to man. Rabbi Solomon Luria *(Yam Shel Shlomoh,* Baba Kamma 8:59) extends this prohibition to the willful destruction of one's own body. An example of this is described in the Talmud (Shabbath 129a) where a footstool was broken up for Rabbah, whereupon Abaye said to Rabbah: "But you are not infringing on *Thou shalt not destroy?*" He retorted: "Thou shalt not destroy in respect of my own body is more important to me."

The prohibition against intentionally wounding oneself is codified by both Rambam in his *Mishneh Torah (Hilchoth Chovel Umazik* 5:1), and R. Karo in his *Shulchan Aruch (Choshen Mishpot* #420:31 and *Orach Chayim* #571). Not only can smoking be considered to constitute wounding oneself or intentionally

injuring one's health, but it may in fact constitute a slow form of
suicide. Suicide, itself, whether slow or rapid, is absolutely
prohibited in Jewish law[10] based upon the biblical phrase *And
surely your blood, the blood of your lives, will I require* (Genesis
9:5).

Some argue that the following two Talmudic principles
mitigate against the imposition of a Rabbinic ban against cigarette
smoking:

a) we must not impose a restrictive decree upon the
   community unless the majority of the community will be
   able to endure it (Baba Kamma 79b).

b) it is better that they should transgress inadvertently rather
   than be deliberate sinners (Shabbath 148b).

Both arguments can be rejected[11] since neither is applicable in
the face of *Pikuach Nefesh* or danger to life. Furthermore, the
smoking of cigarettes is not an inadvertent act (although the sin or
transgression may be inadvertent), but an intentional practice of
oral gratification which can lead to serious illness and even death.

Nearly a century ago, Rabbi Israel Meir Ha-Kohen Kagan
(1838-1933), popularly known as the *Chofetz Chayim*, wrote a
small treatise entitled *Kuntres Zechor Le Miriam* which is appended
at the end of many editions of his famous book *Shemirath
HaLashon*. In this treatise (Chapter 10, p.16), he points out that the
smoking of cigars and cigarettes is "not only harmful to the body
as is well known, but also causes harm to the soul" in that it
causes one to neglect one's study of Torah. He therefore concludes
that one should refrain from smoking for these two reasons.

On the other hand, very few Rabbis have to this day issued a
prohibition against smoking, though most condemn the practice as
foolhardy and dangerous. Rabbi Moshe Feinstein, in his famous
responsa[12], asserts that althout it is proper not to begin smoking,

10. Rosner, F. "Suicide in Biblical, Talmudic and Rabbinic Writings." *Tradition 11*
    (2): 25-40 (Summer) 1970.
11. Aberbach, M. "Smoking and the Halakhah." *Tradition 10(3)* 49-60 (Spring)
    1969.
12. Feinstein, M. *Responsa Iggrot Moshe. Yoreh Deah* Section 2. New York, 1973,
    Balshon. Responsum 149.

one cannot say that it is prohibited because of the danger since many people smoke and the Talmud (Shabbath 129b and Niddah 31a) states that: *The Lord preserveth the simple* (Psalms 116:6). Rabbi Feinstein also points out that many rabbinic scholars from previous generations as well as our own era smoke. Furthermore, even to those who are strict and do not smoke because of their concern about possible danger to health and life, there is no prohibition in lighting the match for those who smoke. Rabbi Feinstein has recently reconfirmed his opinion in writing[13].

Rabbi Feinstein does admit, however[14], that if the exhaled smoke is harmful to others in close proximity to the smokers, the smokers would be obligated to smoke in private or far removed from other people. There is considerable controversy in the medical literature on this point. There is no doubt that maternal smoking affects fetal development, being associated with low birth weight[15],[16], prematurity[17], birth defects[18], increased spontaneous abortions[19], and long-term growth deficiency in the offspring[20]. Thus, in Jewish law, a pregnant woman should be prohibited from smoking because she is endangering the health and life of her child. The suggestion that healthy adult non-smokers may be

---

13. Feinstein, M. Unpublished responsum dated June 10, 1981 addressed to Dr. Fred Rosner.
14. Feinstein, M. Unpublished responsum dated Oct. 6, 1980 addressed to Mr. Reuben Soffer. (Lacking the text of the responsum, we cannot know why Rav Feinstein did not apply the principle "G-d preserveth the simple" to those non-smokers inhaling the smoke.-Ed.)
15. Comstack, G.W., Shah, F.K., Meyer, M.B., Abbey, H. Low birthweight and neonatal mortality rates related to maternal smoking and socioeconomic status. *Amer. J. Obstet. Gynecol. III*: 53-59, 1971.
16. Davies, D.P., Gray, O.P., Ellwood, P.C. Abernethy, M. Cigarette smoking in pregnancy: Association with maternal weight gain a fetal growth. *Lancet I*: 385-387, 1976.
17. Meyer, M.B., Tonascia, J.A. Maternal smoking, pregnancy complications, and perinatal mortality. *Amer. J. Obstet. Gynecol. 128*: 494-502, 1977.
18. Andrews, J., McGarry, J.M. A community study of smoking in pregnancy. *J. Obstet. Gynecol. Br. Commonw. 78*: 1057, 1972.
19. Kline, J., Stein, Z.A., Susser, M., Warburton, D. Smoking: a risk factor for spontaneous abortion. *N. Engl. J. Med. 297*, 793-796, 1977.
20. Butler, N.R., Goldstein, H. Smoking in pregnancy and subsequent child development. *Brit. J. Obstet. Gynecol. 4*: 573-575, 1973.

seriously harmed by other people's smoke is based on four studies, summarized in a recent editorial in the prestigious medical publication LANCET[21]. Each of the studies can be criticized for a variety of statistical reasons[22]. At present, the state of the art seems to be that, although suggestive, the evidence is not sufficient to definitively conclude that passive or involuntary smoking causes lung cancer in non-smokers.

Rabbi J. David Bleich[23] is of the opinion that smoking does not involve an infraction of Jewish law. He explains that certain actions which contain an element of danger, such as crossing the street or riding in an automobile, involve a certain danger yet are certainly permissible because "the multitude has trodden thereon", i.e., these dangers are accepted with equanimity by society at large. Therefore, an individual is granted dispensation to rely upon G-d who "preserves the simple". Rabbi Bleich also quotes Rabbi Yaakov Etlinger (Binyan Zion #137) who distinguishes between an immediate danger which must be eschewed under all circumstances, and future danger, such as that related to cigarette smoking, which may be assumed if, in the majority of cases, no harm will occur. Two correspondents[24] take strong issue with Rabbi Bleich's analysis of the Jewish legal permissibility of smoking. The five points in Jewish law raised by these correspondents are rebutted by Rabbi Bleich[25]. In spite of the technical inability of Rabbi Bleich and others to promulgate a formal binding prohibition against smoking, he does urge Rabbis to use their extensive powers of moral persuasion and exhortation to urge "the eradication of this pernicious and damaging habit"[23]

Dr. Abraham S. Abraham quotes Rabbi Shlomo Zalman Auerbach and Rabbi Ovadiah Yosef as being in agreement with the thesis that smoking cannot be prohibited in Jewish law for the

21. Editorial. Passive Smoking: Forest, Gasp, and Facts. Lancet 1: 548-549 (March 6) 1982.
22. Lee, P.N. Passive Smoking. Lancet 1: 791 (April 3) 1982.
23. Bleich, J.D. Survey of Recent Halakhic Periodical Literature: Smoking. Tradition 16(4): 121-123 (Summer) 1977.
24. Hendel, R.J. and Weiss, Z.I. Smoking. Tradition 17(3): 137-140 (Summer) 1978.
25. Bleich, J.D. ibid. p. 140-142.

reasons cited by R. Feinstein and Rabbi Bleich. Nevertheless, "one should do one's utmost to avoid smoking, since this has been proven medically to be injurious to well being, and dangerous to life"[26].

In regard to marijuana smoking, mounting scientific evidence shows that it is a threat to brain function as well as a respiratory hazard[27]. Acute intoxication impairs learning, memory, intellectual performance and driving ability[28]. Marijuana also has adverse effects on the body's immune, endocrine and reproductive systems.

Because of the above, Rabbi Feinstein prohibits the smoking of marijuana by stating the following: Firstly, marijuana is harmful to the body. Even those people who suffer no physical damage may suffer mental harm in that marijuana confuses the mind and distorts one's abilities of reasoning and comprehension. Such a person is thereby not only preventing himself from studying Torah but also from performing other precepts. Marijuana use, continues R. Feinstein, can also bring on extreme and uncontrollable lusts and desires. Furthermore, since the parents of marijuana users are usually opposed to its use, the users violate the biblical commandment of honoring one's father and mother. Other prohibitions may also be involved in marijuana use and, therefore, concludes R. Feinstein, one must use all one's energies to uproot and eliminate this pernicious habit[29].

Other Rabbis also consider marijuana smoking to be prohibited in Jewish law[30],[31] but very few prohibit cigarette

26. Abraham, A.S. *Medical Halachah for Everyone.* Jerusalem, New York. Feldheim. 1980, p. 6.
27. Dupont, R.L. Marijuana Smoking - A National Epidemic. *Amer. Lung. Assoc. Bull.* 66(7): 2-7 (Sept.) 1980.
28. Willette, R.E. Editor. *Drugs and Driving.* National Institute on Drug Abuse Monograph II. DHEW Pub. No. (ADM) 77-432. National Institute on Drug Abuse, 1977.
29. Feinstein, M. *Responsa Iggrot Moshe. Yoreh Deah.* Section 3, B'nei Brak, Israel. 1981. Yeshiva Ohel Yosef. Responsum #35.
30. Brayer, M.M. Drugs: A Jewish View. in *Jewish Bioethics* F. Rosner and J.D. Bleich (Editors). New York. Sanhedrin Press (Hebrew Pub. Co.) 1979 pp. 242-250.
31. Landman, L. (Editor) *Judaism and Drugs.* New York. Federation of Jewish Philanthropies. 1973. 265 pp.

smoking. Some Rabbis are finally speaking out on the evils of
cigarette smoking and the possible prohibitions involved. Rabbi
Moses Aberbach" writes that

> "the medical and statistical evidence demonstrates that
> smoking is hazardous to health, and can lead to fatal
> diseases. The idea that smoking is liable to shorten a
> person's life is virtually undisputed. It follows, therefore,
> that the numerous *halachic* rules prohibiting dangerous
> activities should be extended to include smoking. This
> extension should be enacted by the leading Rabbinic
> authorities of our times, preferably acting jointly, and with
> due publicity. A general Rabbinic injunction against
> smoking has every chance of being gradually accepted, at
> least in strictly Orthodox circles. Thus, many Jewish lives
> would be saved, and the health of our people would
> substantially improve. Finally, not the least fringe benefit
> would be a demonstration of the relevance of Judaism —
> and especially *halachic* Judaism — to our own times."

Rabbi Nathan Drazin[32] asks "why, indeed, have the great
halachic authorities of our generation been silent concerning the
prohibitions of Jewish law in regard to cigarette smoking?" Citing
a variety of biblical and Talmudic sources, Rabbi Drazin concludes
that

> "it is therefore high time, before more irreparable damage
> is done, that the great *halachic* authorities of our time come
> out openly and declare that the use of narcotic drugs and
> even cigarette smoking are evil practices that are certainly
> forbidden by Jewish law ..."

In 1976, the Sephardic Chief Rabbi of Tel Aviv, Rabbi David
Halevy, declared cigarette smoking to be a violation of Jewish law.
His prohibition on smoking was widely publicized and was

---

32. Drazin, N. Halakhic Attitudes and Conclusions to the Drug Problem and its
    Relationship to Cigarette Smoking. In *Judaism and Drugs* (Leo Landman, edit.)
    New York. Federation of Jewish Philanthropies. 1973. pp. 71-81.

reported on page 2 of the December 11, 1976, issue of the New York Times.

It is my fervent hope that more Rabbis will follow this example and ban smoking. Physicians should urge their patients to stop smoking. Rabbis should deliver sermons urging their congregants to stop smoking, or non-smokers not to begin this evil practice. Physicians and Rabbis must themselves give up smoking in order to practice what they preach and teach by example. Leading Rabbinic authorities should speak out on this subject without timidity. The Jewish community of this nation must marshal its forces in an attack on the promotional activities of the tobacco industry. Judaism must appeal to its people and educate them in the ways of our Torah which regards life and health to be sacred and their preservation a Divine commandment.

Halacha and the Conventional Last Will and Testament

By Judah Dick

Jacob Adler passed away, leaving an estate of $450,000. He expected that in accordance with Jewish law his wife, Jenny, and Dana, his unmarried daughter, would be provided for from a special fund of $50,000. The remaining funds would be divided into four equal portions. Two would be awarded to Rubin, his oldest child, and one portion each (of $100,000) to Simon and Levi his other two surviving sons.

But Mr. Adler did not leave a written will, so the disposition of his estate will probably be quite different. Instead of his expectations being fulfilled, one-third of his estate will be awarded to his wife and the remaining two-thirds divided equally among his four children — in accordance with the State law.

Michael Zoberstein was disappointed with his oldest son, Kenneth, who had become a sculptor. He did not want his handbag business to end up in Kenneth's hands, so Mr. Z. wrote a will leaving him a token inheritance, designating the rest of his estate to be divided equally among his widow, Ruth, his other son, Ralph, and his two sons-in-law, who had joined him in his business.

Mr. Zoberstein's wishes will be carried out by the executor of his will, but failure to adhere to the halachic requirements of

Asst. Corp. Counsel, City of New York:
Smicha, Yeshiva Torah Vodaath

disposition of a person's legacy may invalidate such legacy insofar as Jewish law is concerned. Could something have been done to have his wishes implemented without contravening Torah law?

What are Mr. Zoberstein's heirs to do? Are they obligated to follow Torah law in disposition of his funds, giving his eldest son a double portion, etc., or are they required to "harken to the wishes of the deceased"?

Old Dave Samsonoff was an invalid during his last years. Of all his sons and daughters and their children, only Faige, the oldest child of his daughter Sima, devoted an hour every day to keeping him company. He would like to leave her a share of his fortune, but daughters — and surely granddaughters — do not inherit according to Torah law when sons are present.

Mr. Samsonoff would also like to leave several thousand dollars to the yeshiva, where he was founding president. How can this be achieved?

In the following pages we will seek to elucidate the areas where a will written in accordance with secular law may conflict with the dictates of the halacha; furthermore, we will try to explain what the solutions to these conflicts might be, and the possible difficulties of accepting these solutions:

☐ How may a person dispose of his assets after death in a manner both in accordance with halacha and civil law?

☐ What are the rights of the surviving wife and daughters to the estate of the deceased head of the family?

☐ Are there any ways in which a person can write a legal will, modifying the Torah's prescribed disposition of one's estate, without violating Torah law?

☐ How inviolable are the rights of the bechor — the first born — to a double portion of the estate?

☐ What is the halachic status of wills written according to civil law?

The Basic Rules

The Torah devotes six verses to the laws of inheritance (Bamidbar 27:5-11), setting forth the procedure for disposition of estates:

* When male offspring exist, they are invariably the exclusive heirs of their father's estate.

* The Torah awards women no rights of inheritance as long as there are male heirs in the same class. (Daughters do not inherit if there are sons, nor sisters if there are brothers. Also, only paternal relatives can be considered heirs.)[1]

* In the absence of sons, daughters (and their offspring) are exclusive heirs.

* Children who die before their father are replaced by their qualified heirs.

When a decedent leaves no children, his father is the exclusive heir to his estate.

If his father is no longer living, *his* children (the decedent's paternal brothers) inherit his estate.

* When the first born is a male, he is entitled to two shares of the tangible assets of the estate, by rule of *bechora* (progenitor).

Originally a widow was only entitled to her *kesuba* of 200 silver pieces. By rabbinical ordinance dating to pre-Talmudic times, her needs and living facilities must be provided for from her husband's estate until the time that she claims the lump sum due under the *kesuba*, or until she remarries.

* The Rabbis also made provision for support and maintenance of unmarried daughters (up to physical maturity at the age of 12½), and for a dowry at their time of marriage — which may run as high as ten percent of the total assets left by the decedent.[2] But this does not leave options for changes of the type Mr. Zoberstein or Dave Samsonoff had wanted to offer in their wills.

The Torah concludes this discussion with the term *chukas mishpat* (a statute of judgment). From the use of the word *chuka*, which implies inalienability, the *Rambam* derives a maxim that a person cannot change the order of inheritance described in the Torah — neither *to bequeath a legacy* to a person not entitled to

---

1. *Bava Bathra* 110b; *Rambam*, Laws of Inheritance, Ch. 1(6), *Tur* and *Shulchan Aruch* 276(4).
2. *Kesubos* 52b; *Rambam*, Laws of Marriage, Ch. 20(1) etc. *Tur* and *Shulchan Aruch*, Even Ho'ezer 113(1).

inherit, nor *to disinherit* a person entitled to inherit. In this respect, inheritance differs from the general rule in monetary matters, which allows people to stipulate any conditions or rules of conduct of business they choose *(kol tenai shebemamon kayom)*[3]. The only modification permitted by the halacha is to provide a greater share, or even one's complete estate, to any of the persons entitled to inherit, even though this would disinherit others in the same class, *providing* that a first-born *(bechor)* is not deprived of his right to a double share.[4]

The Sages were generally not in favor of any disinheritance or diminution of inheritance among one's children, even in favor of one child who is a Torah scholar over another who does not conduct himself properly, and they counseled against participation in any such disposition of assets.[5]

So the problem remains: How can a man direct the way his assets will be distributed *after* he has died — at a time when he no longer "owns" his possessions?

The Gift Approach

Talmudic scholars have demonstrated that, by utilizing the laws of gifts and inter-vivos trusts (trusts made during one's lifetime), a Jew can create a halachically acceptable will-substitute. The Torah laws of inheritance only apply to property owned by the

3. *Bava Bathra* 139b; *Rambam*, Laws of Inheritance, Ch. 6(1), *Tur* and *Shulchan Aruch*, Ibid, Ch. 290.

Interestingly, although several ancient civilizations recognized the power to devise property by will, especially Roman Law, English Common Law prior to the enactment of the Statute of Wills in the reign of Henry the Eighth (32 Henry VIII Ch. 1) did not permit devises of real property and restructure devises of personal property. Thus, the courts have held that a state may regulate the disposition of property after death and prohibit devisors to certain classes such as aliens, corporations, and even the United States government. The U.S. Fox 94 U.S. 315, 320 (1876); U.S. Perkins 163 U.S. 625, 628 (1895); see also Bigelow Theory of Post Mortem disposition; Rise of the English Will, II, Harvard Law Review 69 (1897).

4. Ibid, Halachos 2-3, based on *Bava Bathra* 130b; *Tur* and *Shulchan Aruch*, Choshen Mishpat, Ch. 281 (1).

5. *Bava Bathra* 133b; *Rambam*, Ibid, Halacha (II).

person at the time of his death; however, one can made a gift to
absolutely anyone — heir-apparent or otherwise — until the last
conscious moment of one's life. Thus, if the person gave away or
otherwise disposed of his property *during his lifetime*, the
restrictions limiting the inheritance would not have any effect.

(The discussion here will not include *matnas she'chiv me'ra*: a
special rabbinical enactment that permits a person on his death bed
to distribute his assets as he sees fit regardless of laws of
inheritance. The only proviso is that he use the terminologies of
"gift-giving" rather than a "bequest" — or at least use both terms,
in which case it will be presumed that he had intended to give a
gift. Such gifts take effect in the case of death, but are revocable if
the person recovers from his illness.[6] We are primarily interested in
a person of normal health, who desires to draw up a will or
document with the general characteristics of a will recognized by
secular civil law.)

There is a drawback in making an ordinary outright gift, since
the testator (maker of a will) does not wish to part with his
possessions during his lifetime; but halachically one cannot give a
gift during his lifetime to be effective *after* death, since death
divests the testator of title and vests title in his legal (halachic)
heirs.[7]

What we seek here, then, is a means by which the gift-giver
presents the items in his will to his intended heirs while he is still
living; yet he retains full control and possession of his property
during his entire lifetime and the power to revoke or change his
will as long as he lives.

The Method & The Drawback

The technique generally utilized so as the conform both to
halacha and the wishes of the testator is a revocable inter-vivos
trust: technically, the beneficiary takes immediate title to the
property, but the donor retains the right of all income during his

---

6. *Bava Bathra* 148b; *Rambam,* Laws of Bestowals and Gifts, Ch. 8-12.
7. *Bava Bathra* 135b.

lifetime, and may revoke the trust if and when he so desires.[8] The drawback to this method is that a majority of *poskim* (halachic authorities) require a *kinyan* — a formal immediate transfer of title to the property, which is done by the witnesses giving their garment symbolically to the donor. A significant problem inherent to this method is that the *kinyan* is only effective in transferring property (other than currency) which is in the possession of the donor *at the time* of the *kinyan*. It has no effect whatsoever on property yet to be acquired[9]. Yet, a conventional will generally deals with future holdings as well.

There are other methods of transferring currency, such as through *agav*, whereby a movable item — like silver, china, or furniture — can be transferred simultaneously with an interest in real property, which can be accomplished with *kinyan*, but there is no universally accepted means for transferring something which is not as yet in existence *(davar shelo bo le'olam)* or not presently in the testator's possession *(davar she'eino bi'reshuso)*[10]. Thus, if a person acquires new possessions after making his inter-vivos trust, these possessions are not covered by the *kinyan*. His will based on this device is totally ineffective as far as these newly acquired possessions are concerned. Worse yet, the beneficiaries carry the burden of proof to show that the items transferred — that is, covered by the will — were in existence and in possession of the donor at the time the trust was made.[11]

This burden of proof may be difficult to meet and could readily serve to frustrate the intention of the donor. Thus, the inter-vivos trust approach (standing alone) gets poor marks as an all-purpose method of transferring property through the conventional will.

---

8. *Bava Bathra, Tosafos* 136b; *Tur* and *Shulchan Aruch*, Ibid, Ch. 257.
   Our proposed sample will is based in part on text suggested by Rashba in responsum #106 attributed to Ramban.
9. *Bava Metzia* 46a, *Tur* and *Shulchan Aruch*, Choshen Mishpat 203, 209.
10. *Shulchan Aruch*, Choshen Mishpat, Ch. 204(4).
11. Choshen Mishpat 251(2) and 211(6).

"Harken to my wishes ..."

Another technique for making a will is based on the maxim of the rabbis: "Mitzva lekayeim divrei ha'mes — It is a mitzva to fulfill wishes expressed by a person since deceased." Under this rule, although title to the property descends to the legal heirs, as per Torah laws of inheritance; nevertheless, the heirs are under an obligation to carry out the wishes of the decedent and dispose of the property as he indicated.[12] Thus, any intended disposition of assets expressed in a legal will become "the wishes of the deceased," and the heirs are obligated to carry them out.

The drawback to this technique is that it applies only where the decedent addresses his wishes directly to his heirs in their presence in regard to existing property, or when he transfers possession to the property during his lifetime to a trustee, with directions on how it should be distributed.[13] In the ordinary will situation, the testator often does not wish to inform his legal heirs of his testamentary wishes in order to avoid undue pressure and hostility, nor to part with title during his lifetime. Moreover, according to many views this rule applies only to a she'chiv mera[13a].

Creating an Indebtedness

A most original and effective technique of bequeathing one's possessions halachically is to create a theoretical indebtedness in favor of the chosen heirs (such as "Faige," Mrs. Samsonoff's granddaughter). This debt (to Faige) becomes a lien on all the testator's (Mr. Samsonoff's) property — both current and future holdings.

A person may create an indebtedness even if none previously existed, even if no loan or other consideration was ever given,

---

12. *Shulchan Aruch*, Choshen Mishpat 252, based on Kesubos 69b.
13. *Shulchan Aruch*, Choshen Mishpat, Ibid. See also extensive discussion on this subject in Responsa, *Maharsham*, Vol. 2, 224.
13a. See responsa *Binyan Zion* of Rabbi Jacob Ettlinger, addendum #24, and discussion in note 29a intra.

merely by executing a note in favor of another person.[14] In the will situation, a debt for a huge sum well in excess of the total value of the estate is created, but does not mature and is not payable until one hour before death. The huge sum is not going to be paid, but will be used as leverage for carrying out the terms of the will: the note, by its terms, gives to the halachic heirs (Mr. Samsonoff's sons) the option of paying the debt *or* a stated legacy in lieu of such debt. This legacy is the amount willed to the chosen legatee (Faige).

This technique was primarily used to give daughters a half share or full share in one's estate and is known as *shtar chatzi zachor* (half share) or *shtar zachor shaleim* (full share). Such a document was often drawn up and delivered to a daughter at the time of her marriage, and generally excluded real property and holy books.[15] A fictional debt (a personal obligation not subject to the restrictive rules of *kinyan*) was utilized in preference to a direct *chiyuv* since there are problems in dealing with a specific item not yet in existence or in the possession of the donor at the time the *chiyuv* was created. In such case, there is a difference of opinion among authorities as to whether the *chiyuv* is binding on the donor's legal heirs.[16] On the other hand, in the case of fictional debt, the debt is absolute, and the giving of the bequest or legacy is an optional method of satisfying the debt: this technique is definitely binding on the donor's heirs, since non-compliance would trigger the full monetary obligation of the note.

The Charity Bequest

When someone bequests a portion of his estate to a charity, this does not impose a legal (i.e. halachic) obligation on the donor's heirs to carry out this bequest. This is because a bequest is only a personal obligation of the donor, but does not constitute a lien on

---

14. *Shulchan Aruch*, Choshen Mishpat 257(7).
15. *Shulchan Aruch*, Even Ho'ezer 108(3), Choshen Mishpat 281(7).
16. See Tumim, *Kesos Hachoshen* and *Nesivos Hamishpat* on *Shulchan Aruch*, Choshen Mishpat, Ch. 60(6).

his assets (the inheritance).[17] There is a difference of opinion among authorities, however, when the donor makes a bequest of a specific object or a set amount of funds to charity. This is because of a rabbinic rule whereby "a pledge to Heaven (i.e. the Temple) is as if delivered to the recipient," which according to some authorities applies to charity pledges also.[18] The most accepted way of making a charitable legacy enforceable would be in the same manner as an ordinary legacy — such as creating a debt to the charity, as outlined above.

Incidentally, while a person is generally not permitted to contribute more than twenty per cent of his property or income to charity during his lifetime, most authorities agree, one may leave as much as he chooses to charity after his death.[19] People in a high estate-tax bracket may find it advisable to consider a charitable bequest as a means of reducing the estate tax, as well as a benefit for their *neshama*. This can be accomplished by creating a direct charitable bequest or a trust fund with income (and/or principal ultimately) payable to yeshivos and other worthy institutions* which can be named in the will or left to the executor's discretion. One would be well-advised to pursue this matter with one's legal and financial advisors ... The charity bequest should, of course, be made with due consideration for the needs of the survivors.[20]

The Non-Halachic Will

"Law of the Land"

What, indeed, happens when someone (like Mr. Zoberstein, in the opening anecdote) ignores all halachic requirements, and simply writes a will in accordance with civil law? There is a rule that *dina*

---

17. *Ramo*, Choshen Mishpat, Ch. 352(2) and *Kesos Hachoshen*, Ibid.
18. See *Kesos Hachoshen* and *Nesivos Hamishpat*, Ibid., and *Tur*, Yore De'ah 258(13).
19. *Kesubos* 61b; *Ramo*, Yore De'ah 249.
20. *Bach*, on *Tur*, Yore De'ah, Ch. 249, *Aruch Hashulchan*, Choshen Mishpat, 282(3).

*Henry Ford was able to keep Ford Motor Co. in the family by leaving most of the (non-voting) stock he owned to a charitable foundation which perpetuated his name.

d'malchusa dina (the law of the land has halachic validity). One might wonder why this rule would not supersede any halachic requirements for validity of a will and make it effective halachically. Most opinions maintain that this principle pertains primarily to transactions between Jews and the government and/or non-Jews, and does not govern purely intra-Jewish affairs such as family inheritance where no public policy considerations are involved.[21] Therefore, according to this opinion the principle of *dina d'malchusa dina* cannot supersede the *halachos* of inheritance.

It should be noted, however, that Rabbi Moshe Feinstein שליט"א maintains that where the transaction (in this case the will) were only lacking a *kinyan*, then *dina d'malchusa dina* would apply and all of the halachic requirements would have been satisfied.[22]

All would agree, though, that one should pursue all feasible means to write a will incorporating halachically-sanctioned methods of distributing one's property.

"Situmta" — the Prevailing Communal Custom

Others have suggested that the related principle of *situmta*, or custom of the merchants, may resolve the problem. Under this principle, the commercial customs prevailing in a particular city or area supersede any halacha in civil law, since in money matters, people are free to make any agreements as long as they are based on express or implied consensual relationship between the participants.[23] Thus, it has been suggested, where the common practice of the Jewish community is to make wills in accordance

There are some who would limit charitable requests to fifty percent or thirty-three percent — Sheiltot 64, Sheira Knesset Hagedola, Yore De'ah 249. In any event something should always be left for the legal heirs — Shita Mekubetzes, *Kesubos* 50, in the name of Disciples of Rabbi Jonah, and *Meiri*, *Kesubos* 50a.

21. Beth Yosef on *Tur*, Choshen Mishpat 27, citing response of Rashba; *Shach*, Choshen Mishpat, 73(39). See also *Beth Yosef* on *Tur*, Choshen Mishpat 369.
22. *Igrot Moshe*, Even Ho'ezer, 109 (Volume 1).
23. Talmud Yerushalmi, *Bava Metzia*, on Ch. 7, Talmud Bavli, *Bava Metzia*, 74a; *Tur* and *Shulchan Aruch*, Choshen Mishpat, 201(2).

with the legal system of the place where they live, such wills shall be deemed to be in accordance with the rules of wills in halacha, as a transfer by inter-vivos trust effective prior to the testator's death.[24]

The objection to this approach is that the role of *situmta* is actually limited: it can create a substitute mode of *kinyan*; it may create contractual obligations or a *chiyuv*; or it may even, in the view of many authorities, effectively transfer ownership of something not yet in existence;[25] but there seems to be no valid basis for converting the very nature of a legal will, which takes effect only after death, into a *kinyan* that takes place during one's lifetime — which is the element that must be fulfilled.

In other words, although *situmta* may operate to give legal validity through custom and usage to any act which people can voluntarily implement between themselves, it should not be effective to validly change the laws of inheritance, which are designed to take effect immediately upon death, since even an heir cannot waive his future rights to his inheritance.[25a] It seems to be beyond the capacity of *situmta* to effect the transfer of property within one's lifetime with the use of a transaction designed to take effect only *after* death.

The "Death-bed Gift" — Alive and Well

Another possible saving feature of legal wills is based on the view of *Maharam Rotenberg* and the *Mordechai:*[26] that halacha

---

24. Responsum 21 of Rav Yecheskel of Laveda in *Sefer Ikre Hadat* on *Shulchan Aruch*, Orach Chaim. See critique of this view in Responsa Maharsham, Vol. 2 #204. See also responsa of Maharam Mintz, #66.

25. Responsa, *Chasam Sofer*, Choshen Mishpat, 66; Responsa, *Radvaz*; Vol. 2, Ch. 278; Responsa, *Rosh* 13(2); Maharam Rotenberg in *Notes of Mordechai* on Sabbath 472-3.

26. Maharam Rotenberg cited in *Mordechai* on *Bava Bathra*, 591. See also lengthy discussion in Responsum 21, *Ikre Hadat*, Supra. See also responsa Maharil (Rabbi Yaakov Molin) 75, who suggests that Maharam distinguishes between terminology used by testator. In his view, a request for a third person such as "he shall take or receive" is valid, whereas a directive to an agent to give or deliver to a third person is not valid in a will, but may be valid under the rule of *mitzva lekayeim divrei ha'mes*. Maharsham, responsum #224, concurs with this interpretation.

does make provision for a conventional will prepared by a healthy person *(bari)*, allowing it to take effect in the same manner as a *matnas she'chiv me'ra* — the bequest spoken by a person on his death bed. According to their view, the Talmudic reference to a gift by a *bari*, similar in operation to one made by a *she'chiv mera (Bava Bathra* 135b), was intended to permit anyone to make an oral or written will in the presence of witnesses without need for a *kinyan.* All that is required is that the gift announcement be made in contemplation of death and that it dispose of all of the person's possessions.[27] (If any possessions are left out of the disposition, it cannot be a *matnas she'chiv mera).* True, this view is not accepted by most Rishonim and Acharonim, but it may well be that the general custom of treating legal wills as valid may establish this minority view as the halachic norm in those communities. This may be so, because a *minhag* (custom) can generally determine a conflict among *poskim*, especially in monetary matters.[28]

If this approach is relied upon, it would be preferable that the witnesses to the will be halachically competent (kosher), i.e., observant males over thirteen years of age and not related to each other or to any of the parties affected by the will. It should be noted that if the legal heirs do not challenge the signature on the will, the signature in and by itself may be sufficient, dispensing with the need for "witnesses."

Under the laws of New York and many other states, a holographic will which is not witnessed by two persons is not generally accepted. But if there are witnesses who are not "kosher," and the will is legally proper, the will may nevertheless pass the *halachic* standard because of the testator's own signature.[29] Other theories have been advanced to validate legal (non-halachic) wills in accordance with liberal views of some Rishonim, who rule that *mitzva lekayeim divrei ha'mes* is applicable to all situations,

27. Ibid.
28. Responsa, *Perach Mate Aharon*, Vol. 1, 60; Responsa, *Ikre Hadat* 21, Supra; See generally, *Magen Avraham*, Shulchan Aruch, Orach Chaim, Ch. 690(22) and Responsa, *Chasam Sofer*, Orach Chaim 159.
29. Responsa, *Rashba*, Vol. 3, 67, and Vol. 4, 7; *Tur* and *Shulchan Aruch*, Choshen Mishpat 250, (3) based on *Bava Bathra* 149a; Ibid 113(2) and 207(16).

including healthy persons, especially where the testator is a parent
and the respect of parental wishes may be considered as *Kibud Av
ve'Em*. This is espeically so where the executors or legatees under
the will are in actual possession of the estate's assets.[29a]

The Bottom Line

In conclusion, it should be said that it would be far preferable
— and likely be more proper — if a will is prepared in a manner
that meets the strict requirements of halacha, in keeping with the
views of all *poskim*. A sample of such a will is available from this
author upon request. [It should be noted that since the sample
refers to a *kinyan*, it was best implemented if the witnesses made a
symbolic *kinyan* by giving a handkerchief or other chattel of theirs
to the testator before he signed the will. By making such *kinyan*,
they are considered as agents of the legatees mentioned in the
will.[30] Money cannot be transferred by such a *kinyan* but may be
transferred by a *kinyan agav*. This means that the testator
symbolically transfers a piece of real property he owns or rents to
the legatees and, together with it, any money or other chattel he
wishes to transfer.

It is technically possible to avoid the need for any type of
kinyan, by acknowledging that a proper *kinyan* has taken place,
even if it did not in fact occur.[31] The sample will contains such an
acknowledgement so that the omission of an actual *kinyan* would
not invalidate the will. Such an acknowledgement may also resolve
the difficulty of transferring any debt whether oral *(milveh ba'al
peh)* or evidenced by a note *(shtar)*.]

Post facto, if one has made a legal will without conforming to
halachic requirements, it would probably be sanctioned by a *Beth*

29a. See responsa Maharsham, Supra, who collected views of all predecessors and
     suggested novel views on the subject, as well as Responsa *Binyan Zion*, Supra.
     Maharsham also suggests that *Kibud Av* may be considered independent
     grounds for enforcing a will where the legal heirs are the testator's children. He
     also rejects the contention that failure to deliver a will during one's lifetime to a
     third party is fatal to its validity, since that rule only applies to a will signed by
     a scribe and witnesses, on behalf of the testator, but not to one signed by the
     testator himself.
30. *Shulchan Aruch*, Choshen Mishpat, 195(3).
31. *Shulchan Aruch*, Choshen Mishpat, 81(17); 1 Piske Din, Rabbanon, pg. 112.

Din (rabbinical court) in which the will's validity is questioned, on the basis of custom supported by the view of a minority of *poskim*.[32] There is still one stipulation — that the term "give" be utilized rather than only "leave" and "bequeath," because any attempt to interfere directly with the order of inheritance prescribed by the Torah is *ipso facto* invalid, and it is only by way of a "gift" that the halacha permitted even a *shechiv me'ra* to alter the order of inheritance prescribed in the Torah.

Circumventing the *Bechor*

The use of a gift is also an effective means of avoiding the rights of an eldest son *(bechor)* to his additional share, since the rules of *bechora* only govern inheritance and not gifts.[33] Some maintain that it would be best to leave some amount of money or property outside the will, so that the Torah's rules of inheritance apply to at least a portion of one's estate.[34] This can be accomplished by including a special paragraph in the will so stipulating.

For a do-it-yourself-er, a legally valid will can be drawn up by a layman, as long as it is properly signed and witnessed by two persons who are not named in the will as legatees. Thus, anyone writing a will according to one of the halacha forms (such as those in *Otzar Hashtoros* or *Nachlus Shiva*) can make it legally valid. It may be written in any language, but would have to be translated into English before it could be probated in a state court. Wills drafted by laymen have been the source of much litigation and are not recommended for the uninitiated.

In summary, it is important that we explore all aspects of our personal and business lives to rediscover the myriad broad areas and countless fine points that have clearcut halachic requirements and guidelines. Then we must endeavor to change our lives to conform with the halacha ... to bring the *Choshen Mishpot* off the shelf and make it an active source of our conduct, as it is meant to be.

---

32. See published letters of Rabbi Chaim Ozer Grodzinsky, (Michtevei Achiezer) vol. 1, no. 25.
33. *Shulchan Aruch*, Choshen Mishpat 282, based on *Bava Bathra* 133a.
34. Responsa of *Tashbaz*, Vol. 3 No. 147, cited by *Ksos Hachoshen*, 382(2). See also Responsa, *Chasan Sofer*, Choshen Mishpat, 151.

Vegetarianism From A Jewish Perspective

By Rabbi Alfred S. Cohen

"Animals should be seen but not hurt" was the message on the red T-shirt worn by Marcia Pearson, a fashion co-ordinator from Seattle. "For professional athletes, a vegetarian diet can't be beat" was the message of Peter Burwash, a top-ranking tennis player from Canada. Sporting a variety of banners and mouthing numerous slogans, hundreds of vegetarians convened for the fourth annual congress of the North American Vegetarian Society.

The Vegetarian Society is not just another conglomeration of assorted oddballs. As the New York Times reported, there are well over 10 million vegetarians in this country. New York alone is supporting 35 vegetarian restaurants for about 100,000 strict vegetarians, and there are perhaps half a million who are part-time vegetarians. As one said, "There is more glamour and respectability now to vegetarianism, and we love it."[1]

The vegetarian phenomenon is rapidly winning adherents all over the world. Where once a non-meat-eater might be viewed as an anomaly, or possibly be suspected of following some exotic

---

1. Aug. 2, 1978.

Eastern cult, vegetarianism today scarcely merits a raised eyebrow. Not only is it an increasingly familiar phenomenon, but more and more we also find vegetarians putting meat-eaters on the defensive.

A surprising gamut of motives brings individuals to renounce meat and adhere to a diet which is far removed from the American ideal of "a chicken in very pot" or "meat and potatoes" as the typical dinner. The motives include health-consciousness, figure-consciousness, belief in macro-biotics, fear of pollution, and moral, even religious reasons. As with so many other social and ideological movements which sweep American society, Jewish people, particularly young people, are caught up in the wave of enthusiasm. There are many, many Jewish vegetarians, and more than a few are quite Orthodox in the full sense of the word. It therefore becomes a subject of considerable interest to investigate vegetarianism vis-a-vis Judaism and to determine if there is anything in Judaism which might oppose the practice of vegetarianism; conversely, can we find within Judaism positive reinforcement for this way of life?

A cursory appraisal of two thousand years of Jewish literature reveals that our Sages and thinkers have often considered the ethics of meat-eating, and their conclusions have been varied. The Gemara censures Rabbi Judah the Prince for his apparent callousness towards an animal, and more than a thousand year later, Rabbi Moshe Isserless (Ramo) displayed a heightened sensitivity to making a blessing on garments made from animal hides. More recently, the Baal HaTanya had a surprising argument for applauding the consumption of meat, while Chief Rabbi of Israel, Avraham Isaac Kook, shrank from that practice.

It is our intent herein to examine the many references to meat-eating found in our halacha and other religious writings, so that we may arrive at an understanding of how this concept fits in with traditional Jewish teachings. Additionally, and perhaps most important of all, we shall examine the reasons why people adopt a vegetarian regimen, and see if there is anything in these philosophies which is antagonistic to the Jewish *Weltanschauung*.

Vegetarianism and The Sabbath

The suggestion that refraining from eating meat might in any
way be contrary to Jewish law may at first seem absurd. However,
there are in fact certain times when the Jew is *bidden* to eat meat.
The question therefore becomes, how to interpret these halachic
indicators — as imperatives or possibly only as permissives. In
other words, does it say "Thou shalt eat meat" or maybe only
"Thou may"?

The weekly Shabbat is a prime example of how vegetarianism
might be proscribed by Jewish law, for there is a particular mitzva
of *Oneg Shabbat*, pleasure of the Sabbath. Rambam describes the
mitzva: "Eating meat and drinking wine on Shabbat are considered
Oneg Shabbat."[2] Since it is clear that a person must celebrate the
Sabbath with food and drink — specifically meat and wine — can a
vegetarian fulfill the halachic requirements of this mitzva?

Clarifying the mitzva of *Oneg Shabbat*, the Shulchan Aruch
goes so far as to note that it is forbidden to fast on the Sabbath,[3]
with some saying that this stricture derives from the Torah itself[4].
However, the Shulchan Aruch questions whether a person who
feels pain due to eating must in fact eat heartily on Shabbat. For
him, the pleasure is in *not* eating rather than in indulging. If that
be the case, the Shulchan Aruch determines that such a person
does not have to eat much on the Sabbath.

In the Shulchan Aruch, Rabbi Yosef Karo further probes the
ruling that one should eat on Shabbat as part of the mitzva of
Oneg Shabbat:

> A person who fasts each day, and would have
> pain from eating during the Sabbath day, since it
> would be a change in his normal eating schedule —
> there are those who say that they have observed
> several pious persons and men of deeds, who used to

---

2. הלכות שבת פרק ל — הלכה י.
3. אורח חיים רפ"ח ס' א.
4. תשובות הרשב"א תרי"ד.

fast on the Sabbath for just that reason, and they say
that this is what Rabbi Judah the Hasid used to do...[5]

If it is even permissible to *fast* on the Sabbath under these
circumstances, certainly it would be permissible to abstain from
eating meat if there is an aversion to it. Further substantiation for
this can be found in the commentary of Rabbenu Yonah on the
Talmud. In discussing the laws of a mourner, the Gemara teaches
that one whose close relative has died but has not yet been buried,
(called an *Onen*) may not eat meat or drink wine. However, on the
Sabbath the *Onen* eats meat and drinks wine. On this teaching, the
Rabbenu Yonah writes: he is *permitted* to eat meat and drink wine,
if he so wishes, but he is not obligated, for an *Onen* has to observe
all the mitzvot of Shabbat, and eating meat and drinking wine are
not mitzvot of Shabbat...[6]

Later authorities also accept this view.[7] Thus, there seems to
be little halachic controversy concerning vegetarianism and the
Sabbath. If a person is more confortable not eating meat, there
would be no obligation for him to do so on the Sabbath.

YomTov

The application of the halacha of vegetarianism with respect
to YomTov is somewhat more complex than that regarding
Shabbat. Whereas we have shown that on Shabbat one is not
obligated to eat meat if he derives no pleasure from it, that is not
sufficient reason to excuse one from eating meat on YomTov.

On Shabbat, the Jew is bidden to enjoy *Oneg Shabbat*;
however, on YomTov the Torah specifically indicates "*vesamachta
bechagecha*", "you shall rejoice on your Festivals." Consequently,
the Rambam wrote:

A person is obligated to rejoice and be of good

---

5. Ibid.
6. רבנו יונה מועד קטן.
7. דרכי משה, יורה דעה שמ"א.

spirit during the Festival, he, his wife and children,
and all those who are with him ... How is this done?
He gives sweets and nuts to the children ... and the
adults eat meat and drink wine ... and there is no
simcha (joy) *except with meat and wine.*[8]

Following the Rambam's view, therefore, we would have to
state unequivocally that an observant Jew must eat *some* meat
during the Festivals. However, not all halachic authorities accept
the Rambam's explanation. The Beit Yoseph, as a matter of fact,
cites a Talmudic text which specifically counters the Rambam. He
writes:

"Our Rabbis taught that a person is obligated to
bring joy to his wife and children and members of his
household during the Festival. He rejoices with wine
... Rabbi Judah ben Betairah says, in the days when
the Temple was in existence, there was no rejoicing
without meat ... but now that there is no longer the
Temple, there is no rejoicing without *wine...*"[9]

Following the original text in the Talmud, therefore, the Beit
Yoseph rejects the reading of the Rambam. In his authoritative
Code of Jewish Law (Shulchan Aruch), he omits any mention of
the obligation to eat meat on a Festival, as a factor of the mitzva of
"*simcha.*" Bringing the halacha up to date in our own time, the
Chafetz Chaim briefly notes that while the Beit Yoseph does in fact
reject the opinion, other halachic authorities try to bridge the gap
between them.[10] Rabbi Joel Sirkes (the Bach) agreeing that the

---

8. ‏טור אורח חיים תקכ"ט‎.

9. ‏פסחים קח‎.

10. ‏אורח חיים תקכ"ט‎. A study of the first Mishna in Nedarim 66 shows that the
    Rambam once again maintained that one is obligated to eat meat on Saturday
    and Holidays — whereas the other commentaries including the Shulchan Aruch
    only saw fasting as being forbidden.
       It would be interesting to ascertain how the Rambam reconciled his opinion
    with the talmudic text *Hullin* 11B where it is stated that one is obligated to eat
    meat on one Holiday only — namely Passover — when one is obligated to
    partake of the Paschal Lamb.
       See also Rambam ‏פרק ג הלכות דעות‎.

requirement "to rejoice" is fulfilled by drinking wine alone, nevertheless maintains that someone who also eats meat in rejoicing on the Festival has fulfilled a positive mitzva of the Torah.

A further support for the view that eating meat is not necessarily a mitzva on YomTov may be derived from a different source in the Talmud. In Bava Bathra 60b, the Gemara records that after the destruction of the Beit Hamikdash, the Sages were so overcome by the enormity of the disaster which had befallen the Jewish people, that they contemplated forbidding people from getting married or eating meat, as a sign of mourning for the Destruction. (For a number of reasons, these ordinances were not later enacted). Studying this text, the Tosafot ask a simple question — how could the Sages consider forbidding people from getting married, when it is a mitzva in the Torah? The answer to that question need not concern us here; however, from the mere fact that Tosafot *does not ask the same question* concerning the prospective prohibition upon eating meat, we may clearly infer that eating meat, even on a Festival, is not mandated by the halacha.[11]

In summing up this point, it is only proper to note that while in truth the Shulchan Aruch, which is the foundation for normative law for Jews today, does not insist upon the necessity to eat meat as *simchat YomTov* — nevertheless, there are many equally illustrious halachic authorities who maintain that it is certainly desirable, even if not strictly required, and that it is a mitzva to mark the joy of the Jewish Festivals with special meat and drink. In that sense, vegetarianism would be antagonistic to the *spirit* of Jewish thought on YomTov, even if not to the actual letter of the law.

Moral Considerations

The most sensitive area of our inquiry concerns the many per-

---

11. A more definite proof that one is not obligated to eat meat on the Holidays can be found in חולין יא:. This proof is in fact recorded in פתחי תשובה יורה דעה יח-ט.

sons who adopt a vegetarian regimen not from any convictions of its supposed benefits, whether physical, emotional, or psychological, but rather on moral or philosophical grounds. These moral considerations are generally expressed in one of two forms: Either that it is morally wrong to take the life of an animal for so trivial a purpose as eating its flesh; or that it is inhumane for a human being to inflict pain upon another creature.

As we address either of these arguments, let us bear in mind the concomitant question of whether a religious Jew may accept moral values which are not found within Torah or halacha, or approve standards which might oppose the Torah's standards or which imply, at the very least, that the Torah's standards are inferior or less humane. Is it not presumptuousness bordering on blasphemy, to call an act sanctioned by the Torah (and perhaps mandated by halacha), an act of cruelty, of inhumanity? We must first of all respond to this challenge to Jewish tradition, for if there is indeed any lése majesté in accepting the vegetarian credo, that would automatically preclude acceptance of that system for an observant Jew. Where the standards of vegetarianism condemn the values of the Torah or denounce its mitzvot as immoral or distasteful, we must categorically reject vegetarian ideology as aberrant philosophy. We believe that the Torah's ways "are paths of pleasantness" and righteousness; any belief which seeks to negate the Torah's truths is misguided.

Yet Jewish vegetarians often claim that "All the reasons that people become vegetarians are Jewish reasons", claiming two Chief Rabbis of Israel as vegetarians,[12] to quote Jonathan Wolf, leader of

---

12. In response to my telephone inquiry as to the identity of the chief Rabbis, I was told that these are the present incumbent, Rabbi S. Goren, and the first Chief Rabbi, Rav Kook. However, when asked to substantiate this last, Mr. Wolf responded only that it was "common knowledge". I have questioned a number of people who were peripherally involved with Rav Kook and none of them were aware of his alleged vegetarianism. Mr. Wolf then referred me to Rabbi Ben Zion Bokser, who recently published a book on Rav Kook. Rabbi Bosker informed that, as a matter of fact, he had been in direct contact with Rav Kook's son, and the son categorically denied that his father had been a

the North American Jewish Vegetarian Society, whose 300 members are an affiliate of the London-based Jewish Vegetarian Society with members worldwide (New York Times, September 14, 1977).

Jewish vegetarians often quote Rabbinic literature and the Torah for religious legitimacy, and to some extent they are justified. Albeit the Torah mandates animal slaughter in the Temple service, Rav Avraham Isaac Kook wrote that in the Epoch of the Messiah, "the effect of knowledge will spread even to animals ... and sacrifices in the Temple will consist of vegetation, and it will be pleasing to G-d as in days of old..."[13] The implication is that if there will be no animal sacrifice in the Temple, then there will be no animal slaughter whatsoever.

Our Rabbis teach that consumption of meat was not part of the original Divine plan at the world's creation. After the creation of Heaven and Earth and all living creatures, the All-Mighty instructed Man as to his proper relationship with the rest of Creation: (Genesis 1:29) "Behold I have given to you all vegetations ... for food." Since there was a bond interrelating all living things, life was sacred, and Man was not permitted to take life, even for his own sustenance.[14] Ramban explains this stricture "because creatures which possess a moving soul have a certain superiority and in this respect are somewhat similar to those who possess intellect (Man), and they have the power of affecting their welfare and their food and they flee from pain and death."[15] There is a measure of kinship between man and beast, and according to the original design of the world, the beast was to serve and assist mankind, but not to be his food.

---

vegetarian. Those vegetarians who look to Rav Kook as a mentor seem to be relying on a false rumor.

13. עולת ראיה חלק א P. 292.

14. See תו"ס סנהדרין נו: which is of the opinion that Adam was in fact permitted to consume meat; Adam was only forbidden to kill the animal — if the animal however died by itself, then the meat was permitted.

15. בראשית פ' נח.

Now while it is true that the above sources certainly accord with vegetarian claims, it is simply not accurate to base Jewish thought only on the experiences of Adam. There is the entire Torah which has to be considered, and what emerges from that presents a somewhat different picture. A few chapters after the Creation account, the Torah records a major upheaval of the original world-society, in the Deluge wherein all that had been was wiped away. The post-Diluvian world had different standards. Speaking to Noah after he emerged from the Ark, G-d specifically permitted him and his descendants to kill animals in order to eat their flesh (Genesis 9:3). However, even in this permission, there were restrictions, as the Ramban points out: "Although He gave them permission to slaughter and to eat ... yet He did not give them permission regarding the animal's soul and forbade eating a limb cut off from an animal that was still alive, nor the blood of the animal."[16]

We see therefore that although eating meat was now definitely sanctioned,[17] that dispensation was hedged about with limitations. Animal life did not become something negligible; man still had to maintain some respect for the dignity of the animal's life. That obligation still applies to all mankind. As for the Jewish people, the Torah later added many more restrictions upon them, further limiting their ways of eating meat.

In his mystical writings, Rav Avraham Isaac Kook sees the transformation of the relationship between the animal and human kingdoms as a diminution of the spirituality which was in each:

> The free movement of the moral impulse to establish justice for animals generally and the claim of their rights from mankind are hidden in a natural psychic sensibility in the deeper layers of the Torah. In the ancient value system of humanity ... the moral

16. Ibid.
17. Ramban (in Bereshis) and other Torah commentaries explain that after the Flood man's nature was changed and became weaker; therefore he was permitted to eat meat in order to give him more strength.

sense had risen to a point of demanding justice for
animals. "The first man had not been allowed to eat
meat" (Sanhedrin 59b) ... But when humanity, in the
course of its development suffered a setback and was
unable to bear the great light of its illumination (i.e.
the Flood) ... it was withdrawn from the fellowship
with other creatures ... The long road of development,
after man's fall, also needs physical exertion, which
will at times require a meat diet, which is a tax for
passage to a more enlightened epoch, from which
animals are not exempt.[18]

If a person tends toward vegetarianism because he sees it as a
lifestyle consonant with the way the All-Mighty really wanted the
world to be, there can be no denying that he has a valid point of
view. However, to claim that the Torah and Talmud share with
vegetarianism an abhorrence to animal slaughter as a cruel and
inhumane act, is simply false. A truer understanding of Jewish law
and tradition would indicate that many Rabbis viewed the Torah's
license to eat meat as a necessary dispensation, a reluctant
permission as it were, not as an indication that eating meat was a
desirable pursuit. On the other hand, it is quite wrong to view this
reluctance as arising out of a feeling that slaughter is cruel. The
reasoning is quite different. Let us proceed to examine it.

* * *

A talmudic passage often cited in support for the vegetarian
contention that Judaism disapproves of eating meat is found in
Bava Metzia 85a: Rabbi Judah the Prince was a great Rabbi and
supreme teacher, who compiled the Mishna, the basis of the
Talmud and the fundamental redaction of the Oral Law. For many
years of his life, Rabbi Judah suffered from a variety of intestinal
problems which caused him great pain. What had this sainted
scholar done to merit so much pain in his life? The Gemara found
the answer in an episode where Rabbi Judah was walking in the

---

18. תעלה אורות.

marketplace, and suddenly a calf that was being led to the slaughter fled its keepers and ran to hide behind him. However, Rabbi Judah pulled the calf out from its shelter behind his legs and returned it to the slaughterers, admonishing the calf, "Go, for you were created for this purpose." For this callous lack of pity for the animal who was afraid of dying, Rabbi Judah was punished with years of pain.[19]

However, it would be fallacious to interpret this text as indicating that Rabbi Judah was at fault because he condoned the slaughter of an animal. In fact, many Talmudic commentaries are puzzled by the story — after all, what did Rabbi Judah do wrong? Was he not correct in telling the animal to go willingly to its end, for in truth it exists for the benefit of man? The Geonim, however, indicate that while his conclusions cannot be faulted, his *attitude* was lacking in compassion. Here was an animal who had fled to him personally for help — his failure to be moved by its distress bordered on hardness of heart, unbefitting a person suffused with so much Torah knowledge. In a similar vein, the Maharshah notes that the text tells us it was a *calf* being led to its slaughter, not a mature animal. It is one thing to see a mature animal, which has lived a number of years, being taken to slaughter to provide meat for men to eat. It is quite another thing for a tender young calf, who has not even had time to taste of life's joys, to be summarily taken to the slaughter. No, he was not "created for this purpose."[20] Thus, Rabbi Judah erred in lacking pity for the young animal which ran to him for safety.

Let us not misread this episode as an indictment of those who eat meat, for it is not that. On the other hand, it is an excellent illustration of the high level of thoughtfulness for all living creatures which Judaism expects from its adherents.

Elsewhere the Talmud discusses the consumption of animal

---

19. His suffering continued for many years, until by an act of great kindness to a cat, Rabbi Judah evidenced that he had attained a higher level of compassion.
20. ‏בבא מציעא פה.‏

flesh in the light of the Torah's permission to eat it:

> The Torah teaches one the proper way to act: That a person should not eat meat except in certain circumstances ... he should only eat it with appetite. One might think that he should go out to the marketplace to buy meat — but the Torah writes "from your flocks" (i.e. not to go out and seek it and spend extra money for it, but only if it is available from your flocks). The Torah says 'you may slaughter from your flock and from your herds' — this teaches us that *some* of the animals may be slaughtered, but he should not slaughter *all* of them.[21] Rabbi Elazar ben Azariah learned from this that there is a proper proportion of a man's flocks which might be slaughtered, so that only occasionally would a person use his animals for food, and not on a regular basis.

Furthermore, the Hida, writing on this passage, notes: Our Rabbis taught us proper behavior, that a person should not eat meat excpet in certain circumstances, which means that if he does not have a strong and healthy constitution, then he may take money to buy meat.[22] Furthermore, the Maharshal writes that Rabbi Yochanan and Rabbi Nachman taught that one should eat meat for the strengthening of his body and ought not to hurt his body through excessive abstentions; however, he should not do it only for pleasure.

In Bina Bamikra we find a beautifully sensitive citation from Sefer HaChasidim: "And that which the Torah permitted the eating of meat to those who study Torah and observe the mitzva of Tfillin, it is because the Torah and the Tfillin are formed from the hide and the sinews of the animals, and after we have used parts of the animal in order to fulfill the needs of the mitzva, therefore we

---

21. .חולין פד

22. .חיים שאל סימן מ' אות ו'

may find therein justification for using the rest of the animal for
the eating of flesh.[23]

The Torah bids us "Be holy" (Leviticus 19:2), and our Rabbis
have found many ways to understand this mitzva. Perhaps the
most famous lesson was taught by the Ramban: "Be holy by
abstaining from those things which are permitted to you ... For
those who drink wine and eat meat all the time are considered
'scoundrels with a Torah license'."[24] Again we find reinforcement
for the view that albeit the Torah permitted the eating of animal
flesh, this was always understood within the teachings of Jewish
tradition as permission for occasional indulgence, but certainly not
as something to be sought after.

We may therefore conclude that when a vegetarian is loath to
eat meat because he does not want to take an animal's life merely
for his own pleasure, that person is acting well within the spirit of
Jeish belief and philosophy. He is not denigrating a Torah value,
for the Torah does not establish the eating of meat as a desirable
activity, only as something which is not forbidden to do.
Moreover, the less meat eaten, the better, and one who indulges
himself by eating meat too often is "disgusting", though he be
within the technical limits of the Torah.

* * *

Let us now give serious attention to other considerations
which are factors for those who opt to become vegetarians, some of
which stem from what might be termed "spiritual worldviews". An
exponent of such ideas, writing in *Vegetarian Times* (March/April
1978) declares:

> "In Buddhism the first precept is "not to kill but
> to cherish life." To eat the flesh of animals, then, is
> to encourage their slaughter, to be an accessory after
> the fact of their killing. How can anyone who
> professes to abhor violence and the suffering it causes

23. P. 203. בינה במקרא
24. רמב"ן פ' קדושים.

> inflict them on others — in this case animals — either
> by directly destroying them through so-called sport or
> hunting, or indirectly sanctioning their killing by
> buying their flesh and consuming it? We pride
> ourselves on being beyond the low level of morality
> of "might is right," which is universally condemned,
> yet we condone it every time we put into our bellies
> the flesh of helpless animals — animals that for the
> most part have served us and have every right to life
> as we on this planet."

Obviously, Judaism shares this aversion to animal suffering, for the admonition to have respect for the sensitivities even of animals is a basic tenet of our faith, having its origin in the Torah; as our Rabbis teach, the prohibition of causing pain to a living creature derives "d'oraitha", from the Torah itself, and not only from Rabbinic decree. Furthermore, the Torah which forbids destroying a fruit tree even in war time, would never sanction the sheer *waste* (not to speak of the barbarism) of hunting animals simply for the "sport". Commenting on hunting as a sport, Rabbi Yechezkel Landau, the world-famous Nodah BiYehudah, wrote, "I am amazed at the very concept ... we never find such a thing in the Torah other than Nimrod or Esau (both hunters, both infamously wicked), and this is not the way of the children of Abraham, Isaac, and Jacob."[25]

Concern for animal life is a hallmark of Jewish thinking, evident in any number of legal dicta in many areas. For example, Rabbi Moshe Isserles (Ramo) notes that although it is a mitzva to make a blessing when putting on a new garment for the first time, to thank G-d for his bounty, there are those who refrain from reciting the blessing if the garment or shoes are made out of leather, for the verse says "G-d's mercy it upon all his creatures."[26] Although the Ramo notes that this is not a conclusive argument

---

25. נודע ביהודה יורה דעה שאלה י.
26. אורח חיים רכ"ג.

for omitting the blessing (since the animal might have been dead anyway, and not been killed for that purpose), yet he stresses that there are many[27] who will not recite the blessing in such an instance. Ramo seems to approve of the rationale, for "how can a Jewish person kill, with his own hands, a living thing without any purpose and only for beauty or plesaure"?[28]

In embodying the concept of compassion for all living things into actual practice, I do not think there is anywhere a legal or religious system which can compare to the Torah's teachings. According to the Torah, it is forbidden for a person to slaughter an adult animal and its offspring on the same day — it would be just too cruel to wipe out two generations at one time; although the Torah permits taking animal life when it is needed for the benefit of man — yet man may not do this with viciousness. And even if the *animal* cannot be aware that its calf will die on the same day — yet *the Jew* must not allow himself to become callous about spilling blood.

> And therefore the essence of the prohibition is not in not killing that animal and its offspring on one day ... but rather ... the most important is that we should not become cruel...[29]

* * *

Some vegetarians espouse their cause as being the only humane way to act, maintaining that slaughter of an animal is necessarily painful to the creature, and thus always cruel. In *Vegetarian Times* (March/April 1978) we find:

> According to research involving hypnotism even the fast death of decapitation causes pain that lasts for some time after the killing. Years ago at an

---

27. In some editions the word "many" is not found.
28. Ibid.
29. רמב״ן דברים כ״ב פסוק ו.

execution in Paris a hypnotist had his subject
experience the pain of the condemned man;
reportedly it went on for a long time after the head
rolled, just as a chicken runs about for some time
when her head has been cut off. Similarly, alligators
which are dead to all appearances are cut open and
their hearts are still beating; fish which have been
cleaned of all internal organs are known to snap at
those who pass too close. The implications are that
immense suffering goes on in the nervous systems of
animals not only before the slaughter and during it,
but also afterwards.

I do not see why we have to accept these "implications" as
truth, nor act upon them. The fact that animal muscle tissue moves
even after the head is severed is simply the automatic reaction of
the nerve endings. There is no reason to assume that "immense
suffering" is taking place, when the animal is already dead;
whatever movement there is, is just that — automatic movement,
and not the expression of pain.

Nevertheless, Jewish law is extremely careful to assure that
even a momentary pain which might ensue at the instant of
slaughter, be reduced as far as possible.

"The regulations of slaughter, in special
prescriptions, to reduce the pain of the animal
registers a reminder that we are not dealing with
things outside the law, they are not automatons
devoid of life, but with living things."[30]

All the laws of Shechita stress the absolute necessity of
severing the trachea and esophagus so rapidly that the animal can
have no awareness; the slaughter is as painless as it is possible to
make it. That is why shechita requires severing the jugular "for
this is where most of the blood will come out, and also since the
prohibition of causing pain to an animal is proscribed by the

30. עורות "Loc Cit".

Torah; and therefore also the knife may not have any nicks, lest it cause any pain to the animal."[31]

In trying to clarify what the Jewish point of view is on the question of a vegetarian way of life, we have to understand that there is a distinction between supporting a certain point of view and making that point of view the cornerstone of our moral code. In every mitzva, in countless teachings, the Jew is taught to have compassion for all living things — yet that compassion does not override other values which are also fundamental to Judaism.

For all the 613 commandments of the Torah, there is no mention of any reward. The only exceptions are honoring one's parents — and the mitzva of "sending the mother bird from the nest." Certainly this must be one of the most unusual precepts of any religious code:

> If you chance upon a bird's nest on the road, in
> a tree or on the ground, and there are fledglings or
> eggs, and the mother is roosting on the fledglings or
> on the eggs — do not take the mother together with
> her children. You shall surely send away the mother,
> and you may take the fledglings for yourself; so that
> it may be good for you and you will have long life.
> (Deut. 22:6-7)

What is the reason for this commandment, which apparently ranks in importance with the command to honor one's father and mother, which is one of the Ten Commandments? The Gemara debates the question: one view is that just as G-d has pity upon his creatures, so, too, must man emulate Him. Send away the mother bird so that she will not suffer the pain of seeing her chicks taken away from her. There are those who disagree, saying that it is not possible to assert that this is the primary purpose for the command to send away the mother bird. However, even the latter group agrees that while compassion for the bird might not be the *primary*

---

31. פרי מגדים end of Preface to the Laws of Slaughtering.

consideration for the mitzva, it is undoubtedly one of the reasons why we were so commanded.

Compassion for an animal's pain is an important aspect of the Divine commandments; yet it is not the overriding feature of the mitzva. As the Rambam wrote, "If someone cries out in prayer — O, You Who had pity on the mother bird and commanded us not to take the fledglings while the mother is watching; O, You Who forbade us to slaughter an animal and its calf on one day; O, G-d, have mercy on us in the same way" — then, we *silence that person*, because these commandments are simply the decree of the Torah, and are not commanded to us out of pity for the animals, since if it were out of compassion for the animal, the Torah would *not have allowed us to slaughter the animal at all.*"[32]

It would be intellectually dishonest to maintain that Judaism shares with vegetarianism an abhorrence to eating the flesh of animals. We have to treat animals humanely, but as Rambam points out, compassion for animals cannot be the most important aspect of our mitzvot, for were that truly so, we would not be permitted to slaughter them at all. What we are in fact commanded to do is to reduce to the barest possible minimum any measure of pain which may be necessary to inflict upon them.

Nevertheless, a person who feels an emotional or intellectual distaste for the concept of killing an animal in order to satisfy one's appetite, will find support in the writings of our great Rabbis.

Rabbi Kook, the first Chief Rabbi of Israel, approved of many vegetarian attitudes. One time he was asked to comment upon a recommendation to split the two functions involved in animal slaughter between two separate people — the checking of the knife, inspection of the lungs and liver for disease would be carried out by a Rabbi learned in this field, while the actual physical slaughter would be carried out by another man. He applauded the

---

32. רמב"ם פרוש המשניות ברכות לג:.
משנה תורה הלכות תפלה פרק ט הלכה ז.

suggestion, "for this finds great favor in my eyes, and I believe that it accords with the spirit of Israel. For that a learned individual, a spiritually-inclined person, should at the same time be involved with the slaughter of living creatures and taking their souls, does not accord with the sensitivities of a refined heart. Although slaughter and eating of living creatures still has to be accepted in the world, nevertheless it is proper that this kind of work be performed by those people who have not yet reached the level of refined sensitivity. And learned people, men of ethics, knowledge, and religion, they are fit to be supervisors of the technicalities, so that killing the animal should not become barbaric."[33]

* * *

Rabbi Shneur Zalman of Liady, the towering scholar and mystic who founded the major Hasidic movement, Chabad (Lubavitch), expressed his opinions on the slaughter of animals also. However, his view reflects an understanding of the man-animal relationship totally different from what we have discussed heretofore. He writes that all the world exists for the greater glory of the Creator. "If a G-d-fearing individual eats ... meat or drinks wine ... in order to broaden his heart to G-d and His Torah, or in order to fulfill the mitzva of pleasure on Shabbat and YomTov ... then that flesh has been affected by a measure of radiance, and goes up to the All-Mighty as a sacrifice."[34] In other words, if a cow lives and dies a normal life, then — it was just a cow. But if it is slaughtered and then eaten by a G-d-fearing person in the performance of a mitzva, or to give him strength to perform mitzvot, then that cow has been transformed into part of something higher than itself; in giving its life to become food, the cow has been elevated to a higher plane of Divine service. From this point of view, there is no cruelty whatsoever involved in taking the animal's life. On the contrary.

* * *

---

33. Letters of Rabbi A.I. Kook Vol. II P. 230
34. תניא פרק ז.

In summation, I think our investigation well demonstrates that Judaism is a religion which places great emphasis on justice and compassion for all G-d's creatures. The Torah and all our teachings forbid the causation of the slightest unnecessary pain to anyone or to any thing, and include many strict regulations to assure that the slaughter of animals will be carried out in this spirit. And as Judaism seeks at all times to reduce our involvement with the physical and turn our hearts to spiritual pursuits, it recommends reducing the frequency of eating meat. On the other hand, animal sacrifice and consumption of animal flesh are at times mandated by halacha, and we cannot therefore find these activities morally unjust. If we had the wisdom to perceive the mystical unity of all Creation as expressed in the Torah's teachings, in the way Reb Shneur Zalman did, we would appreciate the beauty and compassion of the mitzvot.

In a subjective aside, I wish to concur with the comment of the *Vegetarian Times* (Nov./Dec. 1977, p. 38) that "although many feel that the vegetarian diet is more spiritually oriented than one containing meat, a vegetarian is not necessarily more spiritual or involved than his or her meat-eating neighbor." How painfully true! Let me direct the reader's attention to an ancient Rabbinic dictum: "He who takes pity on the cruel, ends up being cruel to those who ought to be pitied." Vegetarian ideologues who spout allegedly superior moral sensitivities often lack consistency in their ethical beliefs. Unfortunately, there are too many people today who are very much concerned with animal welfare, but who are not in the slightest bit moved by the lack of proper children's shelters, or at the thought of thousands of fetuses aborted annually. Is their pity for life not somewhat misplaced? The Psalmist praises G-d, "for His compassion is upon *all* His creatures." Someone who finds himself committed to a vegetarian regimen out of moral considerations ought to carry that super-sensitive moral refinement into all areas of human activity, and not confine it to the animal kingdom. If he can do that, then he is truly an admirable and ethical human being; otherwise, should we not label him a hypocrite?

Health Motives

Thousands of people become vegetarians for reasons which have nothing to do with the supposed immorality of taking animal life. On a far more pragmatic level, they renounce meat out of a conviction that meat offered on the market today is irretrievably contaminated with chemicals and additives, and that cattle are raised in such a way that meat is an odious, potentially dangerous food to eat. Some of the proof tendered to support this contention paints a truly gruesome picture of the meat-producing business in America, enough to make the most confirmed meat-and-potatoes man blanch at the thought of what he is consuming:

> The life expectancy of a steer, once two to four years, is now eighteen months. A steer is born. The moment he is dry from the womb, he is taken from his mother. The cattleman places him on a "Calf starter ration" consisting of milk powder, synthetic vitamins, minerals, and antibiotics — because suckling temporarily reduces the amount of salable milk produced by the mother. Just 25 pounds of calf food replaces the 225 pounds of milk he would normally drink. The drug-spiked food also reduces the calf's natural desire for activity, thus reducing his need for more energy-sustaining food.

> When the steer arrives at the commercial feedlot, he is forced off the boxcar and through a tank filled with pesticides that cleanses him of worms and flies. He is then confined in a pen continuously lit to encourage him to feed around the clock. Several times a day, his trough is refilled with a feed mixture computer-blended that morning. In addition to starchy, high-protein grains, these ingredients may include urea carbohydrate mixtures and artifical roughage such as ground-up newspaper mixed with molasses, tasteless plastic pellets, feathers, or treated wood mixtures. In fairness, we must state that this is

not a common practice, though it does exist.

Sometimes, the force-feeding of a steer will create a painful liver abscess which can slow his rate of weight gain. But this is no longer a problem for feedlot owners; cattle with abscessed livers are simply treated with 75 milligrams daily of the antibiotic oxytetracycline. During his marathon feeding our steer gains upwards of three pounds of muscle and fat a day.

By now, our steer more resembles a test tube than an animal, but his chemical diet isn't quite complete. He is sprayed and dusted with pesticides from time to time, and he eats the insecticide with his feed. It passes through his digestive system and is eliminated in his manure, where it serves the purpose of keeping flies from breeding. Charcoal may be added to dairy feeds to absorb the pesticide, preventing their excretion into the milk.

After four months of ingesting the equivalent of three huge dinners a day, the steer weighs about 1200 pounds, almost enough for slaughter. During the last three to five days, he is fed a booster of 1,000 milligrams of oxytetracycline or chlortetracycline a day, and given one last shot of streptomycin for the road to the slaughter house.

Meat packers used to hang beef in a refrigerated room for fourteen to twenty-one days to tenderize it. But this lengthy process took up warehouse space, and caused both meat and profits to shrink. Now meat is tenderized on the hoof or dipped in a solution of enzymes prior to freezing.

McClure also describes how meat managers use sodium sulfite, a powerful chemical illegally used to hold the color in meats, to change the color of rotten meat from green to red. Treated ground meats like chuck, round, sirloin, and sausage are especially

dangerous because the chemical is mixed throughout
to completely disguise the rotten odor and color.

The increase of environmental contaminants and
the rise of cancer has made scientists more concerned
with the investigation of long-range toxins —
substances which are toxic over a long period of time.
The damage from some of these toxins may not show
up for twenty or thiry years, while others may wreak
havoc after a year or two. The F.D.A., more
concerned about substances that can cause immediate
damage in humans or in laboratory animals, is
shortsighted about the restriction of chemicals that
may be long-term toxins.[35]

If the nauseating depictions of the vegetarians are indeed true
and the meat we are ingesting is as dangerous to our health as they
claim, it may well be that Jewish law would require us to cease
consuming this dangerous substance.

It is well known that Jewish law places the highest priority
upon the preservation of life; virtually every mitzva of the Torah
can be ignored, if that will save a life. Eating on Yom Kippur,
driving on the Sabbath — almost anything is permitted in order to
preserve life.[36] What is possibly less well-known is the corollary to
that principle of the supreme importance of human life — namely,
that one is forbidden to take any action which can put one's life in
danger, whether immediately or over a long term.[37] The Talmud
warned that it is forbidden to drink from water that was left
uncovered, since it might have been poisoned by a snake. Even if it
is doubtful whether the snake actually deposited its venom in the
water, one must refrain from taking a chance and drinking it.[38]

Similarly, Rabbinic law forbids drinking directly from a

---

35. New Vegetarian P. 72.

36. יומא פב.

37. עבודה זרה ל: — בבא קמא קטו:

38. יורה דעה קט"ז ס"ק ה — חולין ט:

stream of water, lest he swallow a dangerous insect. Even if others had drunk from the stream before him, without harm, he could not take a chance. Our Rabbis further decreed it a violation of a religious precept to walk near an unsteady wall or enter a ruined building, due to the danger of collapse.

Following the many precedents prescribed in the Code of Jewish Law, we would have little difficulty in arriving at the conclusion that, if indeed eating meat is injurious to one's health, it is not only permissible but possibly even mandatory[39] that we reduce our ingestion of an unhealthful product to the minimum level.

Kashruth

A uniquely Jewish reason for becoming a vegetarian is the motivation to follow the laws of kashruth properly. Volumes upon volumes of Jewish Law books detail the myriad requirements involved in observing the kashruth laws. Not only are there minute regulations for the slaughter and preparation of the animal, but there are also many laws forbidding the combination in any way of meat and milk, or the dishes used therefor, or the utensils, etc., etc. A person who avoids eating meat, avoids many of the problems involved in its preparation. Interestingly enough, there is a clear historical precedent for such a course of action:

The Midrash tells us that it is customary for Jews to eat foods prepared with milk on Shavuot, because on the first Shavuot in the

---

39. However, it would be mistaken to conclude that the Jewish law would forbid people from eating these foods altogether. Based on the Talmudic dictum "Shomer Petaim Hashem", "G-d watches over simpletons," our Rabbis have come to the conclusion that, although an act should actually be forbidden because it poses a danger to the individual — yet, if many people do engage in it, we can rely on the fact that the All-Mighty watches over those people, who are not wise enough to watch out for their own welfare. *Nidah* 31a, *Yevamot* 72A and *Shabbat* 129B. Also see *Trumat Hadeshen* #211.

   In our own generation, Rabbi Moshe Feinstein has written that one could not forbid smoking, although smoking may pose a danger to health, following the same reason we have noted. See *Iggerot Moshe, Yoreh Deah* II, #49.

desert, the Jews ate only dairy foods. On that day, Shavuot, the Children of Israel received the Torah from Mount Sinai; however, while they were aware of the prohibitions of kashruth, they were not yet versed in the details of the law. Therefore, since they were not sure if they would be preparing the meat in accordance with halacha, and wished to avoid any doubt, they refrained entirely from any meat, thereby avoiding any possible transgression, even if only inadvertent.

A growing dilemma on the American Jewish scene is the increasing unreliability of kashruth supervision, or, more correctly, the increasing *implications* of such unreliability. It is rumored that even the former bastions of unimpeachable kashruth have had their mishaps and their slip-ups. Rival kashruth-supervisory organizations hurl accusations at one another, seeking to register their reliability by casting doubt upon that of others. Conscientious observant Jews worry about the hundreds of chickens one *shochet* is called upon to slaughter within an hour, about the thousands of tongues and livers which the slaughtering industry must provide to kosher caterers and butchers in seemingly endless quantities.

Disconcerted by all the accusations, and apprehensive about the true kashruth of what they eat, not a few observant Jews have opted to avoid all the problems, like the Children of Israel at Sinai, by avoiding meat altogether.

In Pesachim, the Gemera tells us that Rabbi Judah the Prince taught, "it is forbidden for an ignorant person *(Am Haaretz)* to eat meat since the Torah writes,[40] 'This is the Torah law concerning the (slaughter of) animals ... whoever is involved in learning Torah may eat the flesh of an animal or fowl, but whosoever does not learn the Torah may not eat the flesh of an animal or fowl.' "

Expounding upon this passage, the Maharshah comments that since there are so many laws involved in rendering an animal suitable for consumption, and an *Am Haaretz* is ignorant of the law, he may mistakenly eat meat which is not kosher, and

---

40.   :מט.

therefore must avoid that possibility.[41] (Apparently, in those days, people did not go to butcher stores to purchase kosher meat, but rather had to see to the animal's *shechita* and kosher-rendering personally. Obviously, there would be many occasions where a person ignorant of the law would mistakenly assume the meat was kosher). The Ramo agrees with this opinion, in stating, "The reason that an *Am Haaretz* may not eat meat is that he is not conversant with the laws of Shechita..."[42]

Thus, there is ample precedent for refraining from eating meat in a situation where there is doubt whether that meat is truly kosher within the meaning of halacha. If a person sincerely doubts whether he can rely upon either the knowledge or trustworthiness of the kashruth supervisor, he is then certainly well-justified in deciding not to eat meat at all. In this aspect of his decision, he would not in any way be acting contrary to Jewish law.

However, I do not wish in any way to suggest that this decision is a moral imperative for a conscientious, kashruth-observing Jew. While there are undoubtedly areas of kashruth supervision which could be improved, nevertheless, there are enough kashruth supervisions of sufficient reliability in this country to allow strictly-observant Jews to eat meat without qualms. If this be the rationale for a person's decision to stop eating meat, it seems to have no real justification.

That wisest of men, King Solomon, noted that there is nothing new under the sun. Although vegetarianism has the glamor of a new fad for many people, our research shows that Judaism dealt with these "modern ideas" millenia ago. Once again we are awed by the scope, perceptiveness and sensitivity of our great Sages.

---

41. Ibid.
42. תשובות רמ"א שאלה סה.